The Soul of the Embryo:

An enquiry into the status of the human embryo in the Christian tradition

DAVID ALBERT JONES

continuum
LONDON • NEW YORK

Continuum

The Tower Building
11 York Road
London, SE1 7NX

15 East 26th Street
New York
NY 10010

www.continuumbooks.com

British Library Cataloguing-in-Publication Data
A catalogue record for this book is available from The British Library.

ISBN 0 8264 6296 0

Typeset by BookEns Ltd, Royston, Herts.
Printed and bound in Great Britain by
Antony Rowe Ltd, Chippenham, Wilts.

I would like to thank Fr Michael Hayes, Head of the School of Theology, Philosophy and History at St Mary's College for supporting an ethos of research and scholarship within the School; Robin Baird-Smith of Continuum books for his great patience; and the Linacre Centre for Healthcare Ethics for the use of their excellent library. Also thanks to Professor John Keown, Dr Wendy Hiscox, Dr Agneta Sutton and Mr Anthony McCarthy for suggestions and corrections which have helped sharpen the text in many ways. They bear no responsibility for those weaknesses that remain.

Contents

Abbreviations

AMA   American Medical Association

GA   Aristotle, *On the Generation of Animals*

HA   Aristotle, *On the History of Animals*

IVF   *in vitro* fertilization

MAL   *Middle Assyrian Laws*

NC   Hippocrates, *The Nature of the Child*

NIV   *New International Version* [Bible]

OAP   Offence against the Person [Act]

SCDF   Sacred Congregation for the Doctrine of the Faith

ST   Thomas Aquinas, *Summa Theologiae*

*To my parents
who gave me life
and inspired in me a love of learning.*

Foreword

A recurring theme in contemporary bioethics is the way in which advances in scientific and medical technology have provoked renewed interest in age-old debates of philosophers and theologians. Nowhere is this clearer than at the beginning of life.

In vitro fertilisation, pre-implantation diagnosis, therapeutic & reproductive cloning, germ-line genetic therapy, embryo selection and stem cell technology – the application of these spectacular modern techniques are all profoundly influenced by our understanding of the status and significance of the human embryo. At the same time, confronted by new insights in the nature and development of the embryo, Christian philosophers and theologians have been forced to re-explore their ancient ethical traditions.

Dr Jones combines the skills and insights of a historically informed theologian and philosopher with that of the contemporary bioethicist. Not only does he provide a unique distillation of legal, scientific, philosophical, ethical and theological sources over continuing history of more than two thousand years, he also draws out the multifaceted implications in the ethical and legal fields. His work provides a carefully researched and authoritative response to simplistic and widely publicized assertions about the historical origins of Christian teaching on the embryo.

John Wyatt is Professor of Neonatal Paediatrics
at University College London

Introduction

Begin at the beginning, go on till you come to the end; then stop.
(Lewis Carroll, *Alice's Adventures in Wonderland*)

There was a time when you did not exist. This is a strange thought truly to get your head around. It provokes a certain dizziness. We seem to be a necessary part of our world, of the world seen from here and now, and yet we know that we have not always existed. Reflecting in this way on our previous nonexistence gives a sense of depth to what it means for each of us to be, to be alive, to exist in our own right. Thinking of someone very close to us can bring a similar realization. We might be telling someone of a memory or event and then realize that, at that time, the person in front of us did not even exist! Someone who is real and significant in our lives, who is the centre of his or her own story, his or her own world, once did not exist. If we seriously consider the existence and the beginning of any one particular human being, of ourselves or someone we know well, we realize that it is something strange and profound. Many philosophers have recognized that the existence of the world is something mysterious: 'Not how the world is, but that the world is is the mystery' (Wittgenstein 2001; see also McCabe 2002; Munitz 1965). However, if we truly grasp the existence of any one person we see that this too is mysterious (Crosby 1996). The beginning of each human life thus shows itself to be a matter of religious and philosophical concern, not only something to be thought of in terms of biology or medicine.

The task of 'beginning at the beginning' is nowhere more significant and nowhere more bewildering than in our own case. We are led to ask, when and how does a new human individual come to be? Or, to put it another way: when did *I* begin? Someone

1

might say to us, 'I knew your parents before they met one another, when you were just a twinkle in your mother's eye.' But, of course, a twinkle in the eye is not a human being, and when the twinkle was, we were not.

The question of how to understand the beginning of human existence shapes the attitudes we have, or should have, towards the human embryo. It affects not only the question of whether, and if so in what circumstances, termination of pregnancy could be ethically justified. It also provokes the question of what should *count* as pregnancy. The line between abortion and contraception has been obscured by forms of 'contraception' which actually work by preventing the human embryo from implanting. In the UK, the courts have thought it necessary to rule on whether the morning-after pill 'causes a miscarriage' and thus falls within the terms of the Offences against the Person Act (1861). They ruled that it did not. In the USA in 2001, District Judge Herman Weber ruled that the conscience clause in an Ohio law, designed to protect people who refused to perform or participate in abortion, also applied to pharmacists asked to provide 'emergency contraception'. Other such cases are expected.

Understanding how and when each of us begins to exist also has implications for the treatment of the embryo *outside* the womb. In 1978 Louise Brown became the first child to be delivered successfully after having been conceived in vitro: the first 'test-tube baby'. Subsequently very many couples have accepted in vitro fertilization (IVF) and many have gone on to give birth to healthy children. However, the standard technique for IVF involves conceiving more embryos than will be transferred in a single treatment cycle. One effect of contemporary reproductive technologies has therefore been the creation of thousands of unwanted human embryos.

These frozen embryos have in turn been seen as a potential scientific resource that should not be left to go to waste. In 1985 in the UK the *Warnock Report* recommended that pre-implantation human embryos could be used in experiments to improve fertility treatments and to develop new forms of contraception. This recommendation was enshrined in law in the Human Embryology and Fertilization Act (1990). In 2001 permission to use human embryos was extended to cover a wider range of medical research including stem cell research. This move was approved, after the fact, by the House of Lords Select Committee on Stem Cell Research chaired by the Anglican Bishop of Oxford, The Rt Revd Richard Harries. In the USA experimentation on human embryos is governed by state law and has varied from state to state. South Dakota has a human embryo research statute banning 'non-therapeutic research that destroys a human embryo', while others (such as Louisiana and Michigan) have laws that ban experimentation on live foetuses. These laws could apply to experimentation on human embryos. In 2002, after a great deal of debate, President Bush banned the destruction of embryos to produce stem cells, but allowed research to continue on stem cell lines that had already been generated.

Given the difficulty of understanding what it means for a human being to come to exist, and given the profound significance of this question for law and ethics, any approach which offers to shed some light on the issue should be allowed a fair hearing. In this book, the issue of the beginning of the human life will be pursued by critical engagement with the history of *Christian* thought on the human embryo. Many people should be interested in discovering how the Christian tradition has understood the human embryo. A significant proportion of the world population (around 30 per cent or two billion people) declare themselves to be Christians. Christianity has also exerted a great influence on Western ethical thinking and on the understanding of the human person and has shaped many of the core beliefs of modern society. Even in contemporary Europe, where the practice of Christianity is in decline, the stance of the Christian churches on ethical issues still carries some weight. This is evident, for instance, in the choice of an Anglican bishop to chair the House of Lords Select Committee on Stem Cell Research.

The aim of the present work is to help clarify what the Bible and what the subsequent Christian tradition hold and teach concerning the beginning of human life. That such clarification is necessary can be seen, for example, by comparing recent statements by two leading churchmen. In 1995, in a letter to the whole Church on the Gospel of Life (*Evangelium Vitae*), Pope John Paul II asserted that 'the Church has always taught and continues to teach that the result of human procreation, from the first moment of its existence, must be guaranteed that unconditional respect which is morally due to the human being' (para. 60). According to the Pope, this unconditional respect is a constant feature of Christian history. 'Throughout Christianity's two-thousand-year history, the same doctrine has been constantly taught by the Fathers of the Church and by her Pastors and Doctors' (para. 61). Similar statements may be found in the *Catechism of the Catholic Church* and in other official Catholic documents.

In stark contrast, in a debate in the House of Lords in 2000, the Anglican Bishop of Oxford, Richard Harries, claimed that far from representing 2,000 years of history, the present teaching of the Roman Catholic Church had been established less than 200 years ago (Hansard, 621. 16, cols 35–7). 'I should like to suggest that it was only in the 19th century that the position became firmed up. Earlier Christian thought on this subject indicates an awareness of a developing reality, with developing rights as we would put it.' In opposition to the claims of the Pope and of others, the Bishop asserted that there was 'an alternative Western tradition'. This alternative tradition was said to give the embryo a non-absolute status which would be compatible with using human embryos in experiments. 'If we take a developmental view of the human person, as I believe the Western tradition did until the nineteenth century, the early embryo has a special, though not an absolute, status.'

In order to resolve this issue, what is needed is an investigation which does not rush into dealing with contemporary ethical arguments, but which tells the long and sometimes complex story of Christian reflection on the human embryo. That is the aim of this book. The validity of arguments and the accuracy of evidence will be weighed and criticized as the narrative unfolds. It will be important to consider the discussion of abortion within the tradition, as this is part of that story. However, this is not simply a history of Christian attitudes to abortion (for this see Noonan 1970; Connery 1977; Gorman 1982). Rather, the focus is on the more fundamental question of what it means for a new human being to come to be, and how and when this happens. This will be pursued through legal, scientific, philosophical and ethical discussion as well as specifically theological writings. It will begin with ancient Scriptures and primitive scientific texts and follow the topic through history until it embraces contemporary debates on the status of the human embryo. In this way a sense of historical perspective and of religious vision can combine to illuminate the origin and deeper meaning of human existence.

It is hoped that an explicitly Christian approach to these issues may be of interest for many people who are not themselves Christian but who share with Christians some significant beliefs. People of other religious traditions, whether Jewish, Islamic, Hindu, Sikh or Buddhist, may find more in common with a Christian account of the human soul than with purely secular accounts of what a human being is. Individuals without any strong religious affiliation may find a depth and resonance in Christian discussions that is lacking in the modern secular rhetoric of conflicting rights and cost-benefit analysis. Some may be looking for an alternative approach to these issues and be ready to listen to a neglected but sophisticated tradition. Others will be drawn in by the sheer scope of the story, spanning over 2,500 years of intellectual effort, debate and dialogue from the Hebrew Scriptures and ancient Greek medicine and philosophy to modern embryology, in vitro fertilization and stem cell research. We begin, then, where this story begins, with the creation of the embryo according to the Hebrew Scriptures.

1

Moulded in the Earth

[T]he Creator of all things, visible and invisible, by almighty power from the beginning of time made at once and out of nothing both orders of creatures, the spiritual and the corporeal, that is, the angelic and the earthly, and then the human creature, who as it were has a share in both being composed of spirit and body.

(Fourth Lateran Council, *Symbol of the Lateran*)

Our enquiry begins by examining the theme of the creation of each individual human being according to the Hebrew Scriptures. These ancient writings comprise the chronological beginning of our story, and the foundation not only for Christianity but for much of Western thought. Written between 2,500 and 3,000 years ago, the oldest of the Jewish Scriptures appreciably predate the establishment of Roman law or the foundation of Plato's academy. They have helped shape modern ideas of human equality and universal justice and deserve serious consideration.

For those who believe, both Jews and Christians, the Scriptures are more than inspiring and influential historical texts. They comprise a communication from God of the meaning of human existence. While acknowledging that these books were written at particular times and places and in particular circumstances, believers nevertheless hold them to be holy: the Word of God in the words of human beings. While law, science and philosophy certainly contribute to the understanding of human nature, the initial terms of reference should be taken from the source that can provide the deepest wisdom. An enquiry into the Christian understanding of human life must therefore begin with the sacred page. For a believer, the insights of Hebrew Scriptures are prior to the categories of Greek philosophy and the discoveries of modern embryology not only in time but also in authority.

One of the most eloquent and expressive passages to speak of the human embryo is Psalm 139:13–16.

> 13 For it was you who formed my inward parts;
> you knit me together in my mother's womb.
> 14 I praise you, for I am fearfully and wonderfully made.
> Wonderful are your works;
> that I know very well.
> 15 My frame was not hidden from you
> when I was being made in secret,
> intricately woven in the depths of the earth.
> 16 Your eyes beheld my unformed substance.
> In your book were written
> all the days that were formed for me,
> when none of them as yet existed.*

The basic tenet of this passage is that the formation of the child in the womb is a work of God. The exclamation 'wonderful are your works' brings to mind the works of God in fashioning the whole created order, and in providing for all living creatures, as described in Psalm 104:24, Psalm 145:5 and Job 37:14. The formation of the child in the womb is thus placed in the context of divine creation. The child is said to be formed (*qanah*), knitted (*sakak*) made (*'asah*) intricately woven (*raqam*) or fashioned (*yatzar*) by God. A variety of words is used to evoke the image of God as a craftsman fashioning the human body.

The association of the creation of the world with the forming of each new human being is a recurring theme through a number of scriptural texts. A good example is from the book of Ecclesiastes (11:5): 'Just as you do not know how the breath [*ruah*] comes to the bones in the mother's womb, so you do not know the work of God, who makes everything.' The reference to the breath coming to the bones in the womb echoes the story of God forming the first human being, Adam, and breathing into his nostrils the breath of life: 'Then the Lord God formed man [*ha'adam*] from the dust of the ground, and breathed into his

---

* Quotations from Scripture are unless otherwise indicated from the *New Revised Standard Version*.

nostrils the breath of life; and the man became a living being'
(Genesis 2:7). When talking of the breath or spirit, the writer of
Ecclesiastes seems to have in mind, not the first breath of the
new-born baby but the first signs of life the child exhibits while
still inside the womb, for the text talks of *ruah* coming 'to the
bones *in* the mother's womb'.

The central affirmation of this passage is also the central theme
in Psalm 139: that the coming to be of child is a work of God.
However, here the emphasis is different. In Ecclesiastes reference
is made to God giving life in the womb in order to stress, not divine
knowledge but human ignorance. An important theme in that book
is the vanity of seeking to know what is beyond human
understanding: 'Vanity of vanities! all is vanity' (Ecclesiastes 1:2).
Thus in a mood less of wonder than of intellectual humility, the
writer affirms the mysterious action of God.

In its own manner, Psalm 139 emphasizes the mysteriousness of
God's working. The fashioning is done in secret, 'in the depths of
the earth' (*b'tachtioth arets*). This phrase is illuminated by a
memorable saying of Job, 'naked I came from my mother's womb,
and naked shall I return there' (Job 1:21, see also Sirach 40:1). For
Job, death and burial in the earth are thought of as a return to the
womb. Part of the scriptural context for this is given by Genesis
where Adam is said to be formed from the dust of the earth and his
death is described as a *return* to the dust: 'By the sweat of your face
you shall eat bread until you return to the ground, for out of it you
were taken; you are dust and to dust you shall return' (Genesis
3:19). This return to dust is echoed in Psalm 104:29, 'when you
take away their breath, they die and return to their dust'. And again
in the book of Ecclesiastes 12:7, 'and the dust returns to the earth
(*arets*) as it was and the breath returns to God who gave it'. Psalm
139 and Job add to the theme of a return to the dust, the idea of the
earth as a womb. In Job, burial in the earth is likened to a return to
the womb. In Psalm 139, the forming of the child in the womb is
imagined as happening in the earth (*arets*). In both cases the earth is
seen as the primeval mother: an image which is common to many
peoples and cultures, both ancient and modern. The image of the
embryo being fashioned in 'the depths of the earth' should thus be
understood as combining an allusion to the inner security of the

womb with an echo of the forming of the first human being Adam from the dust of the ground (*adamah*).

According to Psalm 139:16, God beheld the psalmist's 'unformed substance', his *golem*. This seems to refer to the embryonic stage of human existence, before the foetus is fully formed, when development is incomplete or unfinished. It comes from a word meaning to wrap up and implies an enfolded mass. In much later rabbinic writings, well into the Christian era, this word would regularly be used to refer to the first stage of human life after conception. Later still, it would also gain notoriety as the name of a creature of Jewish folklore who is made out of mud and brought to life. This legendary figure has clear links both with the embryo and with the story of Adam. Like Adam, the *golem* is made from dust of the earth and given life. Like the human embryo, the *golem* is unfinished, relatively shapeless. The *golem* of folklore is a slavish monster, not created by God but made by man. It is not, like the embryo, a human-being-in-the-making. It is rather a mindless imitation or caricature of human life. In modern times the *golem* has also given its name to the deformed creature in *The Lord of the Rings* who was once human but whose humanity was distorted by the influence of a malign ring of power. Here, Gollum is not a creature in the making but an unmade creature, not being-formed but de-formed.

In the context of Psalm 139 the *golem* is considered as the hidden beginning of the human being. The focus is on God's knowledge, which is the knowledge that a maker has in mind even before the work is complete. When God sees the human embryo, God already knows what will become of that person, what he or she will do, because it is God who fashions the future. Some commentators suggest a reading of my deeds (*gilay-mi*) instead of my embryo (*golmi*), that is, 'your eyes saw my deeds' (Dahood 1970, p. 295). However, there is no direct evidence for such a variant reading and there seems no requirement to alter the received text in this case. Most scholars agree that 'my embryo' is the original wording (Anderson 1972, p. 910; Allen 1983, p. 252: this is the reading followed by most modern translations including the *New King James Bible*, *New American Bible*, *New Revised Standard Version*). The meaning of the passage is also evident from the use of the word fashion (*yatzar*) to describe how God ordains the future. A contrast is set up between the wrapped-up, hidden and not-yet-fashioned embryo, and the visible deeds of the adult fashioned by God. Hence also the reference to the making of the 'inner parts' and the 'frame'. Emphasis is continually placed on the hidden work of God, not only hidden inside the womb but internal to the developing creature. Throughout the passage the embryo is considered not as unformed but as being-formed and the subject of God's invisible informing activity.

The larger context is given by the overall theme of Psalm 139 as announced in the opening words, 'O Lord you have searched me and known me.' The assertion of God's activity in moulding the human embryo is being used to support the totality of God's knowledge of the person, from beginning to end, from inside to out (cf. Hebrews 4:12–13). It is striking to note that while this psalm talks eloquently of the moulding of the human body, it completely fails to mention the gift of life or breath. This is not made explicit because the emphasis of the passage lies not with the gift of life but with the all-encompassing character of God's knowledge. The focus is on God's intimate personal understanding of the human individual from the very beginning of his or her existence, to the present and into the future.

God's concern for the human being from the womb is also seen in the case of the prophets. They are often said to be called or chosen by God before they were born. For instance, of the prophet Jeremiah it is said: 'Before I formed you in the womb I knew you, and before you were born I consecrated you; I appointed you a prophet to the nations' (Jeremiah 1:5). In this example there is no doubt that the call of God precedes the birth of the prophet. However, this does not of itself establish the reality of the prophet's life in the womb. The prophet is called in order to fulfil the plan of God. The call of God is not a response on the part of the prophet but an initiative by God which precedes any action from the one called. Thus, even before the prophet exists, he can be said to be called by God. Hence Psalm 139:16, 'In your book were written all the days that were formed for me, when *none* of them yet existed' (emphasis added). The pre-existence implied in the call of God is the pre-existence of the divine plan – that is predestination – not the pre-existence of the prophet in the womb. Nevertheless, a parallel verse from the prophet Isaiah makes it clear that the prophet is held to exist in the womb when he is named and called: 'The Lord called me before I was born, while I was in my mother's womb he named me' (Isaiah 49:1). These verses from Isaiah and Jeremiah also suggest an association between being called or chosen and being created. This is made explicit in another verse from the prophet Isaiah, in which it is said that the Lord formed him 'to be his servant' (Isaiah 49:5). Isaiah is created for this purpose. The call is thus implicit in his creation and therefore it is possessed from the first moment of the prophet's existence in the womb. The moulding of the body in the womb, the gift of life and the call from God are here coterminous.

The language of call gives an added dimension to the general theme of God's care for the human being. God not only foresees and fashions the future for each human being but, at least in the case of the prophets, this future is understood in terms of a task given to each one. The person may not seek this role, but it is his or her destiny. This theme is also present in the New Testament. Initially Paul had fiercely opposed the followers of Jesus as a heretical Jewish sect and his conversion from persecutor to apostle was experienced as a radical change of direction in his life. However, he subsequently wrote of his conviction that God had set him apart for this work even before he was born (Galatians 1:15).

The pre-existence of a call from God before a person's birth is also shown by scriptural stories telling of the conception and birth of significant people. The book of Genesis tells how Rebecca was blessed with children as an answer to prayer. When the unborn children seemed to be struggling within her she was told by God that she had conceived twins. They would become two nations who would struggle against one another and the elder would serve the younger. God's choice of Jacob over Esau was set even while they were yet in the womb (Genesis 25:21–4; see also Romans 9:10–13). Another example occurs in the book of Judges where an angel of the Lord appeared to the wife of Manoah to tell her that she would conceive and bear a child whom she must dedicate to the Lord (Judges 13:2–7). The child, Samson, was to be a judge over the people. The conception of the prophet Samuel came as the answer to Hannah's prayer and he, like Samson, was dedicated even before being conceived (1 Samuel 1:1-28). These examples set a pattern followed in the New Testament with the conception and birth of John the Baptist to Elisabeth (Luke 1:5-25, 57-80).

In the book of prophet Isaiah, the language of a divine call from the womb is applied not only to the prophet as an individual but also to the whole people of Israel. The call of the individual prophet sent to the people is thus seen within the context of the destiny of the people as a whole, while the destiny of the people is expressed in terms of the call of a prophet. 'But now hear O Jacob my servant, Israel whom I have chosen! Thus says the Lord who made you, who formed you in the womb and will help you; Do not fear, O Jacob my servant, Jeshurun whom I have chosen' (Isaiah 44:1-2; see also Isaiah 44:24). In this way, both the people as a whole and individuals who have a special role among the people are said to be called, chosen or named by God. This call is, in turn, associated with the origin of the human being in the womb. The idea of someone chosen by God for the sake of the people was to culminate in the new covenant with the coming of the Messiah, the anointed one who would be the Saviour of the people of Israel and the light to the Gentile nations (Matthew 1:18-25, 2:1-23; Luke 1:26-56, 2:1-40). The conception and birth of Jesus, and the understanding of his identity, has profound implications for the Christian understanding of the human embryo. These will be explored in Chapter 9 when discussing the Christian tradition. At this point we should simply notice that the coming of the Messiah fits into a well-established pattern of God calling the chosen one from conception.

The Christian understanding of the Messiah as the fulfilment of the destiny of Israel has a further consequence: the idea of call is universalized. It is still true that there are particular people who have a special role within the Church and who are called as apostles, prophets or martyrs. However, the dominant theme of the Christian message is that *every* person is called to be numbered among the saints of Jesus. The inclusion of the Gentiles within the promises to Israel widens the call of the people to include all the nations. In this way the theme of being called by God, which has been applied first to individual prophets, then to the people of

Israel, then to the Messiah, is applied to all people and fuses with the theme of the concern of God for each person from the time he or she is being created. Thus, in a Christian context, the theme of the call of the prophet while in the womb has relevance to everyone. All are called to life in Christ. Of every human being it can be said that 'while I was in my mother's womb he named me' (Isaiah 49:1) and that the Lord 'formed me in the womb to be his servant' (Isaiah 49:5), just as it is true for everyone that 'your eyes beheld my unformed substance' (Psalm 139:16).

The belief that God has concern for each individual even from his or her formation as an embryo is invoked dramatically in the book of Job (10:8-12).

> 8 Your hands fashioned and made me;
> and now you turn and destroy me.
> 9 Remember that you fashioned me like clay;
> and will you turn me into dust again?
> 10 Did you not pour me out like milk
> and curdle me like cheese?
> 11 You clothed me with skin and flesh,
> and knit me together with bones and sinews.
> 12 You have granted me life and steadfast love,
> and your care has preserved my spirit.

The book of Job expresses the incomprehension that is provoked by the suffering of the innocent. Job does not know the reason for his suffering and expresses his anguish as a series of complaints to God. He seeks to mount an argument against God. It is an argument that will ultimately be resolved in humiliation and homage, but the drama of the book consists in the way it is first allowed to run its course. The theme of God's fashioning of the child in the womb is therefore presented in this book in a way that is coloured by bitter pain and sorrow. Job does not doubt that he was formed by God, given life, taken from the womb and cared for. The affirmation of God's work is as strong here as in Psalm 139. However, the truth of his creation only serves to make his current torment more bewildering. Why create only to destroy? Why give life only to make it wretched? Job goes so far as to wish that he had died while in the womb (Job 10:18). This wish should be seen, along with the rest of Job's words, as an honest expression of anguish of heart which does not adopt any mask or false piety before God. It is a characteristic that makes the book of Job both disturbing and refreshing.

The passage from Job goes into more detail about the process of embryogenesis than any other passage of the Hebrew canon. It begins with a reference to being moulded from clay and returning to the dust: a clear allusion to the creation of Adam (Genesis 2:7, 3:19). Immediately after this scriptural image, the formation of the embryo is likened to the curdling of milk to produce cheese. This analogy was also known elsewhere in the ancient world and occurs in the biological works of Aristotle. It is a vivid image for the condensing of the *golem*. The embryo is then clothed with skin and flesh and knitted with bones and sinews. Verse 12 refers to God granting life, but makes no explicit reference to the entrance of the breath or spirit. Rather, life, steadfast love and spirit seem to be inclusive terms, summing up what God has done in bringing Job into being. The force of this passage, as with Psalm 139, is to trace the human being's existence back to the very beginning in the workmanship of God who moulded and continues to mould that existence. It follows another example of human life being traced back to the first moment of its existence, earlier in the same book: 'Let the day perish on which I was born, and the night that said, 'A man-child is conceived' (Job 3:3). The cursing of the day of birth, like the wish to have been miscarried, is an extreme expression of bitterness and is found both in Job and in the prophecies of Jeremiah (Job 3:3; Jeremiah 20:14; see also Ecclesiastes 4:2-3, 6:3-5). However, Job goes further, also cursing the night on which he was conceived. The beginning of Job's existence is thus pushed back from birth to conception. This verse coheres with Psalm 139:13-16 and with Job 10:8-12 in recognizing the newly conceived *golem* as the beginning of the human being whom God fashions in the womb.

A related verse is found in Psalm 51, where King David is depicted as expressing his remorse by tracing his sinfulness back to his conception: 'Indeed, I was born guilty, a sinner when my mother conceived me' (Psalm 51:5). This text would take centre stage in much later debates among Christians concerning the nature of 'original sin' – a doctrinal issue that would also have a bearing on the question of the origin of the soul. The development of the doctrine of original sin and its relation to the origin of the soul will recur in the context of Reformation debates (see Chapter 10). Most scholars caution against placing too much weight on this one verse. In particular, any interpretation which implies that sexual intercourse is itself sinful or a cause of sin should be resisted. Nevertheless, this verse does seem to point to sin as a universal human condition into which each person is conceived (Tate 1990, pp. 18-20). Furthermore, aside from the question of sin, the verse clearly traces the beginning of a particular human life back to the moment of its conception. In this it conforms with the accounts of the creation of the human being in the womb as given in Psalm 139:13-16 and Job 10:8-12.

At this point it is useful to revisit the opening chapters of the book of Genesis as they constitute an important element of the scriptural context for all passages that consider the beginning of human life in the womb. The story of the making of Adam involves two aspects: that of forming the body, moulding it from the dust of the ground; and that of giving life, breathing into his nostrils the breath of life (Genesis 2:7). In the story, the act of moulding is distinct from and prior to the act of giving life. First the body is formed, afterwards the body is vivified. This order is maintained in the passage from Ecclesiastes (11:5) where the bones seem to be formed first and only then does the spirit come into them (a similar pattern, in a slightly different context is found in Ezekiel 37). For the sake of comparison it is useful to consider a passage from the second book of Maccabees. This is an important work that bears witness to the faith of Jews in a time of intense persecution in the second century BCE. The book is held as sacred by many Christians while others treat it with respect as helpful and instructive. In one place it tells how a mother encouraged her sons to face martyrdom by appealing to the promise of the resurrection.

> I do not know how you came into being in my womb. It was not I who gave you life and breath, nor I who set in order the elements within each of you. Therefore, the creator of the world, who shaped the beginning of humankind and devised the origin of all things, will in his mercy give life and breath back to you again, since you now forget yourselves for the sake of his laws. (2 Maccabees 7:22-3)

As with some of the scriptural passages already discussed, the creative power of God is shown both in the origin of the whole world and in the origin of each human being. It is the Lord who devised the origin of all things, who sets the elements in order in the womb. One interesting feature of this passage is that the giving of new life is referred to *before* the forming of the body: 'It was not I who gave you life and breath, nor I who set in order the elements within each of you.' Should we deduce from this that the giving of life is thought to precede chronologically the ordering of the elements? Surely there has to be some bringing together of elements to have a body at all! It should be clear that there is no need to assume that the order of speech in this passage reflects a temporal sequence of events. If we are looking for a reason why the gift of life is mentioned before the ordering of the elements, we should consider the thrust and function of the passage as a whole. The mother is encouraging her sons to face death by presenting them with the hope of future life. It is the life-giving power of God that is the focus of attention, hence the mention of the gift of life even before referring to the ordering of the elements of the body. Conversely, the thrust of Psalm 139 was the omniscience of God, and there was not even a secondary reference to the gift of life and breath.

These reflections help to clarify an extremely important point. The story of the making of Adam (Genesis 2:7) shows the dual aspects of God's creative action in the origin of the human being: forming the structure or order of the body; and giving life, soul or spirit. However, this story should not be interpreted as giving a particular temporal sequence to the relative appearance or development of these features in the human embryo. Some scriptural passages stress one aspect over the other, depending on the aims or concerns of the account, but both aspects must be recognized as the fruit of God's creative action. It should not be inferred that the order of speech or of imagery in any particular passage necessarily reflect a temporal sequence in the development of the embryo. What is revealed is the action of God as the source of bodily form and as the source of life or spirit and that this action encompasses the whole development of the human being from the very beginning.

To sum up:

- The origin of the human being is a subject treated in several passages in Scripture and touched upon in many more.
- The Scriptures present a coherent account concerned not so much with the biology of reproduction as with the action of God in bringing a new life into existence. This divine action is hidden and beyond human comprehension. The creation of each human being by God is twofold: creating the form, structure or order of the body; and creating the life, soul or spirit.
- God is creatively involved from the very beginning, pictured as the coagulation or condensing of the wrapped-up embryo – the *golem*. The words of Job cursing the day of his conception, and of David tracing his sinfulness back to his conception, conform to a common scriptural pattern in which conception is understood as the beginning of the making of the human being.
- The Scriptures show God calling or naming certain chosen individuals while they are still in the womb. In a Christian context this naming and calling is understood as universal, for all are called by God in Christ. Every human being thus receives a divine call from the first moment he or she begins to be fashioned by God, that is, as a newly conceived embryo.

While the Scriptures bear witness to the action of God in the shaping of the embryo, this should not be taken to imply the rejection of scientific embryology, for the formation of the human body and the transmission of human life are certainly biological processes – even if they are also more than this. Towards the end of the period when the Hebrew Scriptures were being collated, other parts of the ancient world were laying the foundations for a sophisticated biological account of human reproduction and development; an account that was to have a great and lasting effect on generations of Christian thinkers. The next phase of our story requires us to examine two of the most influential figures behind this great achievement: Hippocrates the physician and Aristotle the biologist and philosopher.

2

Curdled Like Cheese

In a higher world it is otherwise; but here below to live is to change,
and to be perfect is to have changed often.

(J.H. Newman, *Essay on the Development of Christian Doctrine*)

The origins of the systematic study of embryology in the West are
associated especially with Hippocrates, the renowned physician
from the Greek Island of Kos who flourished in the fifth century
BCE. Little is known with any certainty of his life or teaching. His
importance resides primarily in the library of approximately 70
medical works which were attributed to him or to the school that
followed him. These writings of the 'Hippocratic corpus' remained
in clinical use until well into the sixteenth century of the Christian
era, over two millennia of medical practice.

The Hippocratic approach to medicine and to nature was strongly
empirical. It tended to focus on immediate material causes and the
consequences and remedies for disease. This approach is evident in
the two-part work on embryology: *The Seed* and *The Nature of the
Child* (*NC*). Here the writer not only made careful observations of
remains from miscarriages but also conducted experiments:

> If you take twenty or more eggs and place them to hatch under two or
> more fowls, and on each day, starting from the second right up until
> the day on which the egg is hatched, you take one egg, break it open
> and examine it, you will find everything is as I have described –
> making allowance of course for the degree to which one can compare
> the growth of a chicken with that of a human being. (*NC* 29)

This simple experiment allowed the development of the chick
embryo to be examined methodically and in detail. It was apparent
that the embryo not only grew but also gradually took shape: the
limbs and organs developing over time. Starting from such
observations the Hippocratic writer sought to account for the

processes of development by appeal to material causes. He considered that the process of generation started with the mixing of male and female seed. The male seed was thought to be secreted from the whole body 'from the hard parts as well as the soft and from the total bodily fluid' (*The Seed* 3) and for this reason could generate all the different parts. The fluid was concentrated in the brain and then passed down the spinal column to the testes. The seed of a woman was identified with moisture secreted into the womb during intercourse and 'sometimes externally as well' (*The Seed* 4). Conception would occur if the mixed seed of male and female were retained in the womb, but would not follow if the seed were expelled immediately after intercourse.

Once in the womb, the seed from both parents was thoroughly mixed together due to the movement of the woman's body 'for the woman of course does not remain still' (*NC* 12). The seed then condensed 'as the result of heat' (ibid.), and the condensed mass acquired air or breath (*pneuma*). When it was saturated with air, the air made 'a passage for itself in the middle of the seed' (ibid.) and escaped, while cool air was in turn drawn in. The seed expanded and formed a membrane around itself rather like the skin formed on the top of bread as it bakes. The author described the six-day-old aborted embryo as looking, 'as though someone had removed the shell from a raw egg' (*NC* 13). While the membrane formed, the blood of the woman was taken into the seed together with the cool air. There the blood coagulated to form the flesh of the embryo. The formation of the different parts of the embryo was explained as being due to the action of the breath which separated out the different elements so that 'like goes to join like' – flesh to flesh, bone to bone, and so on. This action was illustrated by another ingenious experiment.

> Suppose you were to tie a bladder onto the end of a pipe, and insert through the pipe earth, sand, and fine filings of lead. Now pour in water, and blow through the pipe. First all the ingredients will be thoroughly mixed up with the water, but after you have blown for a time, the lead will move towards the lead, the sand towards the sand, and the earth towards the earth. Now allow the ingredients to dry out and examine them by cutting around the bladder: you will find that like ingredients have gone to like. (*NC* 17)

The process of formation of limbs and organs in this way was complete by 42 days in the case of female embryos and 30 in the case of male. This was approximate and would vary somewhat from individual to individual. 'This is the period for articulation in most cases, take or give a little' (*NC* 18). Once the foetus was formed the ends of the limbs, the nails and the hair would start to grow. Only then would the unborn infant begin to move, at around three months for males and four for females (*NC* 21). Having developed the different organs and parts, the growth of the foetus in the womb proceeded in a similar way to the growth of a plant. The author explores this analogy at great length, concluding that 'from beginning to end the process of growth in plants and in humans is the same' (*NC* 27).

There were, then, three major points of transition within Hippocratic embryology: the completion of form, the first felt movement and birth. The articulation of embryonic limbs and organs was complete after around 40 days, the foetus began to move between three and four months, and birth took place at some time between seven and ten months. These figures were generalizations and would vary in the individual case, as is emphasized in a passage from another work.

> For formation, thirty-five days, for movement, seventy days; for completion two hundred and ten days. Others for form, forty-five days; for motion, ninety days; for delivery two hundred and seventy days. Others fifty for form; for the first leap, one hundred; for completion, three hundred days. For distinction of limbs forty; for shifting, eighty; for detachment two hundred and forty. It is not and is. There are found therein both more and less, in respect of both the whole and the parts, but the more is not much more, and the less is not much less. (*On Nutriment* 42)

The Hippocratic writings on the embryo represent a remarkable achievement. By combining careful observation and primitive experimentation they constitute 'the beginnings of systematic embryological knowledge' (Needham 1959, p. 36 – a conclusion still valid even if qualified by King 1990, p. 17). The main elements of this account are that

- The processes of reproduction, development and growth are explicable in material terms.

- The embryo results from the mixing of male and female seed. The seed is secreted from all parts of the body.
- The limbs and organs of the embryo are not present from the beginning but are generated by a process of development and differentiation. The cause of development is the various elements (flesh, bone, blood, etc.) come together, like going to join like, under the influence of breath (*pneuma*). The subsequent process of growth in the embryo is exactly like that in plants.
- The form of the embryo is complete at around 40 days; and the first movement occurs at around three to four months. Variations are to be expected between individuals, but there are typical values for the timing of growth and development.
- The author does not attempt to answer metaphysical questions about the origin of the soul or to identify the philosophical or ethical significance of any particular moment or transition.

While Hippocrates was establishing his school on Kos, the Greek philosophical world was being transformed by Socrates (c. 470–399 BCE). Socrates' interests lay not in the direction of natural philosophy but in the quest for certain and reliable knowledge and in the criticism of concepts and definitions, especially in the area of ethics and politics. He left no writings of his own and his philosophy is known through the works of his most famous pupil, Plato (428–348 BCE). Neither Socrates nor Plato taught anything of significance directly relating to the human embryo. Nevertheless, Plato will go on to play a significant role later in our story because of the influence he exercised upon Christian thinkers on the subject of the soul. Plato believed that the human soul existed before the body was formed and that it survived the death of the body.

Systematic embryology came of age through the work of Plato's greatest student Aristotle (384–322 BCE), who combined conceptual subtlety with inexhaustible empirical curiosity. Aristotle wrote on a vast range of subjects from meteorology, physics and metaphysics to rhetoric, logic, ethics and politics. However, he was especially interested in biology (see for example Thompson 1913; Grene 1963; Nussbaum 1978; Gotthelf 1985; Gotthelf and Lennox 1987; Lennox 2001) and wrote a series of major works on biological topics: on animal behaviour, on physiology, on the soul, on movement in animals and on the generation of animals. In respect of this last work it has been said that, 'the depth of Aristotle's insight into the generation of animals has not been surpassed by any subsequent embryologist, and considering the width of his other interests, cannot have been equalled' (Needham 1959, p. 42).

Before considering his work on embryology it is necessary first to examine the central categories used by Aristotle in his account of physical change: matter (*hule*) and form (*morphe* or *eidos*); and potentiality (*dunamis*) and actuality (*energeiai*). Matter and form are relative terms. If we think of wood being shaped into a statue or a bowl, the *wood* is the material element and the form is the *shape* given by craftsman. However, there is no matter that is completely formless, and material that receives a new form previously had some other form. In Aristotle's view, change occurs because matter receives a new form and loses the form it had before. A second important pair of terms in Aristotle's account of change are potentiality and actuality. Something is potentially X if it can become X. To return to our example, a *potentially* round-shaped thing can become *actually* round-shaped. The potentialities of a thing are rooted in the form it actually has. For example, a piece of wood can be carved into a round shape because of the potentialities it possesses as (actually) wooden.

In his work *On the Soul* Aristotle applies the categories of matter and form, and of potentiality and actuality, to the principle of living things, that is, the soul (*psuche*). He argues that the soul is not a kind of physical stuff or a part of the body but that it is the *form* of the living body. Furthermore, just as the word 'life' covers many different living beings with different powers, so there are different kinds of soul: plants, having only the powers of nutrition and generation possess a *nutritive* soul; simple animals also possessing the senses of touch and taste have an *sensitive* soul; higher animals having in addition smell, sight and hearing, and being able to move location and exhibit complex behaviour possess a *locomotive* soul; finally, human beings, having the power of reason or under-standing, possess a *rational* soul. Among earthly living creatures the higher powers of the soul seem to presuppose all the lower powers:

the rational powers presuppose the locomotive, which presuppose the sensitive, which presuppose the nutritive (*On the Soul* 2.3, 414b).

For Aristotle, the soul is something *actual*, and at the same time, it is the basis of the *potentialities* of the living body. Aristotle explains this using the example of actuality and potentiality in relation to knowledge. The knowledge of mathematics can exist in one way in someone who knows mathematics but who is asleep; in another way in the person who knows mathematics and is awake; and in a further way in the person who is actually doing mathematics (*On the Soul* 2.1, 412a 23; *On the Generation of Animals* [*GA*] 2.1, 735a 11). In this illustration, the knowledge of mathematics is the first actuality, the basis of the potential to *do* mathematics (the second actuality) whether the person is actually doing mathematics or not. In a similar way, Aristotle writes that the soul is 'the first actuality (*entelecheia*) of a natural body having life potentially in it' (*On the Soul* 2.1, 412a 23). Furthermore, just as a person who actually possesses knowledge can be referred to as 'potentially capable of knowing', so a body that actually possesses life can be referred to as having 'life potentially in it' or as being 'potentially capable of living' (*On the Soul* 2.1, 412b 25).

In the case of knowledge and of life, Aristotle can use the term 'potentially X' to refer to something that is actually X (a point emphasized by Freeland 1987 and Balme 1990). In contrast, Aristotle thinks it misleading to say that earth is potentially a human being, even though it is true that human seed is made from earth and that human beings are generated from human seed. 'Is earth potentially a man? No - but rather when it has already become seed - and perhaps not even then' (*Metaphysics* θ.7, 1049a 1-2). The seed is potentially a human being in a sense that common earth is not. Nevertheless, in another way even the seed is not yet potentially a human being, for (male) seed has to combine with the female element and condense before a human being can be produced. There are thus different senses in which something can be said to be potentially something, some further from, others closer to, the actuality. This will be important when we come to Aristotle's account of the development of the human embryo.

Aristotle's main treatise on embryology is *On the Generation of*

Animals, a work in which '(his) thought can be seen integrated as it is nowhere else' (Peck 1942, p. v). Here he considers reproduction not just in human beings but in a great variety of animals: both those without blood (a term roughly corresponding to the modern category of invertebrates: insects, snails, shellfish, etc.) and those with blood (vertebrates). He believed that in some simple bloodless animals generation occurred not from a parent but spontaneously out of earth or water (*GA* 3.11, 762a 18–27, see Lennox 2001, pp. 232–7). This idea would remain influential until the eighteenth century CE. In animals with blood he distinguishes those that lay eggs (such as birds, most fish and most reptiles); those that lay eggs internally but that give rise to live young (vipers and cartilaginous fish); and those that do not lay eggs but generate live young internally (such as horses, dolphins and, of course, human beings).

In living things in which male and female were distinct, what distinguishes male and female, according to Aristotle, is the part each plays in generation. He understood this distinction by reference to his categories of form and matter: 'The male provides the "form" and the "principle of movement", the female provides the body, in other words, the material' (*GA* 1.20, 728a 10–11). He saw this as confirmed by the way that, both in birds and in fish, in order to generate offspring the eggs laid by the female have to be fertilized by a male, even though the male does not add any discernible quantity of matter to the egg. This seemed to imply 'that the contribution which the male makes to the young has to do not with bulk but with specific character' (*GA* 1.21, 730a 24). Later he made it clear that the 'form' or 'specific character' provided by the male is the sensitive soul: 'The male is the factor that produces the sentient soul' (*GA* 2.5, 741a 14).

The male is like the sculptor shaping the statue while the female provides the wood or stone. The seed of the male acts upon the matter provided by the female (the menstrual blood) as rennet acts upon milk, setting it (*GA* 2.4, 739b 23). It is interesting to note that this view seems to have been reflected in Job 10.10, 'Did you not pour me out like milk and curdle me like cheese?' and also in the book of Wisdom 7.2, 'compacted with blood, from the seed of a man'.

The conceptus (*kuema*), formed as a result of the mixing of male and female elements (*GA* 1.20, 728b 33) has the appearance of an egg with the shell taken off (*GA* 3.9, 758b 5, cf. *NC* 13), a stage which lasts for about seven days (*GA* 1.23, 731a 20; *History of Animals* [*HA*] 7.3, 583b 12; *NC* 13). The organs then begin to appear one by one, the heart first of all, then the blood vessels and the umbilical cord. The internal organs are formed before the limbs and the upper part of the embryo before the lower. That the heart is formed first is evident to the senses, but it also accords with reason: as the heart is the principle organ of nutrition it is needed so that the embryo can feed and grow.

However, this sequential account left Aristotle with a difficult problem: are the other organs generated *by* the heart or just *after* the heart? If the former, how can the heart possess the power to generate the liver, for example, when the heart does not possess the powers of the liver? Only what actually possesses a certain form can reproduce that form in another: only hot things pass on heat; only rabbits reproduce rabbits. If the latter (after the heart but not by the heart), what is it that generates the other organs, given that the seed is no longer present? Aristotle's solution to this is to say that it is the male parent who generates; that the seed is an instrument; and that the instrumental power present in the seed is then passed on to the heart. The seed imparts to the embryo a kind of 'movement' which is communicated from part to part transforming the embryo as it goes. 'There is something that fashions the parts of the embryo, but this agent is not a definite individual thing, nor is it present in the semen as something already perfect to begin with' (*GA* 2.1, 734b 18-19). The cause of development is thus in one way from outside (*exothen*) from the power of the parent transmitted in the seed, in another way the cause is within it (*enousa*) (*GA* 2.1, 734b 12, 17). It is analogous to automatic toys that are set going but then keep moving as part moves part, except that in the embryo, this chain reaction involves changes in quality rather than local movement.

So when, according to Aristotle, does the embryo acquire a soul? The soul was defined as the first actuality of a body which is potentially alive, a body of the sort that has organs (*On the Soul* 2.1, 412a 27). The embryo therefore acquires each sort of soul as it acquires the relevant organ of the body. The soul cannot be acquired before the organ takes shape because 'there can, for example, be no walking without feet' (*GA* 2.3, 736b 24). On the other hand, neither can the soul be acquired after the organ takes shape, for it would not be an organ of a living body unless it were informed by a soul.

> Now the semen and the movement and principle it contains are such that as the movement ceases each one of the parts gets formed and acquires soul. (I add acquires soul because there is no such thing as face or flesh either without soul in it). (*GA* 2.1, 734b 22–5; see also *GA* 2.5, 741a 10–12)

The seed of the male contains soul as a power (*dunamis*) to transmit life, and in this sense it possesses every kind of soul 'potentially', whereas the female element, and the initial mixture of male and female elements, possess only a nutritive soul 'potentially'. It is important to distinguish different senses of potentiality here. The male seed is a kind of instrument. It transmits soul to another but it is not itself alive, even potentially, because, according to Aristotle, the matter of the seed contributes nothing to the embryo. On the other hand, the female element in generation is potentially alive and therefore contains soul potentially (*GA* 2.3, 737a 20–35). The mixture of elements, called the conceptus (*kuema*) is 'just as much alive as plants are' (*GA* 2.3, 736a 34), possessing a nutritive soul potentially and, as soon as the heart is formed, actually nourishing itself. Furthermore, according to Aristotle, the heart is not only the fundamental organ of nutrition but also the fundamental organ of touch, of pleasure and of pain. Therefore, at the same time as the embryo begins *actually* living the life of a plant (that is, nourishing itself), it becomes a simple animal *potentially*. Nevertheless, while Aristotle regarded the embryo as an animal, potentially, from the time that it possessed a heart, he did not regard it as any particular sort of animal until it was completely formed.

> It is while they develop that they acquire a sentient soul. I say 'while they develop' for it is not the fact that when an animal is formed at the same moment a human being, or a horse, or any other particular sort of animal is formed, because the end or completion is formed last of all, and that which is peculiar to each thing is at the end of its process of formation. (*GA* 2.3, 736b 1–5)

As the organs appear one after the other the embryo develops from being 'already an imperfect animal, *potentially*' to being 'a locomotive animal, *potentially*' (*GA* 2.4, 740a 24). Aristotle seems to have identified the completion of bodily form with the possession of a locomotive animal soul, that is, with the power of external movement. This identification is driven by theoretical reasons – the wish to unite form and function. However, Aristotle had to square this claim with the physical evidence. The Hippocratic writer had observed that formation was complete at around 40 days, while the first movements were not generally detected until three or four months after insemination. It was perhaps in an attempt to reconcile these divergent observations that Aristotle was led to posit widely different rates of growth in male and female embryos: giving 40 days as the time of formation in males and 90 days as the time for formation in females (an alternative speculation on the origin of these figures is given by Ford 1988, p. 28).

> In the case of male children the first movement usually occurs on the right-hand side of the womb and about the fortieth day, but if the child be a female then on the left-hand side and about the ninetieth day ...
>
> In the case of a male embryo aborted at the fortieth day ... all the limbs are plain to see, including the penis, and the eyes also, which as in other animals are of great size. But the female embryo, if it suffer abortion during the first three months, is as a rule found to be undifferentiated. (*HA* 7.3, 583b 3–5, 15–23)

Some commentators have assumed from this that, according to Aristotle, the rational soul, being the most perfect and most specifically human soul, comes to exist with the completion of bodily form at 40 days for male embryos and 90 days for female embryos. For Aristotle says, 'the end or completion is formed last of all' (*GA* 2.3, 736b 3). However, there is reason to believe that Aristotle had a quite different account of the acquisition of a rational soul.

Aristotle explicitly poses the question: 'At what moment and in what manner, do those creatures which have this principle of reason acquire their share in it, and where does it come from?' (*GA* 2.3, 736b 5–7). He first responds by reasserting the analogy between the different sorts of soul:

To begin with it seems that all things of this sort live the life of a plant. And it is clear we should follow a similar line also in our statements about the sentient and rational soul, since a thing must of necessity possess every one of the sorts of soul *potentially* before it possesses them *in actuality*. (*GA* 2.3, 736b 15)

Yet, immediately after the above quotation Aristotle places the rational soul in a different category by saying that reason alone is not dependent on matter and thus the rational principle comes 'from outside' (*thurathen*) (*GA* 2.3, 736b 28). According to his work *On the Soul*, the act of understanding is not, like sight or walking, the actualization of a bodily organ (*On the Soul* 3.4, 429a 25), therefore the possession of the rational soul potentially does not require the possession or perfection of any organ of the body.

This issue can be approached in another way, by asking when Aristotle regarded the rational soul as exercising its characteristic powers. He held the reason to be *actual* in this way when the child started to *use* his or her reason, that is, one or two years after the child had been born (Charlton 1987; Balme 1990). From what point, then, is the rational soul possessed *potentially?* We should note that the rational principle comes 'from outside' not into the 40-day embryo but with the seed of the male parent (*GA* 2.3, 737a 10; see also Peck 1942, p. 168 n. a; Balme 1990, pp. 27, 30–31 n. 6). It thus seems that, for Aristotle, the embryo possesses a rational soul *potentially* from the time that it is a being in its own right (*GA* 2.4, 740a 7–10, 20), which is when the embryo 'sets' (*GA* 2.4, 739b 21–35) and has the power of development within it (*enousa*) (*GA* 2.1, 734b 12, 17), when it gains a heart (*GA* 2.4, 740a 4) and starts to nourish itself (*GA* 2.1, 735a 15–26), when it becomes 'an animal, potentially, though a simple one' (*GA* 2.4, 740a 24), that is, after the first week or so (Balme 1990, p. 30, cf. *GA* 1.23, 731a 20, *Parts of Animals* 3.4, 665a 35). Before this point, the initial mixture of seed is called a conceptus (*kuema*), but not an embryo (*embrua*) or a living being (*zoon*). Furthermore, the destruction of the conceptus (*kuema*) was not called abortion (*ektroma*) but efflux (*ekruseis*) (*HA* 7.3, 583b 12).

In his work on *Politics* Aristotle advocates a policy of strict population control within the city. No child born with disability is to be permitted to live. Any woman who becomes pregnant having exceeded her quota of offspring is to procure an abortion (*amblosin*). However, this is to happen only before life and sense had begun. 'For what is holy or unholy in these cases depends on the question of life and sense' (*Politics* 7.14, 1335b 25). The phrase 'life and sense' (*tei aisthesei kai to zen*) has commonly been interpreted as referring to the completion of form and the first movements at 40 days for males and 90 days for females. However it should be noted that Aristotle mentions neither form (*eidos, morphe*) nor movement (*kinesis*), but speaks of life (*zen*) and sense (*aisthesei*). In many places in his biological works Aristotle asserts that the heart is the first organ to form, that the heart was the fundamental organ of sense (*aisthetikon*), and that an animal became an animal when it first possessed the power of sensation.

> For the heart is the first of all parts to be formed; and no sooner is it formed than it contains blood. Moreover, the motions of pain and pleasure, and generally of all sensation (*aisthetikon*), plainly have their source in the heart, and find in it their ultimate termination ... no sooner is the embryo formed, than its heart is seen in motion as though it [the heart] were a living creature (*zoon*). (*Parts of Animals* 3.4, 666a 13–23; see also *Youth, Old Age and Death* 3, 468b 27–469a 20; *Movement of Animals* 10, 703a 15)

In his biological writings, Aristotle refers to the appearance of the heart far more frequently than the completion of formation of the body or the first discernible movement. This would seem to imply that what he had in mind in *Politics* 7:14 was abortion during the first week or so before the formation of the heart, and that he understood abortion during this period as somewhat analogous to the modern category of 'emergency contraception'. If this seems improbable it should be noted that the abortion described in *On the Nature of the Child* (a passage Aristotle seemed to have read, as it anticipated the vivid comparison of the embryo to 'a raw egg without its shell' [*NC* 13] see *GA* 3.9, 758b 5) was precisely of this character, being procured after six days. The Hippocratic writer believed that a woman could know she had conceived because in that eventuality the seed would stay inside her and not come out.

For Aristotle, the most significant moment in embryonic development is thus the appearance of the heart, the central organ of nutrition and sense, and this is the first organ to appear, around one week or so after the entry of the male seed. However, the imagination of subsequent generations was captured, not by Aristotle's repeated claims about the heart of the embryo, but by that famous passage from the *History of Animals* in which he gave the figures of 40 days for males and 90 days for females for the completion of form and the first detectable movement.

In summary:

- Aristotle built on the great achievement of the Hippocratic embryologist. Both thought of conception as the mixing of male and female elements, each a fluid, which then 'set' to produce an egg-like being. From the start this egg/embryo was thought to be in the process of rapid change and development. Embryonic development was viewed of as a sort of chain reaction caused by a power of the male parent conveyed by the spirit or breath (*pneuma*) in the seed which became a transforming cause present within (*enousa*) the embryo. The organs were thought to be formed in a progressive development one by one starting with the heart, the brain and the liver. The inner organs were formed before the outer limbs and the upper part of the embryo before the lower. Aristotle argued strongly that the organs of the body did not pre-exist in the seed but were formed during development (a view that would later be termed 'epigenesis'). The shaping of the internal organs and limbs of the embryo from head to toe was thought to be complete at about 40 days after insemination in the case of male embryos.
- Both authors asserted that the female contributed some physical element to generation. Aristotle, for example, explicitly rejected the view that the female contributes nothing to generation but a place (*topos*) where generation may happen (*GA* 1.19, 726b 36). It is therefore 'simply untrue' that he held that the female contributed nothing to inheritance (Balme 1990, p. 30; see also *GA* 4.3, 767b 1–768b 35).
- Aristotle nevertheless felt free to disagree with the Hippocratic writer on a number of points. He claimed that the female analogue to male seed was the menstrual blood and not, as the Hippocratic author had argued, moisture secreted into the womb during intercourse (*GA* 1.19, 727a 26, see *The Seed* 4).

He rejected the idea that the seed was secreted from all parts of the body (*GA* 1.17, 721b 10, see *The Seed* 3). He also rejected the idea that development could be explained by 'like going to join like' (*GA* 2.4, 740a 15, see *NC* 17).

- Most significantly for the later tradition, Aristotle departed from Hippocrates in identifying the moment when the form was complete with the first felt kicks of the child in the womb (quickening) and in placing this transition at 40 days for males and 90 for females (*History of Animals* 7.3, 583b 3–5, 15–23, see *On Nutriment* 42). This identification, combined with the doctrine of a succession of souls, established the view among many of Aristotle's successors that the unformed/formed distinction was *the* fundamental distinction in embryonic development, the transition, in other words, from not-yet-human to human.

- Aristotle's own account of the origin of the rational soul is notoriously obscure, but it seems that the rational principle is given with the seed and is possessed potentially as soon as the embryo is an independent living being, that is, after about seven days when the mixture of seed and blood has set. 'The third question was, "When does the foetus begin to be human?" The answer is, when it begins to be a foetus, at conception ... when the semen has, as he expresses it, "set" the menstrual blood as rennet sets milk' (Balme 1990, p. 30).

The biological accounts of the embryo put forward in the Hippocratic corpus and in the writings of Aristotle, supplemented but little changed by the great physician Galen in the second century CE, had a profound influence on Christian understanding of the embryo. They set the parameters within which Christians asked the question of when human life began, or, to put it another way, when the human being acquired the rational soul. Furthermore, the interpretation of Aristotle's philosophy of the soul was to attain particular importance in the debates of the high Middle Ages when Aristotle's writings were introduced into the universities of Western Europe. However, it would be naïve to pass straight on to such doctrinal discussions as though theory takes shape in a cultural and ethical vacuum. For, to some degree at least, ideas about the origin of the soul and the beginning of life have both shaped and been shaped by ethical attitudes to early human life. Before examining Christian discussion of the question as to when the rational soul was acquired, it is therefore necessary to examine attitudes towards nascent human life among Greeks and Romans, Jews and Christians in the ancient world. In the case of pagan society it is necessary to consider the practice of infanticide, for where children were not granted protection even after birth, it is unlikely that much consideration would be given to the embryo in the womb.

3

Discarded Children

Contrasting the humanity of the present age with the barbarism of
antiquity, great stress has been laid on the savage custom of exposing
the children whom their parents could not maintain.

(Mary Wollstonecraft, *A Vindication of the Rights of Women*)

In contemporary society, most of those who support legal access to
abortion argue that there is an important ethical distinction between
taking the life of a new-born child and taking the life of a foetus.
Even in countries such as the USA and the UK which have
adopted relatively permissive legal frameworks for abortion, it
nevertheless remains a serious criminal offence to kill a child once
it has been born. The deliberate killing of an infant, whether by his
or her parents, by a childminder, by a stranger, or by another child,
is regarded as a shocking crime. The lack of such a sharp
distinction between abortion and infanticide in ancient Greek and
Roman attitudes is striking. By and large, those cultures and writers
who accepted, permitted or advocated abortion, accepted,
permitted or advocated infanticide in equal measure. An illustration of this attitude is provided by a letter written in the first century
CE by a Greek-speaking Roman citizen.

> Know that I am still in Alexandria ... I ask and beg you to take good
> care of our baby son, and as soon as I received payment I shall send
> it up to you. If you are delivered (before I come home), if it is a boy
> keep it, if a girl, discard it. (Lewis 1983, p. 54)

Such a casual acceptance of infanticide seems to have been not the
exception but the rule among both Greeks and Romans in the
centuries immediately preceding the birth of Christ. The Jewish
philosopher Philo claimed that it was a common belief among the
Greeks that a child only became human after it was first fed (*Life of
Moses* 1.11). In Roman law the power of the father over the

household, the *patria potestas*, included the power of life or death for new-born infants. There was no need for a father to justify to anyone else the decision to dispose of one of his own offspring.

One common reason given for killing a new-born child was the presence of deformity or obvious disability. Cicero asserted that the twelve tablets (the basis of Roman law) contained the statute that 'deformed infants shall be killed' (*On the Laws* 3.8). According to Seneca, it was the Roman custom to 'drown children at birth who are weakly and abnormal'. This practice he defended on the basis that 'it is not passion, but reason, to separate the useless from the fit' (*On Anger* 1.15).

Aristotle held that no deformed child should be permitted to live (*Politics* 7:14), while Plato recommended infanticide not only for disabled children but also for the children of parents who were judged unfit to reproduce (*Republic* 5, 461c). Probably the city in the ancient world most notorious for infanticide was Sparta. According to Plutarch (*Lycurgus* 1), the Spartans developed a systematic approach to deciding which children should be reared. The elders of the city would examine the child. If it appeared to be healthy and strong, the father was obliged to rear it. If it was sickly or deformed it was exposed in a ravine called Apothetae. There is reason to be wary of Plutarch's account, for it was written at some historical distance from the customs it relates and may not be reliable. Nevertheless, to the extent that the alleged customs of Sparta show the same fundamental attitude towards eugenic infanticide as that found more generally among Greeks and Romans, Plutarch's account is quite believable.

A good source for common Greek practice is Soranus of Ephesus, a physician who wrote an important early work on gynaecology intended for the instruction of midwives. It includes a revealing section on how to identify which infants are 'worth rearing' (*Gynaecology* 2.6). The midwife would put the child on the ground and examine it to see if it cried vigorously, if its limbs were well formed and if its passages were not blocked. If the child was worth rearing the midwife would lift it up and hand it to the father. Sonarus did not say what was to happen to the infants who were thought unworthy to be reared, but by implication, they were to be disposed of in some way or other.

In addition to such legal, philosophical and medical material, there is other evidence that the attitude to infant death in ancient Rome differed markedly from the attitude to the death of an adult. Given the high rates of infant mortality in the ancient world, there are proportionately very few inscriptions in Rome commemorating the lives of children, and especially few from the higher echelons of society. It is clear that children were not always given a formal interment. Unlike adults, children could be buried inside the city walls and many were actually buried inside the home. These facts are open to different interpretations and their significance has been disputed (Golden 1988). Nevertheless, on the face of it, the lack of formal commemoration seems to imply that the loss of an infant was mourned less than the loss of an adult.

This interpretation receives further support from another piece of ancient Roman legislation. According to Plutarch, 'Numa prescribed rules regulating the days of mourning, according to certain times and ages. As, for example, a child of three years was not to be mourned at all; one older, up to ten years, for as many months as it was years old' (*Numa Pompilius* 12). If we accept this reading of the archaeological evidence, we are not thereby committed to the view that the ancients did not care about their children. Many parents may still have been inconsolable over the death of their child. Nevertheless, their grief would have been deprived of public sanction or acknowledgement, and, in general, the loss even of a wanted child would not have been viewed as meriting the same sympathy as would the death of a parent, a brother or sister, a husband or a wife.

So far we have considered infanticide and the exposure of infants as though they were equivalent. It is likely that in many cases (such as the reported customs of Sparta) the aim was indeed that the child would die of exposure. However, in at least some cases exposing infants should probably be thought of not as intentional killing, but as abandonment, perhaps with the hope that the child might be rescued by someone else. The custom of leaving children at a particular place such as the temple, market-place or the *columna lactaria* in Rome (so called because wet nurses were provided for children abandoned there (Carrick 2001, p. 142 n. 40)) allowed a much higher chance of these infants being found by prospective adopting parents. The practice of exposing infants was also given apparent sanction by many examples from Greek and Roman myth where the children survived to become great figures. Ion, the founder of Ionia, Oedipus, Poseidon and Paris, initiator of the Trojan wars, were all depicted as abandoned children. The very founders of Rome, Romulus and Remus, were supposed to have been thrown into the Tiber, only to survive and to be reared by wolves. Such stories perpetuated the idea that the destiny of the abandoned child lay in the hands of the gods.

It seems likely that people did make a distinction, at least in their own minds, between exposing infants on the one hand and, on the other, active infanticide such as drowning or smothering. For example, the Christian apologist Lactantius commented that, if parents were 'too upright' to strangle their children, they would expose them instead (*Divine Institutions* 6.20). However, both pagan and Christian authors pointed out that the reality facing abandoned infants was likely to be grim indeed. Many children must have died before being found, and those who were found were often taken into slavery or prostitution. The Roman playwright Terence wrote a scene in which a man told his wife to do away with their new-born daughter. The woman disobeyed her husband and had the child exposed, in the hope that someone might find her. When he found this out, the man berated his wife for what he regarded as misguided pity. He feared that his daughter would then be condemned to a life of forced prostitution (*Heauton-timorumenos* Act II, scene v; Carrick 2001, p. 148 n. 38; see also Justin Martyr *Apology* 1.27). Tertullian took this fear a stage further and, perhaps alluding to the story of Oedipus, warned men who exposed their children that they may later find themselves unwittingly making use of their own daughters as prostitutes! (*To the Nations* 1.16).

Given the widespread acceptance of exposure and infanticide, it is no surprise that abortion was also tolerated throughout much of the Graeco-Roman world. Although the reasons for seeking abortion overlapped to a considerable extent with the reasons for resorting to infanticide (as for example in the case of abortion or infanticide to limit the family size), there were none the less important differences. In the days before prenatal screening there was no eugenic abortion. It was only after the child was born that disability could be determined. One reason why a woman might specifically seek abortion was to conceal the fact of having become pregnant – if, for example, the child was conceived out of wedlock or from adultery, or if her husband wanted another child but she did not. Alternatively, abortion might be sought where the pregnancy was thought to pose a health risk to the mother. Abortion and infanticide, though closely analogous from the perspective of disposing of a child, had very different implications for the expectant mother, both in terms of risks and in terms of perceived benefits.

There were various methods of abortion practised in the ancient world. It was generally known that a blow to the abdomen could cause a miscarriage. The Hippocratic text on the nature of the child suggested the use of vigorous movement to produce the same effect (*NC* 13). Soranus also advocated this method (*Gynaecology* 1.19). A related practice was 'womb-binding' – binding cloth tightly around the abdomen. This way of inducing a miscarriage seems to have been used particularly in the third century CE (Hippolytus, *Refutation of all Heresies* 9.7; Origen, *Against Heresies* 9).

Another class of techniques was the use of drugs to induce abortion, either drunk as potions or applied as vaginal suppositories (pessaries). Soranus advocates this approach and suggests several abortifacient recipes (*Gynaecology* 1.19). The prevalence of such techniques is also attested to by ancient pagan authors (Hippocratic Oath; Celsus, *On Medicine* 5.21) and many times by early Christian writers (Hippolytus, *Refutation of all Heresies* 9.7; Clement of Alexandria, *Christ the Educator* 2.10; Basil, *Letters* 188.8; *Jerome*, Letters 22.13; Ambrose, *Hexanneron* 5.18; Augustine, *On Marriage and Concupiscence* 1.17). The great second-century physician Galen was also aware that there were drugs that had the effect of 'rupturing the membranes of the embryo and so destroying it' (*On the Natural Faculties* 3.12), but it is not clear whether he was recommending their use for this purpose or warning against their inadvertent use by women who were pregnant.

Finally there were surgical procedures, but these seem to have been measures of last resort used either when the woman was in grave difficulties during delivery (Soranus, *Gynaecology* 4.3;

Tertullian, *On the Soul* 25; *Mishnah Oholot,* 7.6) or to retrieve the body of a child who had died inside the womb (Celsus, *On Medicine* 7.29; Augustine, *Enchiridion* 86). Prior to the availability of sterilized instruments and general anaesthetic, surgery was very risky and accordingly was usually only applied as a last resort.

There were thus various methods of abortion available in the ancient world, with technical knowledge widespread among midwives as well as physicians. However, there do not seem to have been any methods that were wholly free from risk. According to some authors, women 'frequently' died from the effects of abortion (Jerome, *Letters* 22; Suetonius, *Domitian* 22). This was perhaps one consideration behind Soranus's conviction that abortion should only be procured for serious medical reasons.

No doubt there were many people then, as now, who regarded abortion as being a lesser evil than infanticide. However, there were also reasons why, in the ancient world, someone might find abortion a *greater* evil than infanticide. Abortion did not distinguish between healthy infants and disabled infants. It might be sought for reasons of vanity or might be used to conceal pregnancy and to make decisions without reference to the husband or the father of the child. It could result in serious harm to the mother. In these regards infanticide was more acceptable than abortion and overall it may even have been the more common practice.

Having drawn careful distinctions between the exposure of infants, active infanticide and abortion, it should be borne in mind that the social acceptability of these different actions was shaped by a common underlying attitude. All, if done with the husband's blessing, were legal and relatively acceptable in ancient Greek and Roman society. None carried serious legal, religious or social censure. Human life in its earliest stages was not regarded as worthy of the same respect or protection as the life of an adult and neither did birth generally mark the transition to full legal protection in the way it does in contemporary society. Nevertheless, while the common Graeco-Roman that attitude to abortion, exposure and infanticide was one of tacit approval, there were also important voices of criticism within these societies. Infanticide, though permitted in Rome and in many Greek city-states, was a capital offence in Thebes (Aelian, *Varia Historia*), while in Athens the child was given protection from the time it was ritually received into the community on the tenth day after birth (Carrick 1985, p. 209 n. 8).

From the first century BCE a number of Roman writers began to raise criticisms about abortion: Seneca praised his mother for not crushing 'the hope of children who were being nurtured in her body' (*Consolation to Helvia* 17); Juvenal wrote that the abortionist was paid to 'murder humankind in the womb' (*Satires* 7); and Ovid considered the mother's act of killing her unborn offspring more savage than the tigress or lioness, for they do not devour their own cubs. He thought it justice if she died in the warfare she began (*Amores* 2.14). Cicero appealed to a common Roman sentiment when he criticized abortion as an attack on the future of the republic and on the rights of the father. According to Plutarch, even in the times of the kings abortion without consent from the husband was grounds for divorce, and under Severus and Antoninus in the second century CE this kind of abortion became an offence punishable with exile (Justinian, *Digest* 47, 11, 4). Ulpian makes no mention of the husband's permission, but states baldly that abortion should be punishable by exile (*Digest* 48, 8, 8). At the same time a Roman law against poisoning was being applied to those who gave abortifacient drugs. This was to be punished by exile, or if the woman also died, it was to be treated as murder (*Digest* 48, 19, 38, 5). These developments in Roman law should probably not be interpreted as due to Christian influence upon the law, for at this point Christianity was still very much on the outside of the Roman establishment. They are better seen as a response to falling birth-rates, especially among the higher social classes (Noonan 1965, pp. 20–29). Many Romans feared that Rome herself was in decline and would eventually be overrun by barbarians from the north and east. This concern was reinforced by anxiety about the loss of stability of the family and the subsequent erosion of the authority of the paterfamilias (Connery 1977, p. 32).

From the perspective of the later tradition, one of the most important ancient Greek texts to oppose abortion was the doctor's oath attributed to the great fourth-century physician Hippocrates. Those who took the oath had to swear 'I will give no deadly medicine to anyone if asked, nor suggest any such counsel; and, in like manner I will not give to a woman a pessary to produce abortion' (Jones, 1924). The date and origin of the oath are obscure, and parts of it appear to contradict elements of medical practice found in other Hippocratic writings. As noted above, one Hippocratic physician felt no qualms about recommending vigorous movement to procure a miscarriage (*NC* 13). Could it be that the oath forbade abortion by pessary but allowed abortion by physical exertion? Or was the oath a late addition or alien intrusion into the Hippocratic corpus? What is certain is that by the first century CE the oath was known and was regarded as an ethical authority by a number of physicians. Scribonius Largus praised Hippocrates for prohibiting abortion in the oath. 'For he who considers it a crime to injure future life still in doubt, how much more criminal must he then judge it to harm a full grown human being' (*On Remedies*, Preface). A century later Soranus stated that some of his contemporaries would not prescribe abortive drugs or pessaries.

> For one party banishes abortives, citing the testimony of Hippocrates who says 'I will give to no one an abortive'; moreover, because it is the specific task of medicine to guard and preserve what has been engendered by nature. (*Gynaecology* 1.19)

Soranus himself held that, when it was done to preserve the life and health of the mother, abortion was compatible with the task of medicine, but not if it were sought for reasons of vanity or to conceal adultery.

While the Hippocratic Oath was clear in its prohibition of abortive measures, it was unclear whether the reason for this prohibition rested on the belief that the embryo or foetus was regarded as a human person. The existence of a prohibition on abortion does not necessarily imply that those who first took the Oath held that human life began at conception. The prohibition was compatible both with the view that the embryo was a person from conception and with the view that Nature was not to be thwarted in bringing the not-yet-personal embryo to birth. It is noteworthy that the prohibition of assisted suicide is phrased in terms of the giving of a deadly (*thanasimon*) drug, but the abortive is described not as deadly or homicidal but only as destructive (*phthorion*). This leaves open the possibility that abortion was thought wrong for reasons other than homicide. The reason Soranus gave that some of his contemporaries refused to prescribe abortives was that 'it is the specific task of medicine to guard and preserve what has been engendered by nature' (*Gynaecology* 1.19). If it was the task of medicine to promote and preserve health and to heal disease, acting to assist nature, then it would have been wrong for a physician deliberately to cause ill-health, as is the case in bringing about a miscarriage (a point emphasized by Kass 1988, p. 235). The prohibition could also have stemmed from a respect for the processes of nature and for the life-that-is-coming-to-be.

The influence of the Hippocratic Oath has been truly remarkable. Despite its pagan origin it has been quoted with approval by Christians, Jews and Muslims, and many later oaths have been modelled on it. Generations of physicians found in the Oath an ethical clarity that helped them to understand their role and responsibility. Many centuries in the future, the opposition of the Oath to abortion would encourage nineteenth-century physicians in their campaign for more effective abortion legislation. This will be explored in Chapter 13. At this point it should be noted that the critical stance of the Hippocratic Oath towards abortion seems to represent a minority position in the pagan world.

Abortion and infanticide were accepted by a large part of Greek and Roman society. Nevertheless, this acceptance was generally qualified in some way. Aristotle allowed abortion, but only 'before life and sense begin'. Soranus allowed abortion, but only for medical reasons. Roman law allowed abortion, but only with the consent of the woman's husband. Roman law gave the father the power of life or death over a child, but in Athens infanticide was permitted only before the tenth day, and in Thebes it was a capital crime. Cicero and Seneca approved of infanticide, but only for reason of disability. They were also among a number of voices criticizing the practice of abortion in the Rome of their day. Interestingly, it is also from this period, the first century CE, that we have the first evidence of doctors following the Hippocratic Oath and refusing to procure abortions, and that from the second century CE we see Roman law increasingly restricting abortion and punishing the giving of abortifacient drugs.

In summary, the picture is mixed:

- The exposing of infants, infanticide and abortion were common practices widely accepted for a number of reasons within ancient Greek and Roman society. In particular, infanticide was widely advocated in the case of disabled children. However, the exposure of children was not always intended as infanticide. It was sometimes tantamount to abandonment in the hope that the child would be found and adopted.
- The death even of a wanted child was not thought equivalent to the death of an adult.
- While infanticide and abortion were socially acceptable, this acceptance was subject to various qualifications. The right to procure abortion rested with the husband of the woman, and not with the woman herself. In Rome, abortion against the wishes of the husband was punishable by exile.
- There were a number of methods for procuring abortion attested in the ancient world, but all carried attendant health risks. Not least for this reason abortion may have been less acceptable and less common than exposure and infanticide.
- Certainly from the first century CE, and probably much earlier, there were some ancient physicians who would only induce abortions for medical reasons, and others who would not induce abortions for any reason at all.

Though qualified in various ways, the culture of ancient Greece and Rome was open to abortion, infanticide and the exposure of infants. Thus, there is no precedent from the ancient world for the contemporary distinction between abortion and infanticide, permitting the former while forbidding the latter. If anything, infanticide may have been more widely accepted than abortion. The infanticidal culture of Rome and Greece was the context in which the gospel was first preached and Christian communities were first established. It was also the background to the emergence of rabbinic Judaism in the aftermath of the fall of Jerusalem and the destruction of the Temple. However, as we shall see, Jewish and early Christian attitudes to abortion and infanticide were in the sharpest contrast to those of their pagan contemporaries.

4

Grieving in Ramah

However, the Jews see to it that their numbers increase. It is a deadly sin to kill a born or unborn child, and they think that eternal life is granted to those who die in battle or execution – hence their eagerness to have children, and their contempt for death.

(Tacitus, *Histories*)

The Greeks living within small city-states were often troubled by the perceived threat of overpopulation. This is evident in the writings of Hesiod, Plato, Aristotle, Polybius and others. Rather than resort to infanticide, Aristotle recommended that family size be limited by early abortion 'before life and sense' (*Politics* 7:14). Soranus is credited with being the first to make a clear distinction between abortion and contraception and to seek to develop effective contraceptive measures as an alternative to abortion (*Gynaecology* 1.19). Solutions varied, but there was a recurrent Greek anxiety about overpopulation, family size and control of fertility.

However, when we move from Athens to Jerusalem and from pagan to Jewish mores, there is a clear contrast in attitudes. Far from being a curse, population expansion was seen as a blessing and as a fulfilment of the divine command: 'be fruitful and multiply, and fill the earth and subdue it' (Genesis 1:28). In rabbinic Judaism, this verse came to be regarded as the first of the 613 Commandments of the Torah (Feldman 1974, p. 46; Jakobovits 1988, p. 68). The enumeration of the Commandments in this way was a development subsequent to the parting of the ways of Judaism and Christianity. Nevertheless, to regard this verse as the first and most basic (though not the greatest) commandment is fully in keeping with the spirit of the Hebrew Scriptures. The theme of progeny, offspring and inheritance is essential both to the story of the people of Israel, the progeny of Abraham, and to the story of the human race as a whole, the progeny of Adam and of Eve.

Everywhere in the Hebrew Scriptures fertility is described as a blessing, whereas barrenness is regarded as a curse: Sarah, the wife of Abraham, was blessed with a child in her old age (Genesis 21:2). The Lord had pity on Leah because her husband loved only Rachel, so he gave her children and made Rachel barren (Genesis 29:31). Later God remembered Rachel and she too conceived (Genesis 30:22). The theme of the barren woman crying to God and God granting a child is repeated a number of times. When Hannah was barren, she wept and prayed before the Lord promising that if she conceived, she would consecrate her child to the Lord's service. The Lord answered her prayer and the child she bore was Samuel, the prophet who would anoint Saul and then David as king over Israel (1 Samuel 1:11-20). The blessing of children is one of the rewards promised to those who keep the commandments (Deuteronomy 28:4-11). The man who fears the Lord is promised that 'your wife will be like a fruitful vine within your house; your children will be like olive shoots around your table' (Psalm 128:3). His hope is not only to have children but to see his children's children (Psalm 128:6). Children are thus archetypal of the blessings given by God.

Similarly, there is no worse suffering than to lose a child. The death of the firstborn was the last and worst of the plagues of Egypt (Exodus 12:29). The loss of all his sons and daughters was the first of the sufferings of Job (Job 1:13-21). The book of Deuteronomy promised blessings for those who kept the commandments but curses for those who disobeyed. The curses threatened in Deuteronomy closely anticipated the great catastrophe of 587 BCE when Jerusalem was sacked and the people were taken into exile in Babylon. Deuteronomy thus presented the opposite of the blessing of children not as barrenness but as exile: 'You shall have sons and daughters, but they shall not remain yours, for they shall go into captivity' (Deuteronomy 28:41). The exile was also the setting for a famous passage from the prophet Jeremiah. Here the destruction of Jerusalem and the exile in Babylon, the most traumatic events to befall the kingdom of Judah in its history, were portrayed by the inconsolable grief of a mother weeping over the loss of her children. The woman here was Rachel, wife of Jacob (Genesis 29:28), renamed Israel (Genesis 32:28), weeping over the loss of the children of Israel in exile.

A voice is heard in Ramah,
lamentation and bitter weeping.
Rachel is weeping for her children;
she refuses to be comforted for her children
because they are no more.

(Jeremiah 31:15; see also Matthew 2:18)

There is no evidence from the Hebrew Scriptures of Jews voluntarily resorting to infanticide or abortion to limit their families. However, they suffered from enforced infanticide. While they were slaves in Egypt their Egyptian overlords told the midwives to kill all male children as soon as they were born in order to control their population (Exodus 1:8-22). However, the midwives would not do this because they feared God (Exodus 1:17, 21). Similarly, one of the worst atrocities committed by the enemies of Israel was the ripping open of pregnant women (2 Kings 8:12, 15:16; Hosea 13:16; Amos 1:13). This terrible crime was accompanied by dashing to pieces their little ones (2 Kings 8:12; Hosea 13:16). The only allusion to the regular practice of infanticide by Jews was to the ritual offering of children to the god Molech. However, this activity was explicitly condemned by the Scriptures (Leviticus 18:21, 20:2-5; 2 Kings 23:10; Jeremiah 32:35).

There are no examples of self-induced abortion in the Scriptures. However, there is a passage that Jewish commentators have applied to the question of abortion. It is taken from the story of Noah (Genesis 9:6). The text can be read in two ways because of the ambiguity in the meaning of the Hebrew preposition *be* (either 'by' or 'in'):

(a) Whoever sheds the blood of a human, *by* a human shall that person's blood be shed;
(b) Whoever sheds the blood of a human *in* a human, that person's blood shall be shed.

If this verse is read in the second way (b), it becomes a prohibition of abortion. In this case abortion would be classified as homicide and would be a capital offence. An important passage in the Talmud accepted this interpretation of the verse. 'Who is this "man in man"? It refers to the foetus in the mother's womb' (R. Yishmael in *Babylonian Talmud Sanhedrin* 57b). As this commandment is given to Noah, before the covenant with Moses, the text was read as applying to Gentiles rather than to Jews. This was made explicit much later by Maimonides: 'A "Son of Noah" who killed a person, even a foetus in its mother's womb, is capitally liable' (*Yad, Hilekot Melakim* 9, 4; see Feldman 1974, p. 260). On the face of it, the capital punishment implies that the foetus has the same status as a born child. However, this seems to run counter to other passages in the Talmud in which birth was regarded as giving full legal status to the child. Some rabbis therefore endeavoured to explain the passage from Genesis as a reaction against the excessive practice of abortion among pagans (Feldman 1974, p. 259 n. 45). Nevertheless, when taken at face value, the language of 'a human in a human' (*ha'adam ba'adam*) especially when set alongside the capital penalty, strongly suggests that Rabbi Yishmael regarded the foetus as a true human being.

The importance of this text from Genesis for the tradition is much diminished by the fact that it was regarded by Jews as referring only to Gentiles: the sons of Noah. At the same time it was not taken up by Christians for the simple reason that the common Greek translation used by Christians did not leave open the anti-abortion reading. The Septuagint (LXX) version of the text simply reads: 'Whoever sheds the blood of a man, his blood shall be shed.' Much more important both in Jewish and Christian discussion of abortion is a passage that occurs in the book of Exodus immediately after the giving of the ten commandments. It is useful to quote from Robert Young's translation of 1862, as this gives a more literal reading of the Hebrew than some more recent translations.

> 22. And when men strive, and have smitten a pregnant woman, and her children [*yeled* (pl.)] have come out [*yatsa'*], and there is no mischief ['*ason*], he is certainly fined, as the husband of the woman doth lay upon him, and he hath given through the judges; 23. and if there is mischief, then thou hast given life for life, 24. eye for eye, tooth for tooth, hand for hand, foot for foot, 25. burning for burning, wound for wound, stripe for stripe. (Exodus 21:22-5, *Young's Literal Translation*)

This passage has given rise to a number of different traditions of interpretation, three of which demand particular consideration. For the sake of convenience I shall call these the *rabbinic*, the *Septuagintal* and the *evangelical* interpretations.

According to the *rabbinic interpretation*, this passage should be understood as saying that killing the pregnant woman is a capital offence, whereas causing a miscarriage, and killing the unborn children in the process, only merits a fine. The common rabbinic approach to the text presupposes this reading. In the *Mekilta*, an early Jewish commentary or *midrash* on the Scriptures, it is commented that only the killing of an ensouled human being (*nephesh adam*) is a capital offence (*Mekilta* to Exodus, *Nezikin*, Ch. 8). It seems to be implied that the destruction of the unborn child is not the killing of an ensouled human being. This view also seems to be reflected in the Talmud (*Babylonian Talmud Niddah* 44b, see Feldman 1974, p. 254 n. 17). The same tradition of interpretation was evident in the writing of historian Josephus:

> He that kicks a woman with child, so that the woman miscarry, let him pay a fine in money, as the judges shall determine, as having diminished the multitude by the destruction of what was in her womb; and let money also be given the woman's husband by him that kicked her; but if she die of the stroke, let him also be put to death, the law judging it equitable that life should go for life. (*Antiquities of the Jews* 4.8.33)

If the woman dies the assailant should be put to death because 'life should go for life'. However, a miscarriage, in which the unborn child dies, does not merit 'life for life' but only a fine. Josephus states that causing a miscarriage 'diminishes the multitude by destroying what is in her womb'. There is a real injustice here, not only to the mother but to the foetus and to the human race: what is in the womb is 'destroyed' and the multitude 'diminished'. However, the destruction of what is in the womb is not punished with the death penalty and therefore, arguably, does not seem to amount to homicide in the full sense. In summary, the Talmud and Josephus thus understand the passage as making a distinction between causing a miscarriage (a fine) and causing the death of the woman (life for life) and therefore as punishing abortion differently from homicide.

According to the *Septuagintal interpretation* the passage is to be understood quite differently. The Septuagint translation of the passage reads as follows:

> And if two men are fighting and strike a pregnant woman and her
> infant departs *not fully formed*, he shall be forced to pay a fine:
> according to whatever the woman's husband shall lay upon him, he
> shall give with what is fitting. But if it is *fully formed*, he shall give life
> for life ... (Exodus 21:22-3, LXX, emphasis added)

Rather than a distinction between causing a miscarriage (fine) and
causing the death of the woman (life for life) the Septuagint version
distinguishes death of an 'unformed' infant (fine) from death of a
'formed' infant (life for life). The Septuagintal interpretation is also
expounded by Philo of Alexandria, an older contemporary of
Josephus:

> But if any one has a contest with a woman who is pregnant, and strike
> her a blow on her belly, and she miscarry, if the child which was
> conceived within her is still unfashioned and unformed, he shall be
> punished by a fine, both for the assault which he committed and also
> because he has prevented nature, who was fashioning and preparing
> that most excellent of all creatures, a human being, from bringing him
> into existence. But if the child which was conceived had assumed a
> distinct shape in all its parts, having received all its proper connective
> and distinctive qualities, he shall die. (*On Special Laws* 3.19)

The Septuagint, and the Old Latin translation which was based
on it, were the lens through which the first Christians read the
Scriptures. Even after Jerome's new Vulgate translation in the
fourth century CE, which did not follow the Septuagint version of
Exodus 21:22-3, the Septuagintal interpretation remained popular
thanks to the influence of Scripture commentaries that relied on
the Old Latin (for example Augustine, *Questions on Exodus* 80).
These shaped a tradition of interpretation that was dominant well
into the Christian Middle Ages. However, in more recent times this
approach has fallen out of favour. Since the Reformation, Christian
theologians have increasingly turned to the Hebrew text and have
become increasingly critical of the Septuagint as a translation. The
distinction between unformed and formed is instead generally
believed to reflect the influence of Greek philosophy, and
particularly of Aristotle (see Chapter 2), on the attitudes of
Greek-speaking Jews outside Palestine.

Some differences between the Septuagint and the Hebrew text
were evident even at the time when the books were being

translated. 'Not only this book, but even the Law itself, the Prophets and the rest of the books differ not a little when read in the original' (*Sirach*, Prologue). Nevertheless, we should be wary of thinking of differences between these versions as simple mistakes due to ignorance. Some differences may reflect variant readings of the Hebrew; others may embody alternative interpretations of a text. In each case the basis of the difference needs to be assessed. In the particular case of Exodus 21:22-3, Jakobovits (1965, p. 131 n. 7) has claimed that the translator was ignorant of the Hebrew word '*ason* (mischief) and so substituted the Greek word *exeikonismenon* (formed). On the other hand the word '*ason* occurs elsewhere in the Pentateuch, in Genesis 42:4 and 42:38, where the Septuagint translates it *malakia* (weakness or sickness). Rather than assume that the difference is due to ignorance or scribal error, it is perhaps better seen as a deliberate act of interpretation of the Hebrew text. The key is how to understand the assertion 'her children have come out [but] there is no mischief' (Exodus 21:22). The rabbinic interpretation limited mischief to possible harm to the mother. The translator of the Septuagint offers an alternative possibility - mischief could also refer to harm to the child. However, there would be no harm to the child where there was no child, that is, when the embryo was not yet a child. The word '*ason* did not of itself mean 'formed', but in context it could have been understood to imply that the child was formed.

It should also be noted that the word used for 'formed' (*exeikonismenon*) does not reflect the ordinary vocabulary of Greek philosophy. The translator did not use the Aristotelian terms shape (*morphe*) or species (*eidos*). He used the scriptural term image (*eikon*). The embryo becomes a child when it possesses the image. This evokes the story of the creation of human beings in the image of God (Genesis 1:27) and the begetting of Seth according to the image of Adam (Genesis 5:3). The idea that God forms the embryo in the womb is attested many times in the Hebrew Scriptures (see Chapter 1). Furthermore, the view that the foetus is 'formed' at a certain point (specifically at 40 days) is also found in Talmudic literature (*Babylonian Talmud Niddah* 15b and elsewhere, see Feldman 1974, p. 266 n. 81). The figure of 40 days for a male child (and 80 days for a female child) is taken from the ritual of purification for childbirth (Leviticus 12:2-5). The coincidence between these figures and the times given by Aristotle is striking, but there is no reason to suppose direct reliance of Leviticus upon Greek medicine. In the scriptural case, the figures rest more obviously on the symbolic significance of the number 40.

Thus the claim that the child comes to be when it has been formed 'into the image' while in the womb seems to represent Hebrew theology as much as it does Greek philosophy. Furthermore, the Septuagint should not be always regarded as secondary to the Talmudic tradition simply because it is a translation and emerges in the Greek-speaking diaspora. At least in chronological terms, it is prior to most other witnesses to the Hebrew tradition. It dates from the second or third century BCE, that is, approximately 300 years before Josephus was writing, 400 years earlier than the Talmud and 600 years prior to the composition of the *Mekilta*. It is also worth noting that, at this point, the Septuagint is supported by Samaritan and Karaite interpretations of the text (Feldman 1974, p. 258). The interpretation implicit in the Septuagint translation of Exodus 21:22-5 deserves to be taken more seriously than it generally is.

According to the standard *evangelical interpretation*, the first part of this law does not refer to miscarriage at all, but to premature birth in which the children are born alive. This approach to the interpretation of the text has arisen in more recent times particularly, though not exclusively, within the Christian tradition that emerged from the Reformation. The Reformation brought about a renewed interest among Christians in the Hebrew text of the Scriptures. There was a desire to read the text apart from the lens of traditional interpretations, whether those of the rabbis, the Septuagint or the Fathers of the Church. In approaching the text afresh, many of the Reformers (for example Calvin in his *Commentary on Exodus*) were unwilling to exclude the unborn child from being the victim of mischief ('*ason*). For this would seem to contradict God's care for life in the womb as demonstrated elsewhere in the Scriptures. On the other hand, the Reformers were generally unconvinced by the Septuagintal distinction between the formed and unformed embryo. Thus they faced the question of how to understand 'her children have come out, and there is no mischief' (Exodus 21:22). One possible solution to this problem was to suggest that the phrase 'her children have come out' might not mean miscarriage but could mean premature delivery. The passage could then be read as distinguishing between premature live birth (fine) and miscarriage (life for life). Indeed, this third approach to the text has shaped several modern translations of the Scriptures, for example the New International Version:

> If men who are fighting hit a pregnant woman and she *gives birth prematurely* but there is no serious injury, the offender must be fined whatever the woman's husband demands and the court allows. But if there is serious injury, you are to take life for life ... (Exodus 21:22-3, NIV, emphasis added)

Compare this with the New Revised Standard Version:

> When people who are fighting injure a pregnant woman so that *there is a miscarriage*, and yet no further harm follows, the one responsible shall be fined what the woman's husband demands, paying as much as the judges determine. If any harm follows, then you shall give life for life ... (Exodus 21:22-3, NRSV, emphasis added)

In favour of the NIV interpretation it may be noted that the word *yatsa'* can refer to live birth as well as to stillbirth. Indeed, in the Scriptures it is used far more commonly for live birth (Genesis 25:26, 38:28; Job 3:11, 10:18; Jeremiah 1:5, 20:18) than for stillbirth (Numbers 12:12). Furthermore, there is a more specific word for miscarriage that could have been used (*shokol*) and that occurs only a few chapters later in the book of Exodus (23:26). The use of a word that generally connotes live birth, and the avoidance of a readily available word that unambiguously means miscarriage, gives some credibility to this interpretation.

There is also precedent for imposing a fine in a case where no permanent harm is done, and this occurs only a few verses before the text in question. If someone is injured in a brawl but recovers, the person who caused the injury is liable for the loss of time and for expenses necessary to ensure a recovery (Exodus 21:19). An assault that leads to premature birth would involve a serious risk to the child, trauma for the parents and might also involve the need for extra care for mother and child. These harms are difficult to quantify (Exodus 21:22), but they are certainly harms deserving recompense.

In order to get a better understanding of this text, it can be placed in the context of the law-codes of other ancient Near Eastern civilizations.

In the code and Hammurabi (209–14) a distinction is made between simply causing a miscarriage and the case where the woman also dies. The penalties vary with the status of the woman. Ten, five and two shekels for a miscarriage caused to an upper-class woman, free woman and slave respectively. For the death of the woman the penalties were much harsher: killing the daughter of the assailant (upper-class woman), a fine of half a mina of silver (free woman) and a fine of third of a mina of silver (slave). To the extent that there is a parallel to the text of Exodus here, it supports the rabbinic interpretation, for it distinguishes between miscarriage (a lesser penalty) and the death of the woman (a greater penalty).

A parallel Hittite law (17) does not mention harm to the woman, but the fine is made to vary with the age of the foetus: ten shekels of silver for a ten-month foetus, five shekels for a five-month foetus. This could be seen as giving support to the Septuagintal interpretation, in that it is not directly concerned with harm to the woman, and in that it draws a distinction between early miscarriage (lesser penalty) and later miscarriage (greater penalty).

In the *Middle Assyrian Laws* (*MAL*), self-induced abortion is a capital offence punishable by impaling (*MAL* A 53). The punishment for assault leading to a miscarriage is that 'they shall do to him as he would do to her ... he shall compensate for her unborn child with a life' (*MAL* A 50). It is unclear what this compensatory 'life' refers to, whether the life of the assailant's wife, or the life of his child, or possibly the standard financial compensation for taking a life. If the woman also dies, the assailant is to be put to death (*MAL* A 50). If the woman miscarries and is otherwise unharmed but her husband has no other children, the assailant is to be put to death (*MAL* A 50). If someone assaults a prostitute and causes her to miscarry, 'they shall inflict blow for blow upon him; he shall compensate with a life' (*MAL* A 52). There are distinctions here between penalties, but in general it seems that harm to the unborn child is punished with severity on a par with the punishment for harm to both woman and child. It is reiterated that the death of an unborn child must be 'compensated for with a life' (*MAL* A 50, 52).

This parallel supports the evangelical interpretation in that it regards both the woman and the unborn child as potential victims whose death would be punishable with 'life for life'.

Thus, each of the three divergent interpretations of Exodus finds some parallel in other ancient law-codes. It should also be noticed that the parallels that exist between Exodus and various ancient Near Eastern law-codes are partial at best. The use of vicarious punishment in the code of Hammurabi (killing the daughter of the attacker), and the method of execution in the Middle Assyrian Laws (impaling on a stake), should alert us to the differences between these codes and the Jewish Torah. Also all these codes refer to deliberate attack, whereas the assault in Exodus 21 is indirect. Nevertheless, there are parallels, and the fact that each of three interpretations of Exodus can find some support from one or other ancient code should not be thought a trivial or unhelpful result. While it does not resolve the question of the original meaning of the Exodus text, it does confirm that these three interpretations do not exceed the reasonable limits of the meaning of the text in its ancient context.

There are many other interpretations of Exodus 21:22 (Cassuto 1967; Jackson 1973; and Kline 1977 among others), but the three interpretations outlined above have each played a major role within the Christian tradition and have informed families of Scripture translation accepted within various Christian communities. Each has something to be said for it. Each aims at resolving ambiguities in the text as we have it. Nevertheless, the ambiguities remain. Having said this, there is an important point of agreement between the ancient Septuagint translation and the modern evangelical interpretation embodied in translations such as the NIV. This lies in their refusal to exclude the unborn child from being the possible subject of mischief ('ason). This point is also shared with the diverse interpretations of Cassuto, Kline and Jackson. This is a weakness of the rabbinic interpretation. However, it should also be emphasized that in its ancient context none of these schools of interpretation was thought to justify free access to abortion. This is clear from the remarks of Josephus and Philo. The only explicit permission for abortion is found in the rabbinic tradition and relates to the forcible extraction of the infant to save the mother's life.

> If a woman has difficulty in childbirth, one dismembers the embryo within her limb from limb because her life takes precedence over its life. Once its head (or the greater part) has emerged, it may not be touched, for we do not set aside one life for another. (*Misnah, Oholot* 7.6)

The rabbinic interpretation of Exodus 21:22-5 is evident here in the distinction between unborn child (mother takes precedence) and a partially born child (no setting aside one life for another). As with *Mekilta*, the unborn child is not *nephesh adam*. However, it is only because the mother's life is threatened that this action is justified. In the Talmud it is said that the unborn child cannot be regarded as a pursuer (*rodef*) because it has no harmful intent (*Babylonian Talmud Sanhedrin* 72b). Nevertheless, Moses Maimonides states that the unborn child is a pursuer (Feldman 1974, p. 276, n. 48). Maimonides' intention seems to be to restrict therapeutic abortion by specifying that the child has to be an imminent threat to the mother's life and in this way like a pursuer. The analogous discussion of therapeutic abortion within the Christian tradition will be taken up in detail in Chapter 12.

There is a clear consensus among Jews in the ancient world regarding infanticide. It was viewed as homicide in the full sense. Some Jews also regarded abortion as homicide. Interestingly, Philo seems to regard the scriptural case against abortion as clearer than the case against infanticide, for he argues from the capital penalty for abortion to the homicidal character of infanticide:

> So Moses then, as I have said, implicitly and indirectly forbade the exposure of children, when he pronounced the sentence of death against those who cause the miscarriage of mothers in cases where the foetus is fully formed ... therefore infanticide undoubtedly is murder. (*Special Laws* 3.117-18)

According to Josephus, the killing of a foetus was not the taking of a human life, for it did not require 'life for life'. Nevertheless, in another passage Josephus also describes abortion as murder. This is a good illustration of the tension in ancient Jewish texts between those that make a distinction between foeticide and homicide and those that imply that foeticide is homicide.

> The Law orders us to bring up all our children, and forbids women

to cause abortion of that which is begotten; and if any woman seems to have done so, she will be a murderer of her own child, by destroying a living creature. (*Against Apion* 2:202)

Some further insight into ancient Jewish attitudes to abortion may be gained from considering their attitude to preventing conception. According to Genesis, if a man died without children, his brother had a duty to take his wife and bear children for him. Onan not only refused to do this for his brother but resorted to spilling his seed on the ground (Genesis 38:2–10). This action was regarded by the later Jewish tradition as more than just a failure to be fruitful. It was a form of sexual pollution, and also, as the destruction of the seed (*hash-hatat zera*), it was analogous to killing by anticipation (Feldman 1974, pp. 109–23). The idea that destruction of seed could be analogous to homicide has a parallel in early Christian thought and would later play some part in the development of the canon law of the Church in the Middle Ages. If contraception could be viewed as something like homicide, then the destruction of the early embryo must be even more like homicide.

However, condemnation of the destruction of seed (*hash-hatat zera*) was not regarded as applicable to contraceptive measures taken by women. The Talmud explicitly allowed specific categories of women to use a wool plug (*mok*) in order to prevent conception (*Babylonian Talmud Yevamot* 12b; *Niddah* 45a: see Feldman 1974, pp. 169ff.). This asymmetry between men and women is made even more explicit in another passage in the Talmud. 'A man is not permitted to drink a cup of roots (*kos shel ikkarin*) in order to become sterile, but a woman is permitted to drink a cup of roots to become sterile' (*Tosefta Yevamot*, Ch. 8: Feldman 1974, p. 240). There are various explanations of this asymmetry. It may reflect a primitive biology according to which only the male seed has an active role in generation, with the woman being the passive recipient. Against this, it should be pointed out that Hippocrates, Aristotle and Galen all accepted some female analogue to the male seed and that this is reflected in the mention of female seed in the Talmud (*Babylonian Talmud Niddah* 31a). The asymmetry in prohibitions was more probably shaped by a concern with the physical structure of the act. It may also have reflected an asymmetry in the duty to 'be fruitful and multiply', which was taken to be addressed to the man but not the woman.

In summary:

- For the Jewish people procreation was both a divine blessing and divine commandment. There is no evidence that the practices of infanticide and abortion, widespread among their pagan contemporaries, were prevalent among Jews in the ancient world.
- There are a number of possible interpretations of Exodus 21:22-5, but in the ancient world this text was not regarded as justifying abortion except, for the rabbinic interpretation, to save the mother's life.
- Jews in the first and second century CE regarded infanticide as homicide. Abortion was sometimes regarded as homicide, sometimes not as homicide strictly speaking, but as a serious sin against God and nature.
- The act of destroying the seed (*hash-hatat zera*) was regarded both as a form of sexual pollution and as an act analogous to homicide. However, the use of a wool plug (*mok*) or a cup of roots (*kos shel ikkarin*) by a woman to prevent conception were not regarded as such and could be legitimate in certain cases.

The Christian Church saw itself as the 'ingrafted branch' (Romans 11:24) taken from the pagan world and granted a share in the posterity of Abraham. Christian ethical attitudes were thus shaped far more by their Jewish inheritance than by the ethos of the surrounding ancient pagan society. Nevertheless, the Christian approach was unlike that of ancient Judaism in certain important ways. Christians were not bound by the particular juridical precepts of the Mosaic law. For them, the law is fulfilled in spirit by acting with love and justice towards God and neighbour. Nevertheless, as the Church expanded she found herself having to regulate the behaviour of her members and having to develop a law of her own. However, this canon law did not have the status of divine law and it was subject to variation in different regions and to change and development over time.

5

Medicinal Penalties

The church's curse is not the final word,
for Everlasting Love may still return,
if hope reveals the slightest hint of green.
(Dante Alighieri, *Purgatory*, from *The Divine Comedy*)

The starting-point for Christian ethical reflection on abortion was the characterization of abortion as the killing of a child and its repudiation on this basis. This attitude was in continuity with certain Jewish writings of the period (Philo, *Special Laws* 3.117–18; Josephus, *Against Apion* 2.202). The earliest extant Christian text explicitly dealing with abortion is found in the *Didache* or *Teaching of the Twelve Apostles*, a work generally regarded as having been composed in the first century CE. This verse reflects the characteristic stance of the Early Church: 'You shall not kill a child by abortion nor kill it after it is born' (*Didache* 2:2). The same statement, in the same words, occurs in the early second-century *Letter of Barnabas* (19:5). This may reflect reliance on a common source or the influence of the one text on the other. At this stage in Christian reflection there was no mention of any distinction in seriousness between the abortion of a formed foetus and that of an unformed embryo. That distinction, vital in the Septuagint and in Philo, does not seem to have gained influence in Christian thought until the late fourth century.

The doctrine that 'those women who use drugs to bring about an abortion commit murder' was reiterated in a letter from Athenagoras to Marcus Aurelius written in CE 177. *A Plea for the Christians*, as it was known, was typical of a number of apologetic works produced by Christians in the second and third centuries. They aimed to explain Christian belief and practice for a pagan audience in such a way as to persuade the Roman authorities that the Christian religion was not harmful to morals or to society and therefore that it should be tolerated. One malicious accusation levelled at Christians was that they practised child sacrifice. It was to rebut this claim that Athenagoras stressed that Christians regarded both infanticide and abortion as murder. The same point was made to the same effect 20 years later by Tertullian, 'for us murder is once for all forbidden; so it is not lawful for us to destroy even the child in the womb' (*Apology* 9:8). Minucius Felix in the early third century continued this line of thought, pointing out that it was pagans rather than Christians who treated early human life with indifference.

> It is among you that I see newly-begotten sons at times exposed to wild beasts and birds, or dispatched by the violent death of strangulation; and there are women who, by the use of medicinal potions, destroy the unborn life in their wombs, and murder the child before they bring it forth. (*Octavius* 30:2)

Lactantius, at the turn of the fourth century, added that Christians were forbidden to kill not only in ways that were illegal and socially unacceptable but also in ways that were tolerated or even esteemed in pagan society. This was true of strangling new-born infants and of killing unborn children before they had seen the light of day (*Divine Institutes* 6.20).

From these comments it might be thought that the practice of abortion was the preserve of pagans and was virtually unknown among Christians. However, as sermons and letters from the Early Church attest, then as now Christians often failed to practise what they preached. It is in the third century that there is the first direct evidence of Christians deliberately causing abortion. For example, Cyprian of Carthage accused the schismatic priest Novatus of kicking his wife with his heel in order to cause her to miscarry (Letter 52, to Cornelius). In a similar vein Hippolytus accused Callistus, then bishop of Rome, of recognizing irregular marriages between high-born women and men of low social status, with the result that, out of shame for their state they resort to abortion.

> Women who were reputed to be believers began to take drugs to render themselves sterile, and to bind themselves tightly so as to expel what was being conceived, since they would not, on account of

relatives and excess wealth, want to have a child by a slave or by any insignificant person. (*Refutation of all Heresies* 9.7)

In the fourth century the practice of abortion by Christians seems to have become virtually endemic. It was about Christian virgins that Jerome wrote, 'when they find themselves with child through their sin, they use drugs to procure abortion' (Letter 22:13). Similarly it was about married Christians that Ambrose of Milan lamented, 'even the wealthy, in order that their inheritance may not be divided among several, deny in the very womb their own progeny' (*Hexameron* 5.18.58). And again, John Chrysostom found it necessary to confront the men in his congregation, both single and married, for going to prostitutes. For by doing so they were guilty not only of adultery but also, if the woman became pregnant and then procured an abortion, complicit in murder: 'even if she does the deed, you are the cause of it' (*Homily 24 on Romans*). It would not be difficult to multiply examples of the use of abortion by those 'who were reputed to be believers' in the first centuries of the Christian era.

In response to the practice of abortion by Christians, bishops and teachers continued to emphasize its harmful character. Clement of Alexandria sought to bring out the dehumanizing effect of the act, saying that those who procured abortion 'along with the child destroy all humanity' (*The Teacher* 2:10). Augustine regarded abortion not only as an attack on human life but also as an attack on marriage. If a married couple agreed to abort their child they were not spouses at all (*On Marriage and Concupiscence* 1.17). John Chrysostom referred to abortion as 'something even worse than murder' (*Homily 24 on Romans*) because it made childbearing the occasion for killing and turned the womb into 'a chamber for murder' (ibid.).

Minucius Felix, Cyprian, Lactantius and Ambrose all used the word 'parricide' to refer to abortion or infanticide. They were thereby claiming that abortion was worse than other forms of homicide because it involved killing one's own flesh and blood. However, this use of the term was strange by the standards of the time. For parricide generally referred to killing *of* a parent not to killing *by* a parent. By giving the word this novel sense Christians were in fact effecting a radical inversion of Roman assumptions. In

Roman society there was a particular horror of killing a parent (particularly the father) as this implied an attack on authority. It was like a slave raising his hand against his master or a subject rebelling against his legitimate ruler. However, in Christian terms, the scandalous crime of parricide involved not an attack against authority but an attack against the weak and powerless. The use of the term 'parricide' thus reflected a particularly Christian perspective on wrongness of abortion.

Another theme in early Christian writing and preaching on abortion was the threat of divine judgement. For example, Athenagoras of Athens stated that those who procured abortion were guilty of homicide and would 'have to give an account to God' (*A Plea for the Christians* 35:6). The same theme was also present in a number of writings from the second or third century, including the *Apocalypse of Peter* (26) and the *Apocalypse of Paul* (40). These apocalyptic texts portrayed men and women having to face the children they had caused to be aborted. The threat of judgement was experienced as very real and gave expression to the Christian understanding of abortion as a sin against the child and against God. However, it must not be understood as implying that abortion was regarded as an unforgivable sin. For the Christian, the self-offering of Christ had brought forgiveness of every sin without exception and the hope of reconciliation for sinners. The threat of judgement thus applied only to those who did not accept the forgiveness available in Christ.

In addition to preaching and teaching against abortion, therefore, the Church also responded by providing means of forgiveness and reconciliation for those who had procured abortion. This touched upon a much wider issue for early Christians. According to the gospel, Jesus told his disciples that 'the one who believes and is baptized will be saved' (Mark 16:16). By accepting Christ in baptism the believer was cleansed from all the sins of his or her past life and began a new life in Christ, a life marked not only by an external fulfilment of the commandments but by inner conversion of heart. A major concern for the Early Church was thus how to deal with Christians whose subsequent actions contradicted the faith in which they were baptized. On the one hand, the community could not simply accept such behaviour from people who proclaimed themselves to be Christian. On the other hand, the gospels showed Jesus constantly exhorting his disciples to forgive one another (Matthew 18:21; Luke 6:37, 17:3-4 and elsewhere) and, more significantly, showed Jesus giving the apostles the authority to forgive sins: 'Receive the Holy Spirit. If you forgive the sins of any, they are forgiven them; if you retain the sins of any, they are retained' (John 20:22-3). The practical question of how to effect reconciliation at the same time as upholding Christian discipline was the subject of intense debate.

One important witness to the practice of reconciliation in the Early Church was the highly influential second-century work, *The Shepherd of Hermas*. Hermas stated that the Lord had 'established a means of repentance' for those who had committed sins after baptism and that he himself exercised this ministry of reconciliation (*Shepherd*, Commandment 4.3). This example coheres with what is found in the letter of Ignatius of Antioch to the *Philadelphians* and in the *Letter of Barnabas*, in Tertullian's work *On Penance* and in the letters of Cyprian. However, though the practice of reconciling wayward Christians seems to have been present from the earliest days of the Church, reconciliation after very serious sins, for example publicly renouncing the faith or committing adultery, or even murder, remained controversial. As Tertullian came under the sway of Montanism in *On Modesty* he retracted his earlier view about penance and maintained that certain serious sins, if committed after baptism, could never be forgiven. A similar stance was later taken by the Novatians (in the third century) and the Donatists (in the fourth century).

It was in the face of such opposition that the orthodox Christian view became more explicit. The Church had the power to forgive sins, through the action of the bishop, and publicly to reconcile those who had sinned after baptism. This second offer of forgiveness required a demonstration of repentance (an act of penance) on the part of the person seeking reconciliation. The original focus was on rare and serious sins, and the period of penance was generally prolonged. The foundation of church discipline was thus medicinal or expiatory rather than punitive, acknowledging the reality of sin and setting out a path to reconciliation. The medicinal role of penance provided the context for the ecclesiastical censures, sanctions and penalties prescribed by the Church at various times for various sins. They were not, and are not, intended as obstacles to reconciliation, but rather as the means to reconciliation.

The criticisms of the later Tertullian (*On Modesty* 1) and of Hippolytus (*Refutation of all Heresies* 9.7) imply that, in the early third century, the bishop of Rome was accustomed to reconcile Christians who had repented of serious sins such as adultery or murder and thus, by implication, also abortion. However, there are no records of how this occurred or what was required before full reconciliation. It is at the beginning of the fourth century that we have the earliest extant pieces of church law dealing with abortion. These arose from a church synod held in Elvira in Spain in CE 305. Its 81 canons concerned the order or discipline of the Church, including such issues as the celibacy of the clergy and the administration of the sacraments. There were two canons that dealt directly with abortion.

> *Canon 63* If a woman becomes pregnant by committing adultery while her husband is absent, and after the act she destroys the child, it is proper to keep her from communion until death, because she has doubled her crime.

> *Canon 68* If a catechumen becomes pregnant by committing adultery, and after the act she destroys the child, she can be baptized only at the end of her life.

The penalties prescribed in these canons were very severe: a Christian who first committed adultery and then procured an abortion would not be allowed to receive communion, even on her deathbed. A catechumen who did the same thing would not be allowed to receive baptism until her deathbed. This discipline reflected the concerns of those, like Hippolytus, who feared that if penance were too lenient then Christians would be misled as to the seriousness of the sin. It also reflected a time of persecution when those who publicly professed Christianity faced the threat of torture and execution. The canons on abortion, though severe, were no more or less severe than canons on other subjects accepted at this synod.

The long years of sporadic persecution of Christians by pagan Rome came to an end in CE 313, when the Emperor Constantine declared a policy of religious toleration. The following year a council of bishops was held in Ancyra, in the Roman province of Galatia. It contained one canon on abortion, perhaps referring back to the synod of Elvira.

> *Canon 21* Concerning women who commit fornication, and destroy that which they have conceived, or who are employed in making drugs for abortion, a former decree excluded them until the hour of death, and to this some have assented. Nevertheless, being desirous to use somewhat greater leniency, we have ordained that they fulfil ten years of penance.

This canon expressed the self-conscious desire for more leniency in the application of penance than had been the case in former times. The same attitude was shown in regard to the crime of murder, for which life-long penance was imposed, 'but at the end of life let them be indulged with full communion' (Ancyra, canon 22). This law was reinforced at the first great ecumenical council held at Nicaea in CE 325, 'in the case of anyone whatsoever who is dying and seeks to share in the Eucharist, the bishop upon examining the matter shall give him a share in the offering' (Nicaea, canon 13). Pope Innocent I, commenting some time later (around CE 400) on this shift in attitudes stated that 'the earlier practice was more severe, the later more tempered with mercy' (*Letter to Exuperius*). He also pointed out that even the more severe practice of the past, by imposing penance, was offering a path of hope and salvation and not abandoning the repentant sinner altogether.

It should be noticed that both the Councils of Elvira and Ancyra were concerned with abortion subsequent to adultery, and not with abortion in other circumstances. Also, there was a slight difference between the canons in that Ancyra included in the canon not only the woman who underwent the abortion but also the man or woman responsible for 'making drugs for abortion'. After the legislation of Ancyra, the next significant church legislation regarding abortion was to be found in the canons produced by Basil the Great, written in a series of letters in the later fourth century (c. CE 375). Two were directly concerned with abortion.

> *Canon 2* The woman who purposely destroys her unborn child is guilty of murder. With us there is no nice enquiry as to its being

formed or unformed ...The punishment, however, of these women
should not be for life, but for the term of ten years.

Canon 8 Women also who administer drugs to cause abortion, as
well as those who take poisons to destroy unborn children, are
murderesses.

Basil asserted that whoever underwent an abortion, if done
deliberately, and whoever administered drugs to produce an
abortion, was guilty of murder. However, the penance he imposed
was not the 20 years he laid down as the penalty for intentional
homicide (canon 56), but the ten years given by the Council of
Ancyra. Basil was aware of this apparent contradiction, for he
added that what mattered was 'not the mere lapse of time, but the
character of the repentance' (Letter 188, canon 2). A later
commentator gave as a further reason why Basil treated abortion
more leniently: the psychological state of the woman. Abortion was
more likely to have been undergone out of fear or shame than out
of malice (Balsamon, *Commentary on Basil's Canonical Letters*, canon
2). The disparity between the action itself, which was commonly
regarded as *worse than* simple homicide, and the penance given,
which, while substantial, was significantly *less than* the penance for
simple homicide, seems to reflect some sensitivity to the situation of
the woman. Abortion was murder, but it was felt appropriate to
treat those who procured abortion more leniently that the standard
penalty for murder.

Another significant aspect of Basil's legislation was that it rejected
the relevance of the formed/unformed distinction for the purpose
of penance. This may have been because Basil, like his
contemporary Gregory of Nyssa, thought that the soul was given
at conception, or it may be that he thought that destroying an
unformed embryo was ethically equivalent to destroying a formed
foetus, irrespective of when the soul was infused. Whereas the
earlier legislation of the Councils of Elvira and Ancyra did not
mention whether the embryo was formed or unformed, Basil
represented a development in that he explicitly considered and
explicitly rejected the relevance of this distinction.

The distinction that Basil rejected, while already present in the
Septuagint and Philo, did not begin to make itself felt among
Christians until the fourth and fifth centuries. The *Apostolic*

Constitutions was a late fourth-century work which drew on much earlier material. The seventh book closely followed the *Didache*, but added a gloss that seemed to apply the teaching only to the formed foetus. 'You shall not kill a child by abortion nor kill it after it is born. For *everything that is shaped and has received a soul from God*, if killed, shall be avenged, as having been unjustly destroyed' (*Apostolic Constitutions* 7.3, emphasis added). Though this work used earlier material it was not itself apostolic and was not received as a work of genuine apostolic authority. Its was explicitly rejected by the Sixth Ecumenical Council in Trullo in 692 (canon 2) as an unreliable account of the original apostolic teaching. Nevertheless, this document was not alone in claiming that only the killing of a formed foetus constituted homicide. This opinion can be found in Jerome (Letter 121.4), in Augustine's commentary on Exodus (*Questions on Exodus* 80), and in the Pseudo-Augustinian work *Questions on the Old and New Testaments* (23). In this last work, as in the *Apostolic Constitutions*, the completion of formation was identified as the moment when God gave the spiritual soul. The timing of ensoulment was still controversial in the patristic period, and these texts did not have any immediate effect on church law or discipline, but they would become much more important in the later Middle Ages.

Basil's canons were influential in their own time and were later incorporated, along with the legislation of Ancyra, into the canons of Trullo (canon 2). Trullo also added its own canon on abortion: '*Canon 91* Those who give drugs procuring abortion and those who receive poisons to kill the foetus are subjected to the penalty of murder.'

This canon was in turn incorporated into the great canon legal collection of Photius, the *nomocanon* in 883. The canons of Ancyra, Basil and Trullo thus continue to inform canon law in the Orthodox Church to the present day. Abortion is regarded as homicide, though to be treated with a certain leniency and sensitivity to the circumstances. At no point in its canonical history has the Eastern Church embraced an ethical or legal distinction between early and late abortion.

Between the canons of Basil and the Council of Trullo, legislation on abortion was also given at various local Western synods. The Council of Ledira in Spain in 524 distinguished those who sinned by adultery, even if that sin led to abortion, from those who gave poisons (*venefici*) to produce an abortion. The former were to receive a penance of seven years, but the latter were to receive a lifelong penance. The focus on those who administered drugs may reflect the contemporary practice of abortion, but it also drew upon the Roman criminal law which punished *venefici* who gave potentially lethal drugs for non-medical reasons, either as aphrodisiacs, contraceptives or abortifacients (see Chapter 3).

A second important Western council was held at Braga in Portugal in 572, at which Martin promulgated various canons translated from earlier Eastern councils, among them the Council of Ancyra. However, his translation altered the canon on abortion to include those who sought to prevent conception together with those who committed infanticide and abortion (*Braga*, canon 78). This seems to imply that contraception was regarded as in some way analogous to homicide. There was some precedent among Christians for this attitude. It had already been expressed by Jerome (Letter 22:13) and by Caesarius of Arles 'as often as she could have conceived or given birth, of that many homicides she will be held guilty' (Sermon 1:12). The comparison of contraception to homicide brings to mind the Talmudic characterization of the destruction of seed as homicide, as discussed in the previous chapter. However, there are important differences between the two cases. In the Talmud it was the practice of spilling seed that was condemned, while women were permitted to take sterilizing drugs. In Jerome, Caesarius and Martin the immediate focus of condemnation was providing drugs that produced sterility. This context provided an element of continuity in that the same drug might cause sterility or cause abortion and might also endanger the life of the woman who took it. The condemnation of abortion and contraception together was thus subsumed under the heading of poisoning, *veneficium* or *maleficium*, a category taken from Roman law. This characterization of contraception as quasi-homicide was to have a long history, coming to particular prominence due to a canon in Regio of Prum's *Book of Synods* (book 2, canon 89) in the early tenth century.

At the same time as Martin of Braga was promulgating the

canons of the Eastern Church for a Western audience, important changes in the pattern of church discipline were beginning to develop in the Church in Ireland, changes that would spread first to Anglo-Saxon Britain and then to Frankish Gaul. The relative dominance of monasticism in the Celtic and Anglo-Saxon churches gave rise to a practice of penance and reconciliation that was defined not primarily by length of time away from communion but by time spent fasting and abstaining from meat and alcohol. Defined in this way, penances tended to be shorter but more arduous than the previous canonical penances. In this semi-monastic context penance and reconciliation were also more private in character and could be repeated several times. To support these developments a new form of literature emerged, the penitential, giving the different tariffs appropriate to different sins. One of the earliest known Irish penitentials was that of Finnian from the early sixth century. It dealt with abortion as *maleficium*, imposing penance of six months bread and water plus two years abstinence from meat and alcohol on the person who caused the abortion. As with the earlier canonical tradition there was no variation according to the age of the embryo, and, as with Basil and Ancyra, the penalty, while significant, was lower than that for the sin of murder. Finnian's penitential was followed by Columban in the late sixth century and this, in turn, influenced others.

A later tradition represented by the Irish canons (late seventh century), the Bigotian Penitential (early eighth century) and the Old Irish Penitential (early ninth century) made a distinction between penances depending on the age of the foetus. For example, the Old Irish Penitential gave three and a half years penance for abortion after the pregnancy had become established, but seven years if the flesh had formed and fourteen years if the soul had entered. Thus this tradition, in marked contrast to Basil, related penance directly to the stage of the embryo. It was also remarkable in reflecting not a two-stage but a three-stage process. In the first stage the embryo was unformed 'like water'; in the second stage the flesh was formed but had no soul; in the third stage the foetus gained a soul. This threefold pattern is not found in Aristotle or the Septuagint, but something like it can be found in Hippocrates and there are parallels in the Talmud and in the Koran. It may simply reflect the re-emergence of the distinction between formation and quickening. If this interpretation is correct then, for these writers, abortion was not true homicide if done before the first signs of movement of the child in the womb. Nevertheless, early abortion was still regarded as a serious sin and required three and a half years' arduous penance.

The first Anglo-Saxon penitentials were written in the late seventh century and associated with Theodore, Archbishop of Canterbury. These also made a distinction depending on the age of the embryo: before 40 days the penance was one year; after 40 days it was the same as the penance for homicide – three years. Bede followed Theodore, adopting the same distinction at 40 days and the same penalties of one and three years respectively. However, Bede also stressed the need for the situation and motivation of the woman to be taken into consideration in setting the level of penance. In this way the theme of leniency towards the woman received a much sharper focus, depending on the extent to which the action had been constrained by the circumstances. This theme would be taken up by later writers.

As the influence of Celtic and Anglo-Saxon penitentials became felt in Gaul and Spain they came in direct conflict with the older model of public penance in accordance to canons adopted by local churches. At the Council of Toledo (589) the new penitentials were condemned as an abuse. Nevertheless, increasing numbers of these handbooks of penance were written in the seventh and eighth centuries in mainland Europe. On the question of abortion, most of these followed the earlier Irish tradition and made no distinction for penance according to the age of the embryo, but others followed the Irish canons or the Anglo-Saxon penitentials. The multiplication of different books giving different penances for the same sin and without any firm legal or ecclesiastical authority behind them was regarded with increasing frustration in the late eighth and early ninth centuries, the period of the Carolingian reform. There was a series of attempts to revive the ancient system of public penance, but these revivals failed to take root as the customs and attitudes of Western Christians seem to have shifted irreversibly in the direction of regular private penance. Nevertheless, these attempts had the effect of causing the demise of the penitential literature that had characterized the Irish and Anglo-

Saxon churches. What gradually emerged in the Middle Ages was a two-tier system in which most sins were dealt with by private penance while a limited number of specified sins attracted public canonical penalties.

The development of canon law in the West from the eleventh century onwards looked not to the penitentials but to collections of early canons and to the Fathers of the Church. Opinions were taken from the letters, sermons and treatises of authorities such as Augustine, Jerome and Ambrose. On this basis there were three possible positions that could be held with respect to abortion:

- abortion was homicide whatever the stage of pregnancy
- abortion was homicide only after formation/ensoulment
- contraception was homicide as was abortion whatever the stage of pregnancy.

The first claim represents the dominant tradition from the *Didache* to Trullo reaffirmed in the West in CE 848 at the Council of Worms (canon 35). Nevertheless, from the late fourth century both the second and third opinions became increasingly influential. It is noticeable that these later alternatives, while seemingly contradictory, gained strength simultaneously and could often be found espoused by the same author. Jerome was an important authority for both lines of thought (Letters 121 and 22 respectively).

In the eleventh century, Ivo of Chartres in his *Decretum* cited Jerome (Letter 121.4), Augustine (*Questions on the Heptateuch* 2.80) and Pseudo-Augustine (*Questions on the Old and New Testaments* 23) as support for the assertion that abortion before ensoulment was not homicide. The same set of texts was taken up in the twelfth century by Gratian in his *Concordance of Discordant Canons* and by Peter Lombard in the *Sentences*. The intellectual influence of these two works in the medieval West cannot be overstated. Together they comprised the foundation of church law and theology for the whole of the Middle Ages.

In the thirteenth century, the Dominican Raymond of Pennaforte produced a new collection of canon law for Gregory IX, the *Decretals*. As well as using Ivo and Gratian, he also followed the *Decretum* of Burchard of Worms in regarding both contraception and abortion as homicide (*Decretals* V, tit. 12, can. 5). As authority for this Raymond cited the Council of Worms, though his canon seems to stem more from Martin of Braga and Regio of Prum. However, in addition to this canon, Raymond also included in the *Decretals* a famous decision made by Innocent III on the case of a monk who had accidentally caused a woman to miscarry while 'acting with levity' (*Decretals* V, tit. 12, can. 20). The issue related not to the monk's level of guilt, or to the imposition of penance, but to the question of his clerical status, for it was held at the time that a cleric was irregular if he shed blood, irrespective of his guilt or innocence (see for example Thomas Aquinas *ST* IIaIIae *q*. 64 art. 7 ad 3). Innocent III decreed that the monk should be suspended from the clerical state only if the foetus was living (*vivificatus*). This text gave added authority to the view that only the destruction of a formed foetus was homicide, strictly speaking.

Medieval canon lawyers were therefore faced with an apparent contradiction. Some canons implied that the destruction of an unformed embryo was actual homicide (*Decretals* V, tit. 12, can. 5), but others implied that the destruction of an unformed embryo was not actual homicide (*Decretals* V, tit. 12, can. 20). One way to resolve this contradiction was to say that the killing of an unformed embryo was not homicide in the strict and technical sense, but that it was ethically equivalent of homicide, and could be treated as homicide for some legal purposes. Magister Rufinus (d. 1190) claimed that abortion before ensoulment had the guilt (*reatum*) of homicide but not the act (*actum*). Similarly, Roland Bandinelli (d. 1181) claimed that abortion involved the same intention whether or not ensoulment had occurred and was therefore homicide in *intention* even when it was not actual homicide. The same position was taken by the Franciscan theologian Bonaventure (d. 1274) in his *Commentary on the Sentences of Peter Lombard* (IV, D. 31, Q. 4). The solution of Raymond of Pennaforte, who had included in the *Decretals* canons supporting both positions, was to say that the moment of ensoulment defined homicide for technical questions such as irregularity (where guilt was not in question), but that with respect to guilt and penance, early and late abortion and contraception were all to be classed as homicide (*Summa de Poenitentia* II, tit. 1, n. 4). Many authors took abortion of an embryo prior to formation and ensoulment to be just as serious a sin as abortion of an ensouled embryo. Those, such as Thomas Aquinas, who explicitly thought that contraception and early abortion were less serious sins than homicide, held that they were second only to homicide, 'after the sin of murder, whereby a human nature already in actual existence is destroyed, this sort of sin seems to hold the second place, whereby the generation of human nature is precluded' (*Summa Contra Gentiles* III, Q. 122; see also *Commentary on the Sentences* IV, D. 31, Q. 4). What was common to all the writers of this period was their classification of abortion of the early human embryo as mortal sin and as something at least analogous to homicide: intentional, moral or spiritual homicide.

The universal condemnation of the practice of abortion during this period was reflected in the imposition of excommunication for abortion by local synods in Riez (1234), Lille (1288), Avignon (1326) and Lavaur (1368) (see Connery 1977, p. 148). Excommunication had once been part of the discipline of penance (for penance was at first defined by time away from communion), but as reconciliation began to anticipate the completion of penance, excommunication ceased to be a normal element in the sacrament. It was reintroduced as part of the two-tier system of church discipline to emerge in the Middle Ages.

In 1588, in a decree called *Effraennatam*, Pope Sixtus V invoked the power of excommunication in an attempt to restrain the growing practice of abortion during the Renaissance. As his model he took the *Decretals* V.12.5 and imposed the sanction not only for abortion but also for administering contraceptive drugs. He also reserved the ability to lift the excommunication to the pope alone. The condemnation of abortion as homicide was not in any way novel. However, several aspects of the excommunication were novel: it was promulgated to the whole Church (not just in one diocese or region); it was reserved to the pope to be able to lift the excommunication (not to a local bishop); and it included contraception as well as abortion. This meant that any abortion and any use of contraception anywhere in the Church had to be reconciled personally by the pope. Unsurprisingly, such a discipline proved wholly unworkable. Three years later Pope

Gregory XIV in his constitution *Sedes Apostolicae* greatly reduced the scope of this excommunication: placing the power to lift it with the local bishop, abandoning the attempt to include contraception and narrowing the excommunication so that it covered only abortion of a formed foetus. Gregory's legislation remained in place until 1869 when Pope Pius IX removed the distinction between formed and unformed. The excommunication for abortion was repeated in the Code of Canon Law of 1917 and the new Code of Canon Law of 1983.

In recent years it has been alleged that the canonical change brought in by Pius IX in 1869 represented the introduction of an entirely novel attitude on the part of the Catholic Church, and that before that point the Church had not been as concerned to protect the unformed embryo as it had to protect the formed embryo. This interpretation of events was put forward by, among others, the Anglican theologian G.R. Dunstan. '[T]he claim to absolute protection for the human embryo "from the beginning" is a novelty in the western, Christian and specifically Roman Catholic moral traditions. It is virtually a creation of the later nineteenth century' (Dunstan 1988, p. 40). The phrase 'absolute protection for the human embryo "from the beginning"' can be taken to mean that deliberately and directly destroying an unformed embryo is absolutely forbidden. It need not imply that destroying the embryo is homicide in a technical sense, but such absolute protection seems to imply that destroying the embryo would be at least analogous to homicide.

In the light of the evidence set out in this chapter, it is very difficult to sustain Dunstan's thesis that the legislative changes of 1869 represent 'a novelty' and 'virtually a creation' in the great sweep of the 'Christian and specifically Roman Catholic moral traditions'. On the contrary, the Christian ethical and legal tradition as outlined here gives very strong support and precedence for the stance of Pius IX.

- The earliest witness to the Christian ethical tradition from the *Didache, Letter of Barnabas, Apocalypse of Peter* and *Apocalypse of Paul* to the writings of Athenagoras, Tertullian, Minucius Felix, Clement, Cyprian and Hippolytus, to the canons of Elvira, Ancyra and Basil, treated the abortion as homicide *without distinction* as to formed or unformed. Basil explicitly rejected such a distinction as irrelevant or sophistical.

- The canons of Ancyra and Basil shaped later Eastern canon law, and exercised considerable influence also on Western canon law. The most authoritative statement in this canonical tradition was expressed at the Sixth Ecumenical Council of the Church at Trullo in 692: 'Those who give drugs procuring abortion ... are subjected to the penalty of murder.'

- The strand of Christian tradition that made an ethical distinction between abortion of an unformed embryo and abortion of a formed embryo emerged only in the late fourth and early fifth centuries. At the same time, Christian theologians showed an increasing tendency to characterize contraception as homicide. The medieval Church accepted both these tendencies, which resulted in an apparent contradiction within the *Decretals* of Pope Gregory IX and in the contradictory policies of Pope Sixtus V and Pope Gregory XIV.

- From a medieval perspective what was most unusual about Pius IX's legislation of 1869 was that the excommunication covered early and late abortion but did not extend to contraception. Pius IX did not uphold Sixtus V against Gregory XIV or vice versa. Rather, he revived an earlier canonical tradition.

- Those medieval Christians who did not regard the destruction of the unformed embryo as homicide in the technical sense none the less regarded it as ethically equivalent to homicide or as closely analogous to homicide (a point clearly expressed by, for example, Raymond of Pennaforte and Bonaventure). Abortion at any stage of pregnancy, excepting certain procedures undertaken to save the mother's life (see Chapter 12) was always regarded as mortal sin.

- What has varied through history is the way in which the Church has combined the defence of unborn human life with the demand to be a community of forgiveness and reconciliation. The discipline of penance in its various forms, including the sanction of excommunication, bore witness to the reality of sin while having as its ultimate aim the reconciliation of the repentant sinner.

The fundamental flaw in Dunstan's argument lies in its attempt to move from varying legal penalties to ethical judgements about the status of the embryo. In general, it is a fallacy to think that where one offence is sometimes punished less severely than another then this act is only 'relatively' offensive and that it may be ethically justified by the right circumstances. It is as if the heavier punishment applied to murder were thought to suggest that attempted murder, sexual assault or racially aggravated assault were only 'relatively' criminal and could therefore sometimes be recommended as courses of action. In regard to such cases it is better to say that comparisons are odious.

The constant and consistent Christian tradition from the Early Church to the nineteenth century repudiated abortion at any stage of pregnancy, while offering different penances as a means to reconciliation. This is certainly a noteworthy phenomenon. It provides an important historical context for a Christian, or for someone sympathetic to the spirit of Christianity, who is reflecting on the ethical status of the embryo. Nevertheless, on its own, appeal to tradition is a very weak form of argument, for to apply a tradition, it is necessary to understand not only its conclusions but also its rationale. One important consideration in Christian ethical and legal discussion of the human embryo has been the theological issue of when a human being acquires a soul, or to put the matter another way, what kind of soul is possessed by the embryo. However, before examining this issue it is necessary to address a more fundamental question: What is it that Christians have meant by the word 'soul'?

6

Soul Talk

It is not a notion that can be accommodated *within* the concepts of Aristotelian philosophy, it represents a breakdown of these concepts in the face of mystery. This is not, in my opinion, a reason for ditching Aristotelian philosophy (there may be good reasons for doing this, but this is not one of them) for I believe that important theological ideas are invariably expressed through the breakdown of philosophical concepts. Theology is not done within a philosophical system but at its margin.

(Herbert McCabe, *God Matters*)

In modern usage the word 'soul' has a peculiarly religious feel. It is seldom used by philosophers and scarcely ever by scientists. Where 'soul' has found a modern use it is as a metaphor: soul-music, the life and soul of the party, soul-destroying monotony. However, while the metaphor continues to thrive, the literal meaning has been lost from ordinary speech. Serious talk of the nature of the soul is thus bound to appear arcane or esoteric. Nevertheless, Christian discussion of the nature of the human being has long been conducted in the language of the soul and it continues to be an important category in theology. It is therefore necessary to ask what Christians have meant by the term.

The first definition of soul in the *Oxford English Dictionary* is 'The principle of life in man or animals; animate existence. *Obs.* (freq. in OE. in Scriptural passages).' The meaning is said to be obsolete. However, this Old English use of 'soul' appears similar to the ancient Hebrew *nephesh* in some important ways. The very first use of that word refers not to a human being but to sea creatures: 'And God said, "Let the waters bring forth swarms of living creatures" [*nephesh*]' (Genesis 1:20). The context here gives some sense of the connotations of *nephesh*. The waters are teeming with life. The first meaning of *nephesh* is then that which is alive. The same meaning is present in the creation of land animals a few verses later (Genesis 1:26). It is not until the second chapter of Genesis that the word *nephesh* is applied to a human being, namely Adam, the first human being: 'Then the Lord God formed man of dust from the ground, and breathed into his nostrils the breath of life; and the man became a living being [*nephesh*]' (Genesis 2:7).

These examples show *nephesh* being used to refer to a living being as a whole. However, there are many other cases where *nephesh* is used to refer to the aspect of a living being concerned with appetite: 'His *soul* was drawn to Dinah' (Genesis 34.3); 'The righteous have enough to satisfy their *appetite*' (Proverbs 13:25); 'All human toil is for the mouth yet the *appetite* is not satisfied' (Ecclesiastes 6:7).

Nephesh is also used to refer to the life of a person, especially when that life is in danger or has been rescued from danger: 'my *life* may be spared on your account' (Genesis 12:13); 'Turn, O Lord, save my *life*' (Psalm 6:4). This gives the context for an important use of *nephesh* in the Scriptures as that which is saved by God from going down to the land of the dead: 'He has redeemed my soul from going down to the pit' (Job 33:28); 'O Lord, you brought up my soul from Sheol, restored me to life from among those who had gone down to the pit' (Psalm 30:3); 'If the Lord had not been my help, my soul would soon have lived in the land of silence' (Psalm 94:17).

The word *nephesh* thus refers primarily to the living being as a whole and it can refer to other animals as much as to human beings. However, the language of the *nephesh* going down to the Sheol (Psalm 30:3 and elsewhere) suggests the possibility of a disembodied soul, a ghostly shade or spirit dwelling in the land of the dead. The possibility of such separate existence is still more apparent in the use of another term, closely associated with *nephesh*, the word *ruah* meaning breath or spirit. This also has a range of meanings, from 'the east wind' (Exodus 10:13) to 'the Spirit of God' (1 Samuel 10:10). In the context of human beings, the word can be used in parallel to *nephesh*, as for instance in the book of Job: 'In his hand is the life [*nephesh*] of every living thing and the breath [*ruah*] of all mankind' (Job 12:10). This brings to mind the story of forming Adam from the dust and breathing into him the breath of life (Genesis 2:7). The same image lies behind the famous description of death in the book of Ecclesiastes: 'The dust returns to the earth as it was, and the spirit [*ruah*] returns to God who gave it' (Ecclesiastes 12:7). These two quotations may encourage the view that, whereas *nephesh* refers to all living beings, *ruah* is specific to human beings, but this idea is easily dispelled by other verses. In the story of Noah, God determines to destroy all life on earth, except for what is to be saved in the ark. Of all the different species of animals it is said 'they went into the ark with Noah, two and two of all flesh in which there was the breath [*ruah*] of life' (Genesis 7:15; see also Genesis 7:21-2). Every living thing that breathes possesses *ruah*, and furthermore, in every case, this *ruah* is given by God. It is not only Adam who is composed of dust and breath, but the same goes for all the animals. This is clear from the Psalm, which says in reference to all living creatures:

> When you hide your face, they are dismayed;
> when you take away their breath [*ruah*], they die
> and return to their dust.
> When you send forth your Spirit [*ruah*], they are created;
> and you renew the face of the ground.
>
> (Psalm 104:29-30)

In many ways *nephesh* and *ruah* are used interchangeably. Both refer to the life of a living being. Both can refer to inner feelings, to the heart or mind. Both are used of human beings and of other animals. However, the imagery of God breathing his spirit into the dust of the earth makes spirit [*ruah*] more naturally a *constituent* of the creature, the principle of life, rather than something that refers to the living being taken as a whole. Moreover, the human *ruah* can be thought to have a different a different destiny to the *ruah* of other animals.

> All go to one place; all are from the dust, and all turn to
> dust again.
> Who knows whether the human spirit [*ruah*] of man goes upwards
> and the spirit
> [*ruah*] of animals goes downwards to the earth? (Ecclesiastes
> 3:20-21)

There is little evidence of hope for life beyond the grave in the earliest writings of the Hebrew Scriptures. That which does occur (for example in Isaiah 25:8, 26:19; Hosea 13:14) seems to express a later development within Judaism. Before this point the dead were depicted going down to Sheol, to the pit, into the silent darkness. Nevertheless, even in this earlier strand of tradition it seems that the spirits of the dead were not thought to be wholly extinguished. A striking illustration of this is the story of Saul's use of a medium to consult the spirit [*ruah*] of the dead prophet Samuel (1 Samuel 28:5–25). In consulting a medium, Saul was contravening the Law (Leviticus 19:31; Deuteronomy 18:10) and his own principles (1 Samuel 28:3). Nevertheless, while it was held to be wrong to 'consult the dead on behalf of the living' (Isaiah 8:19) there is no suggestion that such a course of action was impossible.

In the period from the Maccabean revolt in the second century BCE to the time of Jesus there grew up a far more vivid and explicit hope of life beyond the grave. For some, this hope took the form of a purely spiritual life with God. However, the dominant expression of this hope was as a belief in a general resurrection in the body for all those who had died (Daniel 12:2–3; 2 Maccabees 7:8–29). Such a belief, common in first-century Judaism, is clearly expressed in John's gospel: 'For the hour is coming when all who are in their graves will hear his voice and will come forth, those who have done good, to the resurrection of life, and those who have done evil, to the resurrection of condemnation' (John 5:28–9). Christianity inherited from Judaism a belief that human beings were a unity of spirit and flesh, and that their hope lay in a resurrection of the flesh. However, when Hebrew concepts expressed by *nephesh* and *ruah* were rendered by the Greek *psuche* and *pneuma*, they took on new connotations. These were shaped, at least in part, by Greek philosophy which influenced both Greek-speaking Jews (such as Philo of Alexandria and the writer of the Book of Wisdom) and Christians. In this context two philosophers who cannot be ignored are Plato and Aristotle.

Plato was perhaps the most significant ancient philosopher to promote the idea that the soul was an entity distinct from the body and was united to it as if imprisoned in a tomb or chained to a dead weight. The soul moved the body, the body weighed down the soul. In one of his most famous dialogues, Plato portrayed the last hours of Socrates as he faced execution. Crito asked Socrates how he would like to be buried. Socrates replied, 'Any way that you like, that is, if you can catch me first and I don't slip away from you' (*Phaedo* 115c). The reply is illustrative of the view that the real Socrates was not to be identified with the body that would be buried, but with the soul 'the invisible part, which goes away to a place that is, like itself, glorious, pure and invisible' (*Phaedo* 80d).

Plato's doctrine of the soul was explicitly ethical and religious. The soul did not simply enjoy a natural immortality. Rather, the destiny of the soul was described by reference to a dramatic myth of judgement. Souls who had lived a pure life while they were in the body would be rewarded, but those who had been gluttonous, for example, 'would pass into asses and animals of that sort' (*Phaedo* 81e). Souls who had been neither good nor bad would be reincarnated again as human beings and those who had committed murder or other terrible crimes would be flung into the abyss of Tartarus, 'from whence they emerge no more' (*Phaedo* 113e).

By identifying the true person with a soul that could inhabit a series of bodies, animal as well as human, Plato made the relation of body and soul appear accidental. If Plato was to be taken seriously, the souls of different animals were not different in kind but only in character (lions more ruthless, asses more gluttonous, etc.). Such a view was heavily criticized by Aristotle, Plato's most talented student. According to Aristotle, the great weakness of all philosophical accounts of the soul prior to his was that they did not take sufficient account of what sort of body it was that possessed a soul and they did not distinguish sufficiently the different functions of the soul.

In his work *On the Soul* Aristotle surveyed the many and varied theories of the soul that different philosophers of the past had put forward. Some thought that the soul was a kind of body, perhaps composed of very subtle atoms which caused the living body to move about. The supposed explanatory force of such theories was to account for the self-movement of living things. However, while this might explain why an animal moved, it would not explain why the same animal stopped or came to rest. For what characterizes animal movement is the appearance of choice and some sort of deliberative process, hence the animal rests when it has got what it wants. Deliberate movement (as opposed to haphazard movement) cannot be explained by the presence of 'smooth spherical atoms' (the theory of Democritus) or anything of that sort. Whatever the soul is, it does not seem to be a kind of material stuff.

As outlined above (Chapter 2), Aristotle's own account of the soul was to say that the soul was not itself a body or a part of the body but that it was the *form* of the living body. Furthermore, the word soul had more than one meaning. It covered many different living beings with different powers: *nutritive* (or plant) powers; *sensitive* (or animal) powers; *locomotive* powers (possessed by higher animals with the sense of sight and hearing); and finally *rational* powers, (possessed by human beings). In each case, the higher powers did not exist without the lower powers but presupposed and, as it were, included them (*On the Soul* 2.3, 414b). It is not enough, then, to say that plants, simple animals, higher animals and rational animals all possess a soul. From an Aristotelian perspective, it is necessary also to say what *kind* of soul they possess, what powers they have and what kind of bodily form this presupposes.

Whereas Plato had emphasized the priority and separate existence of the soul, Aristotle strongly emphasized the unity of body and soul as one being. The soul was not just a motor that moved the body but the actuality of a particular living form. The soul of this particular plant or animal has existence only as the principle of life of this particular plant or animal. It is thus possible to portray Plato and Aristotle as polar opposites. One could even attempt to categorize all subsequent philosophers as following Plato (dualists) or Aristotle (monists).

The problem with such grand sweeping categories is that they tend to obscure as much as they illuminate. Thinking of Aristotle as the opposite of Plato obscures important areas of continuity between the two thinkers. While Aristotle held that plant and animal souls were wholly inseparable from the living plant or animal, the rational soul was an exception. 'The case of mind is different; it seems to be an independent substance implanted within the soul and to be incapable of being destroyed' (*On the Soul* 1.4, 408b). Aristotle's account of the nature of the human mind seems very Platonic (*On the Soul* 2.1, 413a 13ff.). Reason is separable; it is divine; it is not the activity of any bodily organ and is not generated by biological–physical causes; it comes from outside. 'It remains, then, that Reason (*nous*) alone enters in, as an additional factor, from outside, and that it alone is divine, because physical activity has nothing whatever to do with the activity of Reason' (*GA* 136b 28–9).

Another important point of similarity is that both thinkers accepted the ordinary meaning of soul (*psuche*) as 'the principle of life', that is, whatever it is that makes living things alive. This definition provided Plato with the starting-points for one of his arguments for the immortality of the soul. If the soul brings life then by definition it cannot coexist with the opposite of life, that is death. Therefore the soul, of itself, cannot die and is immortal (*Phaedo* 105c–d). Whatever the merits of this argument, it is clear that it starts with a definition of the soul not as mind but as *life*. Plato and Aristotle were therefore in agreement in attributing soul to all living beings. However, Aristotle regarded Plato as being misled by thinking that soul was an univocal term: that the principle of life in plants, non-rational animals and human beings was essentially the same. According to Aristotle, one should distinguish nutritive, sensitive, locomotive and rational souls.

No account of the soul supplied by a pagan philosopher could be accepted by a Christian theologian without qualification. Nevertheless, some accounts were clearly better than others, and it was the philosophy of Plato that most enjoyed the favour of Christians from the second century CE onwards. His approach had the advantage of being ethically serious and overtly religious. In comparison, other schools of philosophy seemed either over-materialistic or ethically dubious, tainted with scepticism or with outright hedonism (a claim commonly levelled, whether fairly or not, against the Epicureans). When assessing the merits of different philosophies, the Christian theologian Justin Martyr claimed that the insights of Greek philosophy in general, and of Plato in particular, had come from the prior influence of Jewish thought (*Apology* 1.59). In the same vein Clement of Alexandria in the second century quoted with approval the pagan philosopher Numenius as saying 'What is Plato but Moses speaking Attic Greek?' (*Stromata* 1.22). The unlikely claim that Plato had been influenced by reading Moses was at once an expression by

Christians of the high regard with which they viewed Plato's philosophy, and an assertion of the priority of divine revelation over all philosophical systems. If there was truth in Plato, it had been said by Moses first.

Platonic and Neo-Platonic philosophy was well regarded by Christian theologians from the second to the fourth century (that is, from Clement of Alexandria and Origen to Gregory of Nyssa, Ambrose of Milan and the early Augustine). Nevertheless, as Plato's philosophy came into closer contact with Christian theology it was subject to more and more criticisms. Early in the third century, Origen embraced Plato's doctrine that the soul was united to a body in punishment for a primeval fall. Origen's account had the virtue of combining the biblical story of the Fall of Adam and Eve with what Plato had to say about the origin of the soul. The question of the origin of the soul (whether it pre-existed, or was generated by the parents, or was created immediately by God) will be examined in some detail in the next chapter. At this point it is enough to say that later Christians came to regard Origen's synthesis as incompatible with the scriptural doctrine of creation. It was widely believed that in his desire to follow Plato he had distorted Christian teaching.

The Platonic Christians of the fourth century (that is, of Gregory, Ambrose and Augustine) had to be more nuanced than Origen in how they combined Plato's philosophy with Christian theology. Gregory of Nyssa could no longer identify the Garden of Eden with the pre-existence of the soul, but he could and did present Eden as a quasi-angelic state. In defence of this he quoted the saying of Jesus that in the resurrection, 'they neither marry, nor are given in marriage neither can they die any more, for they are equal to the angels' (Luke 20:35-6 quoted in *On the Making of Man* 17.2). According to Gregory, one of the implications of this is that in Eden, had Adam and Eve not sinned, they would have been multiplied without sexual union (*On the Making of Man* 17.2). This approach helped foster a negative attitude to marriage and to the body. It is seen in even more striking terms in Ambrose, another theologian steeped in Christian Platonism. He was not embarrassed to call the body the enemy of the soul.

Therefore [the apostle] rightly devalued and dishonoured this body, and called it 'the body of death ... Let us not trust ourselves to this body, let us not join our soul with it. Join your soul with a friend not with an enemy. Your enemy is your body, which "wars against your mind'. (*On Death as a Good Thing* 3.11, 7.26, quoting Romans 7.24, 7.23)

Ambrose went so far as to say that the soul would be better off without the body. For this reason death could be thought of as a good thing in itself, not only the moment of reunion with God in Christ, but the time when soul was finally separated from the contagions of the body.

In Gregory and Ambrose, Platonic philosophy was fused with Christian doctrine. This had an impact not only on the understanding of the soul but also on attitudes to marriage and virginity, to the body in general, and to death and dying.

Augustine's faith journey much helped by Platonic philosophy. It was this philosophy that helped him see the flaws of the system of the Manichees, a religious sect with which he became involved as a young man. The Manichees believed that matter was itself evil and the work of an evil god. They also practised astrology and developed a complex system for explaining various human and worldly phenomena. Platonic philosophy convinced him that the Manichees were wrong in thinking that good and evil were equal and opposite forces. Rather, he came to believe that everything that exists comes from One who is supremely good. Augustine rejected Manichaean doctrine and astrology in favour of philosophical contemplation. This nourished in him a desire for wisdom and for union with the One from whom all things come, and ultimately led him to embrace Christian faith.

Augustine owed a debt to Plato and continued to have a high regard for Platonic philosophy. However, as his thought developed he came to be critical of certain fundamental points of Platonic thought, one might even say of Platonic piety. Unlike Ambrose, he could not regard the body as an enemy or a burden. This would contradict not only the truth of creation but also the mysterious truths of the incarnation and of the resurrection of the flesh. Christian doctrine envisaged a redemption of the body. In Jesus, 'the word was made flesh' (John 1:14). Augustine realized early in his Christian life that nothing like this occurred in the books of the

Platonists (*Confessions* 7.9). He came to see that while Platonism was not as crude as the dualism of the Manichees it also harboured attitudes that were incompatible with Christian doctrine.

> The Platonists, indeed, are not so foolish as, with the Manichaeans, to detest our present bodies as an evil nature; for they attribute all the elements of which this visible and tangible world is compacted, with all their qualities, to God their Creator. Nevertheless, they believe the soul is so affected from the death-infected members and earthly construction of the body, that there originated in it the diseases of desires, and fears, and joy, and sorrow. (*City of God* 14.5)

According to Plato, the body was responsible for the disorderly passions that lead to bad actions. However, as Augustine pointed out, the Platonists also held that the union with the body was the result of morbid desires within the soul. However, the desire that causes the union of body and soul cannot be the result of the union of body and soul. Thus, even on the Platonists' own account, at least some evil inclinations are due to the soul itself and not to its union with the body.

For Augustine, the paradigm of sin was not found in bodily desire or in the mixing of body and soul. It was found, rather, in the rebellion of the will of the creature against the creator. Augustine strongly distinguished bodiliness from sinfulness. There were sins that only a bodily creature could commit (such as gluttony), but there were other sins that purely immaterial beings could commit (such as envy, pride or malice). There were immaterial beings that had sinned (the devil and his angels) and there were bodily beings that were without sin (Jesus, Adam before the Fall, the saints in the resurrection). The Platonists were therefore wrong to believe that the perfection of the soul required a disembodied state (*City of God* 13:16).

Augustine therefore asserted, against Gregory of Nyssa, that had Adam and Eve not fallen they would still have produced children by sexual intercourse (*City of God* 14.23). He also asserted, against Ambrose, that 'the death of the body, the separation of the soul from the body is not [in itself] good for anyone' (*City of God* 13.6). Similarly, he was far more circumspect than Gregory or Ambrose in his praise of virginity (*On the Good of Marriage and On Holy Virginity*). He recognized virginity as a way of life especially esteemed by Christians, but for this very reason warned virgins of the danger of pride. The highest Christian virtue lies not in overcoming the flesh through chastity, but in overcoming pride through faith, hope and love.

In his mature thought, as evident in the *City of God*, Augustine presented a fundamental challenge to those Christians who derived their doctrine of the soul from Plato. From a Christian perspective, no account of the soul was adequate that made the union of body and soul either the consequence or the cause of sin. That the union of soul and body was good and natural was proved by the original union of soul and body in Adam, by the union of body and soul with the Word, and by the reunion of soul and body in the resurrection. While Augustine criticized the Platonic account of the soul he did not offer an alternative philosophy. Nevertheless, the theology of Augustine effectively paved the way for a renewed interest in the approach of Aristotle as a philosophy that could do better justice to the essential unity of soul and body.

In the late patristic period, some elements of Aristotle's philosophy were used and thereby promoted by Boethius (c. CE 480–524), by John Philoponus (mid sixth century) and, later, by John Damascene (CE 675–749). However, the philosophy of Aristotle gained influence in the Middle Ages initially among Islamic thinkers such as al-Farabi (c. 878–950), Ibn Sina (980–1037) and Ibn Rushd (1126–98) and later the great Jewish thinker Moses Maimonides (1135–1204). It was during the thirteenth century that the new Christian universities of Bologna, Paris and Oxford first began to engage with texts of Aristotle and commentaries translated from Arabic sources. Christian scholars were confronted with an intellectual tradition that was already well developed and represented the best scientific and medical knowledge available (Euclid and Ptolemy, Hippocrates, Aristotle and Galen). It was also a tradition in which others, especially Ibn Sina and Maimonides had already made great efforts to reconcile Aristotle with a theistic world-view.

Several Christian thinkers attempted to integrate this new Aristotelian learning with the received theological account of the world. Among these the most renowned was Thomas Aquinas (1226–74), a Dominican friar whose involvement in the intellectual controversies at the University of Paris was also shaped by a keen pastoral concern. The Order of Preachers or Dominicans had been founded in 1216 in the wake of the Fourth Lateran Council (1215) and in the context of a political and doctrinal crisis in the south of France the focus of which was the cathedral city of Albi. The Albigensians seem to have regarded the body as evil, rejected the sacraments and preached a purely spiritual form of salvation. They appeared to their contemporaries to have revived the system of the Manichees. In opposition to this neo-Manichaean heresy, Catholic theologians such Thomas Aquinas emphasized the goodness of the body, the natural unity of body and soul and the necessity of the sacraments.

Thomas considered the nature of the human soul in many places, but in particular in two questions in the first part of the *Summa Theologiae* (Ia Q.75-6). His enquiry begins by asking whether the soul is itself a kind of body (*ST* Ia Q.75 art. 1). What makes living things alive is not simply the fact of having a body, or all bodies would be alive. It must therefore be due to some quality or perfection of the body. The question then arises: if the human soul is not a body, is it just a quality that cannot exist apart from the body, like size or shape? Or is the soul something that exists in its own right, like an angel? (*ST* Ia Q.75 art. 2) Thomas argues that the soul is a subsistent thing (*subsistens*) because it has some activity that is proper to it: the activity of thought. In this he follows Aristotle (*On the Soul* 3.4, 429a 15-30). The human rational soul is therefore incorruptible and can survive the death of the body. However, Thomas is unwilling to call the soul a person (*ST* Ia Q.75 art. 4). On its own, the soul is not a human being, and neither is it a person because it lacks the complete nature of its species. Furthermore, the soul only possesses sense or imagination when it is united with the body, for these acts are not purely intellectual. They have a material aspect. Thus, while a soul that is separated from the body by death can survive in isolation, it is reduced to an incomplete thing. In this regard the human soul is by nature a different sort of thing from any angel, for angels have no essential relation to matter.

Having established to his own satisfaction the possibility of the soul subsisting in a disembodied state, Thomas turns to the union of soul and body (*ST* Ia Q.76). Here Thomas argues that the intellectual soul is joined to the body as the first principle of a living human being. There can only be one *first* principle and this must be the first principle of all the vital activities of the person: intellectual and bodily. The principle of the life of the body cannot be another body, so it must be the form of the body, a term Thomas takes from the philosophy of Aristotle. Thus we arrive at the formula: 'the intellectual soul is united to the body as its substantial form' (*ST* Ia Q.76 art. 6). The whole of Thomas's teaching on the soul can be summarized by saying that the soul is both a *subsistent* thing and the substantial *form* of the human being.

The views of Thomas Aquinas were controversial at the time. To some, such as his fellow Dominican, Robert Kilwardby, Archbishop of Canterbury, he seemed to have embraced Aristotle too closely. They were troubled by the doctrine of the soul as the form of the body. It seemed to endanger the spiritual character of the soul. Such theologians preferred an account of the soul that was more Platonic and based on the thought of Augustine – though how close the medieval 'Augustinian' account of the soul was to Augustine's own account is a matter of debate. Others criticized Thomas for allegedly misrepresenting Aristotle in his desire to conform the pagan philosopher to the strictures of Christian doctrine. One of the most influential medieval interpretations of Aristotle was that of Ibn Rushd, known in the Latin-speaking world as Averroes. He claimed that the unchanging and semi-divine element of the soul, the active intellect, was not multiplied according to the number of bodies, but there was only one intellect common to all human beings. This contradicted Thomas's interpretation of Aristotle, according to which there were as many active intellects as there were human beings.

Thomas expended much energy arguing against conservative Augustinian theologians among the clergy and against Latin Averroists in the arts faculties of the universities. He urged his fellow theologians to accept the doctrine that the soul is the form of the body as the only way adequately to secure the unity of the human being. Similarly, he challenged Averroists, who argued that there was but one intellect active in all human beings, to explain how the intellect could then be said to be a power of the soul, as

Aristotle clearly thought it was. More fundamentally, Thomas held it to be demonstrable both from philosophy and from experience that, if people think at all, they think for themselves. Someone else cannot think our thoughts for us.

Thomas Aquinas, like Augustine before him, drew on the best philosophical tradition available to him, but criticized that tradition in the light of Christian revelation. Despite great differences, stemming from the differences between the Platonic and Aristotelian concepts on which they drew, there are remarkable similarities. Both held that the soul was naturally related to the body as the principle of life, that it was immaterial in character, that it could survive the body and that, in the separated state, it was incomplete until it could be reunited with the body by the resurrection.

Thomas aimed to be a faithful interpreter of Aristotle, but he worked in a different context and had access to concepts that would have been alien to Aristotle. Thomas could relieve some of the tension between soul as principle of thought and soul as principle of life because both soul and body were understood within a larger context, in relation to the creator God. The soul could both transcend the body and be the form of the body because it was *created* directly by God *to be* the form of the body. Similarly, the soul could survive without the body, even though it was the form of the body, because it was destined to be reunited with the body in the resurrection. Thomas thus resolved tensions in Aristotle's account of the soul by appeal to the creation of the soul by God and the reunion of the soul with the resurrected body by the power of God.

The doctrine that the soul is the form of the body gained strength throughout the Middle Ages. In 1311 the Council of Vienne invoked this teaching against the perceived threat of Franciscan 'spiritualism'. The Council defined the proposition that the rational or intellectual soul is, truly and of itself, the form of the human body. However, from the fifteenth century, with the decline of the influence of Aristotle in renaissance culture and in early modern science, the account of the soul given by Thomas Aquinas fell from prominence. It came to be eclipsed by the philosophy of René Descartes and a dramatically new account of the human being.

Descartes rejected Aristotle's view that living things possess a life-principle. He claimed that living things are complex pieces of machinery designed and created by God. Descartes thought that mechanical causes could explain the processes of growth and account for the simple behaviour patterns of animals, but that they could not account for the phenomenon of consciousness. He acknowledged a principle of thought (or consciousness) which was independent of matter, but this was to be found only in human beings and not in other animals. Thus he combined a mechanical view of the universe with a radically subjective account of the self. In various ways these two elements were to persist through the philosophies of Malebranche and Leibniz, Locke, Hume and Kant. Even today the idea of the human being as a subjective consciousness in control of a mechanical body is more familiar to people than the idea of a principle of life. The dualism of mind and machine is also prominent in popular culture and especially in science fiction. Nevertheless, it is important to see that the modern conception of the body as a machine represents a radical break from a tradition that extends from Plato and Aristotle to Augustine and Aquinas. All of these earlier thinkers understood the soul as the principle not only of thought but also of *life*.

Throughout the twentieth century Descartes' portrayal of the mind as 'a ghost inside a machine' (Ryle 1949) was subject to rigorous intellectual criticism. Philosophers such as Wittgenstein and Heidegger argued that, since Descartes, philosophy had placed a chasm between the self and the world which there was no way to bridge. The only solution to this problem was to re-examine the starting-point and to realize that there was something wrong with the idea of an immaterial self trapped within a soulless material world. Some theologians went so far as to say that the doctrine of the immortality of the soul was not a scriptural or a Christian doctrine, and that Christians should reject the language of the soul in order to retrieve a sense of the importance of the body (a good example is Oscar Cullman in *The Immorality of the Soul or the Resurrection of the Body?*).

Taking a longer historical perspective, the rejection of the language of the soul by many Christian theologians of the twentieth century should be seen not as a rejection of the earlier patristic and medieval conception of the soul but as a reaction against an intellectual tradition that had its roots in the early modern period. It was only with Descartes in the seventeenth century that Christian reflection on the soul became dissociated from reflection on the life of the body.

The older tradition represented by, for example, Thomas Aquinas was the fruit of many centuries of intellectual effort, as theologians gradually reshaped Platonic and Aristotelian ideas in the light of the Christian doctrines of creation, the incarnation of Jesus and the resurrection of the dead. The same process of testing, developing and reshaping must be expected of the insights of modern philosophy. There is much to be learned from Wittgenstein and other modern thinkers. Some elements of twentieth-century philosophy may help us retrieve a classic vision of the unity of body and soul, but other elements will raise new questions and make new intellectual demands that will have to be critically assessed (see Kerr 1986; Braine 1993; Crosby 1996). Christian engagement with philosophical ideas is an ongoing task.

In a Christian context, then, it remains possible to use the language of the soul, and by doing so to invoke a substantial and sophisticated intellectual tradition. Indeed, soul talk has a great advantage over talk of self or consciousness, in that it places mental life within the larger context of biological life (Kenny 1973; Teichman 1974; Midgley 1979). It reclaims the meaning of 'life' as an analogous concept used to refer to different but related realities. This also reaffirms the communality of human beings with other animals, without denying the simultaneous presence of discontinuity.

In summary:

- The scriptural language of *nephesh* and *ruah* calls attention to the unity of the human being as a living animal. The classical Greek and Latin terms *psuche* and *anima* retain this same link of self and life. Most Jews believed that the soul or spirit can survive the death of the body, but the hope of life after death rests on a resurrection of the whole person by the power of God.
- There were many aspects of Plato's philosophy that were attractive to Christians. He held there was one ultimate and good

source of all things and that all human beings would be judged at death. Nevertheless, Christians became increasingly critical of other aspects of Plato's thought, particularly the way he seemed to alienate the soul from the body.

- Christians at first hesitated to embrace Aristotle's ideas as they seemed too secular and irreligious. However, in the Middle Ages the philosophy of Aristotle was rediscovered by Christians and formed the basis of an impressive synthesis of faith and reason. Aristotle's ideas about the soul were transformed by the Christian philosopher and theologian Thomas Aquinas.
- The seventeenth century saw a radical break in the philosophical tradition so that it became inhospitable to soul talk. However, in the twentieth century this movement was itself subject to heavy criticism. It is now much more defensible to use the classical definition of the soul as 'the principle of life'. This is the meaning given to the term 'soul' in the present work.

Having reflected on soul talk it is necessary to ask when soul talk becomes appropriate, that is, when a human soul can be ascribed to the body. However, before addressing this question it is first necessary to ask where the soul comes from. For whence affects when.

7

Whence the Soul?

[A] sparrow flies swiftly in through one door of the hall and out through another. While he is inside, he is safe from the winter storm; but after a few moments of comfort, he vanishes from sight into the wintry world from which he came. Even so, man appears on earth for a little while, but of what went before this life or of what follows, we know nothing.

(Bede, *The Ecclesiastical History of the English People*)

There was a great deal of consensus in the Early Church about the fate of human beings after death. Those who were saved by the grace of Christ would share in his resurrection when all rise from the dead at the end of time (John 11:23–6 and elsewhere). This was emphatically a *bodily* resurrection, but the body would be transformed or glorified. It would be, in the paradoxical words of Paul, a 'spiritual body' (*soma pneumaticon*: 1 Corinthians 15:44). Those who had sinned and had not accepted forgiveness in Christ faced a far grimmer fate. They would also be raised in the body (Daniel 12:2; John 5:28–9; Revelation 20:13) but in their case so as to be punished in the body with everlasting torment. Between the death of each individual and the end of the world, the soul would be disembodied, and in this state would await the general resurrection and its final reunion with the body.

Immediately after death, even before the resurrection, the soul was believed to be subject to judgement and to experience the beginning of its reward or punishment. The immediacy of reward or punishment seemed to be implied by the parable of the rich man and Lazarus (Luke 16:19–31) and also by the words of Christ to the penitent thief on the cross, 'Truly I tell you, today you will be with me in paradise' (Luke 23:43). According to Josephus, this pattern of death as the separation of soul and body, followed by a period when the soul existed alone without the body, until the time when soul and body would be reunited in a resurrection, was also the view of the Pharisees (*Jewish Wars* 2, 154, 163; see Barr 1992, p. 44 n. 32). The same overall scheme was agreed by ancient Christian writers from Justin Martyr (*Fragments on the Resurrection*), Irenaeus (*Against Heresies* Book II, c. 34), Athenagoras (*On the Resurrection of the Dead*) and Tertullian (*On the Resurrection of the Flesh*) onwards.

This confident consensus on the fate of the soul after death was in the sharpest contrast to early Christian uncertainty about the origin of the soul before birth. The writings of the New Testament were primarily concerned with human salvation through the person and action of Jesus. The focus was on the message of eternal life in and after this life and not specifically on how human life came to be. Neither did the writings of the Hebrew Scriptures contain clear and unequivocal teaching on the origin of the soul. The question of where, when and how the soul originated was a subject of speculation. The Early Church was divided between those who held that the soul was generated by the parents and those who held that it was given by God from outside, as it were. 'But with respect to the soul, whether it is derived from the seed by a process of traducianism ... or whether bestowed upon the body from without ... is not distinguished with sufficient clearness in the teaching of the Church' (Origen, *On First Principles* Preface 5).

In assessing these alternatives Christians readily turned to philosophy. Plato's account of the origin of the soul proved highly influential. In several of his dialogues (*Meno, Phaedo, Phaedrus*) Plato argued that the soul pre-existed the body, so that its original and natural existence was not joined to a body. In this separate state the soul was able to perceive truth directly without the hindrance of the senses. The soul was depicted mythically as a chariot pulled by winged horses. If it kept a clear vision of the truth it retained its wings and remained free, but if in struggling with other souls it lost hold of this vision it would lose its wings and fall to earth.

> Thus when [the soul] is perfect and winged it journeys on high and controls the whole world, but one that has shed its wings sinks down until it can fasten on something solid, and settling there it takes to itself an earthy body which seems by reason of the soul's power to move itself. The composite structure of the soul and body is called a living being and is further termed 'mortal' ... (*Phaedrus* 246c)

The union of body and soul was thus regarded not as natural or original but rather as the result of some failure on the part of the soul, a failure to follow the gods and see the whole of being. Furthermore, the extent of the failure of the disembodied soul was reflected in the state of life into which the soul was born, whether philosopher, king, statesman, physician, prophet, poet, artisan, sophist or tyrant (*Phaedrus* 248d-e). It thus helped to explain the cause and natural justice behind the diversity of states of life. The doctrine of the pre-existence of the soul was also used by Plato in his account of learning and of knowledge (*Phaedo* 74b-d; *Meno* 85c-86b) and to support his belief in the soul's immortality.

Among Greek-speaking Jewish writers in the centuries immediately preceding and subsequent to the birth of Jesus, Philo of Alexandria was by far the most strongly influenced by Plato, as reflected in his interpretation of Jacob's dream in which angels ascend and descend on a ladder between earth and heaven (Genesis 28:12).

> [The air is] like a populous city, it is full of imperishable and immortal citizens, souls equal in number to the stars. Now of these souls some descend upon the earth with a view to be bound up in mortal bodies, those namely which are most nearly connected with the earth, and which are lovers of the body. But some soar upwards, being again distinguished according to the definitions and times which have been appointed by nature. Of these, those which are influenced by a desire for mortal life, and which have been familiarised to it, again return to it. (*On Dreams* I. XXII, 137-9)

The passage clearly asserts some kind of pre-existence of the soul. More extraordinarily, it also seems to allude to reincarnation: 'those which are influenced by a desire for mortal life and which have been familiarised to it, again return to it'. The passage goes on to describe the body, again in the most Platonic terms, as both 'a prison and a grave' (*On Dreams* I. XXII, 139). Nevertheless, if Philo could be regarded as the Jewish Plato, he was far from alone among his Jewish contemporaries in positing some sort of pre-existence of the soul.

The doctrine also seems to be implied in the book of Wisdom, a Jewish work written in Greek, again probably in Alexandria, perhaps in the first century BCE. It was commonly included with the Septuagint translation of the Hebrew Scriptures and for this reason came to be included in the Catholic canon of the Old Testament. Here the writer, represented as King Solomon, described himself as entering into an undefiled body.

> As a child I was naturally gifted,
> and a good soul fell to my lot;
> or rather, being good, I entered an undefiled body
>
> (Wisdom 8:19–20)

This verse not only seems to give temporal priority to the soul, but also identifies the not-yet-embodied soul with the person, '*I* entered ...' Later in the same work the author described the moment of death as when the human beings 'go to the earth from which all mortals are taken, when the time comes to return the souls that were borrowed.' (Wisdom 15:8). This echoed a well-known verse from the book of Ecclesiastes, 'the dust returns to the earth as it was, and the spirit returns to God who gave it' (Ecclesiastes 12:7). If the soul was said to *return* to God after death, did this imply that the soul dwelt with God before entering a body? Was it returning to a state in which it existed before birth?

According to Josephus, the sect of the Essenes (now commonly associated with the community of Qumran by the Dead Sea) also believed in the pre-existence of souls: 'Emanating from the finest ether, these souls become entangled, as it were, in the prison house of the body, to which they are dragged down by a sort of natural spell' (*Jewish Wars* 2:154). The language here is unmistakeably Platonic, but Josephus may have been presenting the views of the Essenes in a way familiar to Greek-speakers.

The Dead Sea Scrolls, if indeed these were Essene writings, do not contain any clear reference to the pre-existence of souls. However, in several places (especially in the *Hymns of Thanksgiving*) they do show a pronounced emphasis on God's foreknowledge and predestination. The link between a strong doctrine of divine foreknowledge and a concept of pre-existence can be seen in Jewish apocalyptic works of the same period. In one example, God shows Abraham a picture of the divine plan in which everything that will come to exist already has existence. When Abraham asks about one group of people in the picture he is told, 'these are the ones I have prepared to be born of you and to be called my people'

(*Apocalypse of Abraham* 22.5). Another allusion to the pre-existence, again closely associated with divine foreknowledge, occurs in the Book of Enoch, 'Sit and write all the souls of mankind, however many of them are born, and the places prepared for them to eternity; for all souls are prepared to eternity, before the formation of the world' (*Slavonic Book of Enoch* 23:2). In these passages the primary theological point is that God foreknows those who will be born. However, the imagery easily suggests that the souls of future people somehow already exist.

In certain writings of the Talmud there are clear references to the real pre-existence of souls waiting to be born. One passage described *Arabot*, the last of the seven heavens, as holding 'the spirits and the souls which are yet to be born' (*Chagigah* 12b). In another passage it was said that the Messiah would not come till all the souls in the *guf* (literally 'the body') had been born on earth (*Avodah Zarah* 5a, see also *Nedarim* 13b, *Yevamot* 62a). These passages imply that all the souls who will be born are created at the beginning of time and are kept safe in a treasury called *Arabot* or the *guf*. When all the souls that will be born have been born the Messiah will come and bring the world to an end. In another Talmudic passage it is stated explicitly that all souls were created in the first six days of creation and that God calls each soul to enter a body at conception.

> Each and every soul which shall be from Adam until the end of the world, was formed during the six days of Creation and was in paradise ... At the time of conception God commands the angel who is the guardian of the spirits, saying: 'Bring Me such a spirit which is in paradise and hath such a name and such a form'.... God says to the soul, 'the world into which you enter is more beautiful than this; and when I made you I intended you only for this drop of seed.' (*Midrash Tanhuma Pekude* 3, see Ginzberg 1909–38)

There are great similarities between this passage and a fragment preserved by, or appended to the works of, Clement of Alexandria from an earlier Christian writer: 'The soul entering into the womb after it has been by cleansing prepared for conception [is] introduced by one of the angels who preside over generation' (*Excerpts from Theodotus* [also called *Prophetic Eclogues*] 50).

It is improbable that belief in the pre-existence of the soul was universal among Jews at this period. Josephus and the New Testament bear clear witness that not even on the question of life *after* death was there universal agreement (divergent views being held by Pharisees, Saducees and Essenes). Nevertheless, the books of Wisdom, Enoch, the Apocalypse of Abraham and various passages from the Talmud do comprise a coherent strand of thought favouring a form of pre-existence of the soul. According to this perspective, souls were created before bodies and were later united to bodies in what was a single and unified plan of God. Indeed, within ancient Judaism it was precisely the eternal plan of God that seems to have encouraged the idea of the pre-existence of souls. A related concern, introduced in the *Midrash Tanhuma Pekude*, was the interpretation of Genesis 2:1-2, in which it was said that the work of creation was complete on the sixth day.

If we move from Enoch and the Talmud to Philo and the Essenes (at least according to the account Josephus gave of them) we see a quite different role for pre-existence. Philo regarded the entrance of the soul into the body as a *fall*, due to some failure on the part of the particular soul. The soul was not called by God into a particular body for its good and in accordance to the divine plan (as symbolized by the involvement of a ministering angel). It was imprisoned in a body as a result of its own morbid desires. Philo's conception of the pre-existence of the soul was at once much more Platonic and, from a theological point of view, more problematic than that envisioned in the Talmud.

At least one Christian theologian seems to have followed Philo in this regard. Origen of Alexandria was writing against Gnostic Christians who believed in a variety of creators and a variety of souls, distinguishing different human beings as material, animal or spiritual in nature. (A detailed outline of such a Gnostic system is given by Irenaeus in his *Against Heresies* book I.) In opposition to this, Origen stressed the unity and justice of the Creator, and the free will of all rational agents. No one could be damned simply for possessing a material soul, nor saved merely for possessing a spiritual soul. God punished and rewarded people according to their merits. It was this overriding concern for God's justice that led Origen to suggest that the soul pre-existed the body. In his view, God's justice demanded that all rational creatures were created equal. The reason that some were angels, others demons and others human beings, and that human beings varied in character and in state of life, was wholly due to free will. '[T]his freedom of will incited each one either to progress by imitation of God, or to fail through negligence. And this, as we have already stated, is the cause of the diversity among rational creatures' (*On First Principles* II, 9.6). Origen, like Plato, used the idea of a pre-existent fall to explain the entrance of the soul into the body. However, there were also significant differences between Origen's vision and that of Plato. The entrance of the soul into the body was not simply due to a kind of spiritual gravity, an attraction to the flesh, it was rather the result of divine judgement (*On First Principles* II, 9.8). Origen was aware that the Church had no clear teaching on the origin of the soul (*On First Principles* Preface 5) and therefore, put forward his views tentatively as the speculations of a theologian. Nevertheless, he pointed out that it was necessary for Christians to believe that the devil was an angel who had fallen (*On First Principles* I, 4.2), and if it was merit that was the cause of the differentiation of angels and demons, perhaps merit determined the diversity between human beings, angels and demons, and also the diversity among human beings. Furthermore, the choice of Jacob over Esau in the womb 'not on grounds of justice and according to their deserts; but undeservedly' (*On First Principles* I, 7.4) seemed to Origen to contradict the scriptural truth that 'God shows no partiality' (Romans 2:11).

Origen's ideas on the pre-existence of souls were chiefly put forward in one book: *On First Principles*. This book was unusual among his writing. He was better known at the time for having produced a parallel text of six different versions of the Old Testament: the Hebrew text in Hebrew characters, the Hebrew text transliterated into Greek, and four different Greek translations, including the Septuagint. He was the most renowned of all interpreters of Scripture and was read and appreciated by most of the later Church Fathers. This helps to explain the enduring influence of Origen, and also shows why it is misleading to take certain of his speculations as though these were the centre of his thought. Origen was highly regarded for his work on the Scriptures but his account of a pre-existent fall of souls was accepted only by the most ardent of his disciples (Evagrius, Dydimus the Blind, and perhaps Rufinus). Other writers, including the most significant theologians of their generation, wrote vigorously against the teachings contained in *On First Principles*, for example Augustine of Hippo (*City of God* XI, 23), Jerome (*Apology against Rufinus* and elsewhere) and, not least, Gregory of Nyssa (*On the Making of Man* 28).

Gregory of Nyssa was a great admirer of Origen, but he rejected outright the theory of the pre-existence of the soul. This seemed to Gregory altogether too close to the 'fabulous doctrines of the heathen' concerning reincarnation. If the soul was originally separate from the body and fell into a body on account of its desires, then why could it not transmigrate from body to body, as Plato thought? Origen did not explicitly espouse reincarnation. In fact, in another work, written many years after *On First Principles*, Origen explicitly repudiated reincarnation (*Commentary on Matthew* 17:10–13). Nevertheless, the idea of a pre-existent fall of souls into bodies as put forward by Origen in *On First Principles* and by Philo in *On Dreams*, naturally tended in the direction of reincarnation, to cycles of ascending and descending states without limit. 'Thus this doctrine of theirs, which maintains that souls have a life by themselves before their life in the flesh, and that they are by reason of wickedness bound to their bodies, is shown to have neither beginning nor conclusion' (*On the Making of Man* 28.7).

An account of the pre-existence of the soul that implied a fall of the soul into a body, was thus widely rejected by the subsequent Christian tradition. This rejection culminated in the sixth century, at the fifth ecumenical council of the Church: the Second Council of Constantinople (CE 553). Though the Council was primarily concerned with the nature of Christ and not with the pre-existence of souls, it also contained a condemnation of Origen and his 'impious writings' (canon 11). A list of erroneous statements taken from the works of Origen had previously been drawn up by the Emperor Justinian, who convoked the Council, and a slightly longer list was promulgated at a later occasion, perhaps, though this is not clear, at the Council itself. The first of fifteen condemned propositions concerned the pre-existence of the soul: 'If anyone asserts the fabulous pre-existence of souls ... let him be anathema.'

In his preface to *On First Principles* Origen mentioned two possible sources of the soul: that it was generated by the parents; or that it was bestowed upon the body from outside. However, he only discussed the latter possibility. The former view was developed by another important Christian theologian writing in Latin North Africa a generation or so earlier than Origen. Tertullian, in his work *On the Soul*, endorsed a qualified Stoic view of the soul according to which the soul was corporeal (*On the Soul* 5). Tertullian saw this as confirmed by the gospels, and in particular, the story of the rich man and Lazarus (Luke 16:19–31). There the souls of the rich man and Lazarus were both described in corporeal terms, for the rich man asked for a drop of water to cool his tongue (*On the Soul* 7). However, Tertullian strongly opposed the Stoic (and Platonic) idea that the soul was received from outside with the first breath and departed with the last breath (*On the Soul* 25).

Tertullian maintained that the soul was generated from the parents, and that the seed of the soul was given with, and at the same time as, the seed of the body. As evidence for this he cited the way that not only physical features but also intellectual and spiritual features could be passed from parent to child (*On the Soul* 25). The dominant metaphor in Tertullian's thought was the seed: the seed that contained the plant within it, and so contained the future plants that would spring from it, not as though the plants were actually in existence already, but because of the power that was in it. 'In the seed lies the promise and earnest of the crop' (*On the Soul* 27). For this reason it could be said that the whole human race was produced from that one human being, or that every soul had been produced from one (ibid.). In this scheme the woman was reduced to the 'appointed seed-plot' (ibid.) fertilized by the male. The seed of the soul was thus drawn from the soul of its (male) parent, as the seed of the body was drawn from the body. 'The soul-producing seed ... arises at once from the out-drip of the soul, just as that fluid is the body-producing seed which proceeds from the drainage of the flesh' (ibid.).

Tertullian's strong rejection of Platonic ideas of pre-existence and reincarnation, and his own reading of the Scriptures, led him to regard the soul as immortal and as a gift of God, but at the same time to see this gift as originally given to Adam and then passed on by propagation. 'The soul, then, we define to be sprung from the breath of God, immortal ... rational, supreme, endued with an instinct of presentiment, evolved out of one (archetypal soul)' (*On the Soul* 22). Gregory of Nyssa, having criticized Origen's account, followed Tertullian in tracing the soul back to the generating seed. In the same way, he appealed to the potential found in the seed of a plant, 'in wheat, or in any other grain, the whole form of the plant is potentially included' (*On the Making of Man* 29.3). Similarly, he applied this to the case of human generation, 'the human germ possesses the potentiality of its nature, sown with it at the first start of its existence' (ibid.). Again, like Tertullian, Gregory considered the (male) seed to contain potentially both the body and the soul of the new human being, 'of the part which belongs to the soul, the elements of rationality, and desire, and anger, and all the powers of the soul are not yet visible [in the seed]; yet we assert that they have their place in it' (*On the Making of Man* 29.6).

By the late fourth century it was possible to delineate at least five theories as to the origin of the soul. These were listed in one of Jerome's letters:

> In regard to the origin of the soul: (1) does it descend from heaven, as the philosopher Pythagoras and all the Platonists and Origen think? (2) or is it part of the essence of the Deity, as the Stoics, the Manichees, and the Priscillianists of Spain imagine? (3) or are souls kept in a divine treasure house wherein they were stored of old as some ecclesiastics, foolishly misled, believe? (4) or are they daily created by God and sent into bodies, according to what is written in the gospel, 'My Father is working still, and I am working'? (5) or are souls really produced, as Tertullian, Apollinarius, and the majority of the Western divines conjecture, by propagation, so that as the body is the offspring of body, the soul is the offspring of soul ...? (Jerome, Letter 126.1)

Of these five possibilities, Christians found it easiest to reject the second. This view contradicted the fundamental distinction between God and creatures. With regard to the other four theories, each had its defenders. However, Jerome was convinced that both the views of Origen and those of Tertullian should be rejected. Origen seemed to make the union of body and soul a punishment, and to open the door to reincarnation, while Tertullian seemed guilty of the opposite mistake of making the origin of the soul too much like the origin of the body, and thus endangering the spiritual and immortal character of the human soul. Having also excluded the 'foolish' belief that souls were kept in a treasure house (the doctrine of the Talmud and perhaps also of Clement of Alexandria), Jerome's choice became clear: human souls were created individually by God at the same time as the body was formed in the womb.

Jerome set out his views concerning the origin of the soul at length in an early work (*Apology against Rufinus* II, 4, 8–10, III, 28–31). He later stated his position more succinctly (*Letter to Pammachius against John of Jerusalem*) when he reduced from five to three the possible accounts of the orgin of soul, and placed creationism between the opposite errors of traducianism (Tertullian's view) and pre-existence (Origen's view). This schema was so powerful that it would eventually become the standard characterization of the problem from the Middle Ages up to the present day.

So confident was Jerome of his own view that he characterized it as what 'the Church teaches in accordance to the Saviour's words' (*Letter to Pammachius*, 22). In contrast, Augustine approached the question in quite a different spirit. From his earliest writing as a Christian (*On the Happy Life* 1.5, c. CE 386) to his review of his life's writings, written only three years before he died (*Retractions*, 2.56, c. CE 427), Augustine expressed his inability to solve this problem. It was one he returned to many times. In his book *On the Freedom of the Will* (c. CE 395), Augustine listed four possible origins of the soul: '(1) whether all souls are derived by propagation from the first; (2) or are in the case of each individual specially created; (3) or being created apart from the body are sent into it; (4) or introduce themselves into it of their own accord ...' (*On the Freedom of the Will* 3.20). These comprised four of the five possibilities later to be mentioned by Jerome (5, 4, 3 and 1 respectively). However, unlike Jerome, Augustine did not attempt to adjudicate between the rival accounts. This reticence caused so much dismay to his readers that he found it necessary to write a further defence of his agnosticism on this subject. There he stated, that 'if any one is able to produce such [conclusive] arguments in discussing the very obscure question of the soul's origin, let him help me in my ignorance; but if he cannot do this, let him forbear from blaming my hesitation on the question' (*Letter* 143.11).

While he refrained from defending any one particular view on the origin of the soul, Augustine's thought on the matter shifted significantly over the course of his career. At the time of his conversion to Christianity he was very strongly influenced by Platonic philosophy. He referred with approval to Plato's theory of learning as memory, which presupposed the pre-existence of the soul (Letter 7 c. CE 389). The same doctrine seems to lie behind a passage in the *Confessions* (c. CE 397) where he wrote, 'But what, O God, my Joy, preceded *that* period of life [in the womb]? Was I, indeed, anywhere, or anybody? No one can explain these things to me, neither father nor mother, nor the experience of others, nor my own memory' (*Confessions* VI.9). In contrast, in his letter to Jerome (CE 415), Augustine explicitly rejected the Platonic view that 'souls sin in another earlier life, and that for their sins in that state of being they are cast down into bodies as prisons' (Letter 166.26). In his writings from this period (Letter 166 and *A Literal Commentary of Genesis* book 10) there seem only two serious possibilities for the origin of the soul: either souls were created immediately by God or they were propagated from the first human being. Augustine was inclined to prefer the first option, creationism, but he was unwilling to accept it unreservedly because it threatened to contradict the justice of God. If every new soul was created afresh in a way that was unconnected with Adam, then it seemed unfair (to Augustine) that a newly conceived child should contract original sin and be punished for Adam's fault.

Augustine returned to the question in CE 420 with his most sustained treatment of the subject: *On the Soul and its Origin*. This work was a reply to a book by Vincentius Victor who, like others before him, was critical of Augustine's failure to advocate a single account of the origin of the soul. Augustine took time and care to answer the book though he found it confused in its argumentation and rash in its assertions. Vincentius argued that, though itself innocent, the soul deserved to be tainted by sin simply because it was infused into a body. The justice of God in condemning unbaptized infants, was, in turn, explained by reference to divine foreknowledge: God condemned according to what he knew the infant *would have done*. This supposed explanation struck Augustine as both unfounded and unjust, and went to the root of his misgivings about creationism. In the face of such questions, Augustine advocated the honest admission of ignorance. '[B]etter for a man to confess his ignorance of what he knows nothing about, than either to run into heresy which has been already condemned, or to found some new heresy ...' (*On the Soul and its Origin* 1.34).

To the end Augustine remained unwilling to adopt whole-heartedly the position advocated by Jerome: that souls were not propagated by the human parents but were created immediately by God as the human body was formed in the womb. He pointed out that Scripture did not resolve the question. For example, the text from Ecclesiastes, 'the dust returns to the earth as it was, and the spirit returns to God who gave it' (Ecclesiastes 12:7) did necessarily imply that that God gave the spirit in the sense of individually creating each new soul. The reference to the dust is a clear allusion to the fashioning of the first human being, so also the giving of spirit echoes the giving of the breath of life to the first human being. The soul would be no less a gift of God if it were passed on from parent to child by generation. Again, the use of the word 'return' could be invoked in support of the view that the soul pre-existed with God before entering a body. Nevertheless, in metaphorical terms, being made by God can be thought of as going forth from God and returning as turning towards the source of being (Letter 143.8–10, Letter 166.26). In a similar fashion other scriptural texts relevant to the origin of the soul were open to more than one interpretation.

Augustine strongly affirmed the spiritual character of the soul, an attitude that once inclined him to favour pre-existence and later inclined him to favour direct creation. Nevertheless, he was uncertain how much weight to place on philosophical arguments in an area so deeply mysterious as the human soul. Augustine invited Jerome to provide a demonstration to settle the issue (Letter 166), but Jerome was unable to do so. Augustine, Jerome and the later tradition rejected the form of material traducianism put forward by Tertullian. They also rejected the opinion of Plato, Philo and Origen that the fall of the pre-existent soul explained its union with the body. This view was incompatible with a deeper Christian understanding of the creation, of the goodness of the body and of the bodily resurrection (see for example, *City of God* XI.23, XIII.16–20, XXII.11–21). Nevertheless, there could be forms of traducianism (or 'generationism') more sophisticated than that of Tertullian, and forms of pre-existence (such as that implied in the Talmud and Clement) which did not suffer from the same problems as the version put forward by Origen. Furthermore, while creationism was the most satisfying account available in the fourth or fifth century, it had theological problems of its own, not least how it was compatible with the doctrine of original sin as Christians then understood it.

In the Middle Ages it was Jerome's confidence rather than Augustine's scepticism that was destined to win out. This was helped somewhat by the influence of a work thought to be by Augustine, now universally attributed to Gennadius, a follower of Jerome, which clearly stated that the soul was directly created by God together with the body (*On the Dogmas of the Church* 14). Furthermore, the pattern put forward by Jerome, of creationism as the middle way between the errors of pre-existence and traducianism had a great appeal to the medieval mind. All the major Scholastic theologians, with the exception of Hugh of St Victor and Alexander of Hales, held creationism to be absolutely certain and even they regarded creationism to be the more probable opinion. The two greatest theological textbooks of the Middle Ages, the *Sentences* of Peter Lombard and the *Summa Theologiae* of Thomas Aquinas, both characterized creationism as a dogma of the Church (*Sentences* II, D. 18; *ST* Ia Q. 188. art. 2). It was a doctrine that cohered neatly with the medieval Christian–Aristotelian account of the development of the embryo. Nevertheless, there was never a time when the Catholic Church formally defined its teaching on the origin of the soul. 'It should, however, be noted that ... there are no such explicit definitions authoritatively put forth by the Church as would warrant our calling the doctrine of Creationism *de fide*' (Siegfried 1913).

The immediate creation of the soul by God, though it has been the dominant view among Christians from the Middle Ages to the present day, has not been held universally. In the twelfth century, Hildegard of Bingen felt free to use the imagery of pre-existent souls crying out as they were swept down into bodies by invisible currents (*Liber Scivias*). During the Reformation the issue of the origin of the soul was revived with Martin Luther, and many later

Lutheran theologians favoured traducianism (see Chapter 10). In the nineteenth century a number of Catholic theologians also began to question the received opinion, so that in 1857 Rome felt obliged to censure a book by Froschammer arguing for a version of traducianism. In 1887 Rome also acted against Antonio Rosmini, condemning, among other things, a proposition relating to the origin of the soul and thought to be semi-traducianist. However, the condemnation of these propositions was lifted in 2001 by the Congregation for the Doctrine of the Faith. This reversal was made explicit in order to pave the way for the eventual beatification of Rosmini, but it also serves as a reminder that the question of the origin of the soul is viewed as a more open question in 2001 than it appeared to be in 1887. Furthermore, while Origenist pre-existence has been rejected by the tradition, it should be remembered that the form of pre-existence found in Jewish sources had its roots in the pre-existence of all creatures in the mind of God, and that doctrine retains its place in Christian theology.

For contemporary Catholic theologians, doubts about creationism have been less concerned with original sin (the problem for Augustine) and more concerned with the way that, at least in some simplistic forms, the doctrine of the special creation of the soul seems to negate human parenthood. It seems to reduce the human parents to the fathers and mothers of animals which God subsequently transforms into children, or even the fathers and mothers of vegetables which later become animals and which God finally transforms into children. This was a point made long ago by Maximus the Confessor. In an effort to find a middle way, Karl Rahner has argued that divine creative causality should be seen as a transcendent cause and therefore not as being in competition with natural causes. If such a view is acceptable then children could be seen both as the true offspring of their parents and as the newly created gift of God.

Rahner's view, and similar views put forward by other twentieth-century theologians, stands midway between traducianism and creationism. It is possible to affirm that God is involved in some particular and intimate way in the creation of each human soul and that the soul is not reducible to material causes, and yet also to hold that God gives parents a true role in generation of the new human person. Only God can create (*ex nihilo*) but parents can cooperate in this action such that 'in the sexual union, man and woman under God become procreators' (*The Way Supplement* 25 (1975): 12, cited by the *Oxford English Dictionary* as an example of a new use of the term 'procreator'). An acute and well-balanced assessment of the various theories of the origin of the soul was given by the nineteenth-century Early Church historian Philip Schaff.

> The three theories of the origin of the soul, we may remark by way of concluding criticism, admit of a reconciliation. Each of them contains an element of truth, and is wrong only when exclusively held. Every human soul has an ideal pre-existence in the divine mind, the divine will, and we may add, in the divine life; and every human soul as well as every human body is the product of the united agency of God and the parents. Pre-existentianism errs in confounding an ideal with a concrete, self-conscious, individual pre-existence; traducianism, in ignoring the creative divine agency without which no being, least of all an immortal mind, can come into existence, and in favoring a materialistic conception of the soul; creationism, in denying the human agency, and thus placing the soul in a merely accidental relation to the body. (Schaff, *History of the Christian Church*, Vol. III § 154)

In summary:

- In the course of history Christians have come to reject definitively a number of theories concerning the origin of the soul. The soul is not a part of God, nor is the soul joined to a body because of sins committed in a previous life. No account can be accepted that would contradict the natural union of body and soul. Neither can an account be accepted that would contradict the individual, spiritual and immortal character of the soul.
- The dominant view among Western Catholic Christians since the fifth century has been that the soul is immediately created by God and infused into the new human being that is formed in the womb. However, this has never been formally defined by the Church by a pope or an ecumenical council.
- The caution of Augustine and his willingness to admit ignorance on this issue, in particular between the competing theories of

traducianism and creationism, has more to commend it to contemporary theologians than the brash confidence of Jerome.

- While the soul is certainly created by God 'out of nothing' (for this is true of everything that is not God) there is ongoing reflection and discussion among Catholic theologians concerning how to interpret the doctrine of the creation of the soul of each new individual and, in particular, what theological role the parents play in the generation of a new human life.

The question of the *origin* of the soul is theologically interesting in its own right. Furthermore, it is also relevant to the question of *when* soul comes to be in the embryo. Recent discussion among Catholic and Reformed theologians seems increasingly to favour the view that the parents have a true role in the generation of the whole human being, notwithstanding the necessity of a special creative act of God to enable such an act of generation, a position midway between materialistic traducianism and simple creationism. This would seem to suggest that the soul is present when the embryo is generated by the parents, i.e. from the time that male and female elements fuse at conception. However, while most of those who hold that the soul is generated by the parents also hold that it is present from conception, some theologians (Rosmini, Rahner) have sought to combine a form of traducianism with delayed 'hominization'. Determining the origin of the soul is thus not enough, on its own, to settle the issue of when the soul is acquired. The timing of ensoulment is a question that needs to be addressed directly.

8

The Timing of Ensoulment

The Bill, as it has come to us from another place, proposes research
up to 14 days. My first question is, 14 days after what? Something must
have started 14 days previously to enable us to begin evaluating time.

(Sir Bernard Braine, House of Commons
Hansard Debates, *2 April 1990*)

There are, broadly speaking, four possibilities as to when a human
being may be said to acquire a rational soul, or, to put the matter in
another way, four possibilities as to when the life of a human being
may be said to begin. A human being may acquire a soul (1) at the
moment of conception, (2) some time between conception and
birth, (3) at the moment of birth, or (4) some time after birth. Each
of these possibilities found some support in the ancient world.

- Some ancient authors argued that the human being began *at
  conception*, thought to be the moment when the seed-mixture 'set'
  to produce a living embryo, a few days after insemination. This
  position is associated with the Pythagoreans, but it may well also
  have been the view of Aristotle.
- Another view was that the human being began sometime *between
  conception and birth*, either when the form was complete
  (formation) or when the foetus started to move about
  (quickening). This position is associated particularly with
  Aristotelians and seems also to have been the view of Philo of
  Alexandria.
- There were many who argued that the human being began
  immediately after birth when the foetus was physically separate
  from his or her mother and began to breathe air. This fourth
  view is associated with the Stoics and the Platonists, though what
  Plato himself thought is unclear.
- There were also attitudes and practices common in the ancient

world (most notably the toleration of infanticide) that might seem to imply that even *long after birth*, a child was not considered to have full status as a human being. Nevertheless, ancient writers did not seem to have understood this in terms of the delayed acquisition of the soul. It was simply that young children, like women, slaves and barbarians, did not have the legal or ethical status that depended on free citizenship.

Opinions among Jews in the ancient world were also divided. Several texts in early Judaism imply that the soul was given with the seed at the moment of conception, or even before. One example has already been mentioned in reference to Jewish belief in the pre-existence of the soul: 'At the time of *conception* God commands the angel who is the guardian of the spirits … God says to the soul, "when I made you I intended you only for this *drop of seed*"' (*Midrash Tanhuma Pekude* 3). Another important text recounts a conversation between Rabbi Judah and Emperor Antoninus (possibly Marcus Aurelius).

> Antoninus said to Rabbi, 'From when is the soul endowed in man, from the time of conception [literally visitation *p'kidah*] or from the time of [the embryo's] formation?' Rabbi replied: 'From the time of formation.' The emperor demurred: 'Can meat remain three days without salt and not putrefy? You must concede that the soul enters at conception.' Rabbi [later] said, 'Antoninus taught me this, and Scripture supports him, as it is said, "And thy visitation hath preserved my spirit"' (Job 10:12). (*Babylonian Talmud Sanhedrin* 91b, see Feldman 1974, p. 271)

The argument that meat cannot stay fresh for three days without salt seems to refer to the three days that the process of conception was thought to take (see, for example, *Babylonian Talmud Berakoth* 60a). The soul is like the salt. It is the element that keeps the seed from putrefying while the process of conception is occurring. This text thus supports the view that the soul is given at the very beginning of the process of conception.

While some ancient Jewish texts express the view that the soul is given at the very beginning, others take the moment of birth as the ethically significant point. This is evident from a passage in the Mishnah.

> If a woman has difficulty in childbirth, one dismembers the embryo within her limb from limb because her life takes precedence over its life. Once its head (or the greater part) has emerged, it may not be touched, for we do not set aside one life for another. (*Mishnah, Oholot* 7.6; see also *Babylonian Talmud Sanhedrin* 72b)

The killing of the child is not permitted once the head has emerged for 'we do not set aside one life (*nephesh*) for another'. By implication, it seems, the foetus is not yet counted as a living person (*nephesh adam*). This conforms to the common rabbinic interpretation of Exodus 21:22–5 as outlined above (Chapter 4). It also conforms to the teaching that, at least for certain purposes, the embryo is regarded as 'part of the mother' (*Babylonian Talmud Hullin* 58a; *Babylonian Talmud Gittin* 23b). Nevertheless, it is in some tension with the judgement that 'A "Son of Noah" who killed a person, even a foetus in its mother's womb, is capitally liable' (Maimonides, *Yad, Hilekot Melakim* 9:4; see also *Babylonian Talmud Sanhedrin* 57b).

In addition to these two incompatible views (soul at conception and soul at birth) there are many passages in the Talmud that support the view that 40 days marks the transition from unformed embryo to human being (for the derivation of the figure of 40 days see Leviticus 12:2–5). Until this time the embryo is neither male nor female (*Babylonian Talmud Berakoth* 60a). If the woman miscarries before the 41st day it is not a valid childbirth (*Babylonian Talmud Niddah* 30a–b). In another place the embryo before 40 days is described as mere fluid: '[She] may eat *terumah* only until the fortieth day. For if she is not found pregnant she never was pregnant; and if she is found pregnant, the semen, until the fortieth day, is only a mere fluid' (*Babylonian Talmud Berakoth* 60a). This third possibility also seems to be reflected in the Septuagint translation of Exodus 21:22–5 and in the opinion of Philo that the image of God is present from formation and from that time abortion is homicide (*On Special Laws* 3.19).

What is to be made of the presence of these disparate Jewish views on the timing of ensoulment? It may be possible to harmonize some of the disagreement (for example, by referring to more than one kind of soul), but this does not resolve all the problems and there is no consensus among Jewish scholars as to this question. Feldman summarizes the rabbinic outlook by saying that the timing of ensoulment is something that belongs to the 'secrets of God' (Feldman 1974, p. 273). In summary, different Talmudic texts support different views as to when a human being receives a soul: at conception; at formation (40 days after insemination); or at birth. This breadth of opinion in rabbinic Judaism provides a helpful context within which to understand Christian accounts of ensoulment. Among Christians in the ancient world there was unanimity in rejecting the view that the soul was given at or after birth. Christians were certain that the living foetus had a soul. However, there was no consensus as to precisely when during pregnancy it acquired a soul.

The earliest Christian speculation of the time of ensoulment is found among the works of Clement of Alexandria from the mid second century.

> An ancient said that the embryo is a living thing; for that the soul entering into the womb after it has been by cleansing prepared for conception, and introduced by one of the angels who preside over generation, and who knows the time for conception, moves the woman to intercourse; and that, on the seed being deposited, the spirit, which is in the seed, is, so to speak, appropriated, and is thus assumed into conjunction in the process of formation. He cited as a proof to all, how, when the angels give glad tidings to the barren, they introduce souls before conception. And in the Gospel 'the babe leapt' (Luke 1:44) as a living thing. (*Excerpts from Theodotus* [also called *Prophetic Eclogues*] 50)

The collection of excerpts in which this occurs is coloured by Gnostic Christianity (for example n. 37: 'For Gnostic virtue everywhere makes man good') and doubt has been cast on whether Clement collated this material himself. Nevertheless, among the Fathers of the Church, Clement perhaps did more than any to present orthodox Christianity in such a way as would appeal to Gnostic Christians (for example, 'He who is conversant with all kinds of wisdom will be pre-eminently a Gnostic' *Stromata* 1:13). In any case, this passage should be assessed on its merits. Of itself it does not imply any specifically Gnostic teaching but seems rather to reflect contemporary Jewish influence. It is strikingly similar to the text from *Midrash Tanhuma Pekude* quoted above and is defended by reference to the appearance of angels to the barren (Genesis 18:1-14; Judges 31:2; Luke 1:11-24, 1:26-36) and by the leaping of John the Baptist in his mother's womb (Luke 1:44). It seems to envisage the pre-existence of souls which are then introduced into bodies by the ministry of angels. This dovetails with what is known of Clement's anthropology.

Elsewhere in the second century the first systematic Christian account of the soul was being written by Tertullian. Central to Tertullian's account is the claim that the soul is corporeal and that it does not come from outside but is generated by the parents (or more particularly, by the father). It is for this reason that children resemble their parents in disposition and not only in physical stature (*On the Soul* 25). However, if the soul is generated by the parents then it seems obvious that it is present from the beginning.

> We indeed maintain that both [body and soul] are conceived, and formed, and perfectly simultaneously ... Now we allow that life begins with conception, because we contend that the soul also begins from conception; life taking its commencement at the same moment and place that the soul does. (*On the Soul* 27)

The soul is present from the beginning and life is present from the beginning. Tertullian is aware that the embryo is at first relatively unformed and comes to attain its various powers gradually. Nevertheless, while 'all the natural properties of the soul which relate to sense and intelligence are inherent in its very substance ... they advance by a gradual growth through the stages of life and develop themselves in different ways' (*On the Soul* 38). There is, then, a development and formation of the soul that mirrors the development and formation of the body, but this development is itself based on the existence of the soul that is given with the seed. This helps shed light on a famous passage by Tertullian from his *Apology*.

> [M]urder being once for all forbidden, we may not destroy even the foetus in the womb ... to hinder a birth is merely a speedier man-killing; nor does it matter whether you take away a life that is born, or destroy one that is coming to the birth. That is a man which is going to be one; you have the fruit already in its seed. (*Apology* 9)

The saying 'that is a man which is going to be one' (*homo est, et qui futurus est*) reflects the idea that the basis of the human being, the seed of body and soul, is already present in the embryo. The living being that will become a recognizable human being is already a human being, because he or she already possesses what makes a human being.

Coming from different perspectives with regard to the origin of the soul (pre-existence and traducianism), Clement and Tertullian agree that the soul is present from the moment of conception. The prevalence of this view is also suggested by the general tendency of second-century Christians to characterize abortion as homicide. 'Those women who use drugs to bring about an abortion commit murder' (Athenagoras, *A Plea for the Christians*; see also *Didache*, *Letter of Barnabas*, *Apocalypse of Peter*, Minucius Felix and Clement). This is an impressive consensus. However, already in Tertullian was the hint of a second tradition.

> The embryo therefore becomes a human being in the womb from the moment that its *form is completed*. The law of Moses, indeed, punishes with due penalties the man who shall cause abortion, inasmuch as there exists already the rudiment of a human being. (*On the Soul* 37, emphasis added)

Tertullian seems untroubled at the apparent contradiction between this and the earlier passage in the same work where he asserted 'the soul also begins from conception' (*On the Soul* 27) or with the dictum that 'that is a man who is going to be one' (*Apology* 9). In order to reconcile these views we might suggest that the soul is present from conception, but the embryo only technically becomes a human being (*homo*) when the form of body and soul is complete. On this basis killing an early embryo would not be homicide technically speaking, but it would be the equivalent of homicide, as it would kill a human embryo which already possessed a human soul.

Tertullian's account of the soul was controversial not least because he asserted that 'the soul is corporeal' (*On the Soul* 5). However, some elements of Tertullian's account were taken up by Gregory of Nyssa in a form far more acceptable to many Christians. Gregory said that the soul was spiritual and not physical, but he also held that the soul and body were both given through generation and were given at the same time. Like Tertullian, Gregory argued that the soul was not prior to the body, nor the body to the soul, but both had a common cause.

But as man is one, the being consisting of soul and body, we are to suppose that the beginning of his existence is one, common to both parts, so that he should not be found to be antecedent and posterior to himself, if the bodily element were first in point of time, and the other were a later addition; but we are to say that in the power of God's foreknowledge ... all the fullness of human nature had pre-existence. (*On the Making of Man* 29.1)

In this passage Gregory invokes two arguments. First he says that as the human being is a unity of body and soul, so the soul should not come before the body, nor the body before the soul, but both should be produced together. This is an important argument that would be taken up later in the tradition. Secondly, Gregory invokes the theme of divine foreknowledge of the future human being. The reasoning seems to rest on the idea that because God already has in mind the one he is creating then that human being is present from the beginning of God's action. The link made here between divine foreknowledge and ensoulment at conception is not indisputable but it is a connection others have made, and perhaps lies behind the assumption of the Talmud and Clement that the pre-existent soul would be joined to the seed from conception. The theme of divine foreknowledge and predestination would return to prominence in the sixteenth century in the theology of the Reformation. In this much later context it would again shape reflection on the human embryo (see Chapter 10).

Having argued that the soul must be present from the first, Gregory goes on to argue that the soul is present from the beginning in the unformed embryo even though it has to wait for a necessary sequence of events before it is made manifest.

For just as no one would doubt that the thing so implanted [the unformed embryo] is fashioned into the different varieties of limbs and interior organs, not by the importation of any other power from without, but by the power which resides in it transforming it to this manifestation of energy, – so also we may by like reasoning equally suppose in the case of the soul that even if it is not visibly recognized by any manifestations of activity it none the less is there; for even the form of the future man is there potentially. (*On the Making of Man* 29.4)

The phrase 'the form of the future man is there potentially' closely echoes the dictum of Tertullian that 'that is a man who is going to be one'. However, Gregory is clearer in his argument. It is because the form of the body and the manifestation of the soul is produced not from 'any other power from without' but by a power inherent in the embryo that the future man may be said to be present already. The view set out in *On the Making of Man* is reiterated in another work of Gregory's: 'No one who can reflect will imagine ... that the soul is younger than the moulding of the body; for ... there is no question about that which is bred in the uterus both growing and moving from place to place' (*On the Soul and the Resurrection*). Nevertheless, like Tertullian, Gregory also sometimes reserves the term human being (*anthropos*) for a formed foetus.

> For just as it would not be possible to style the unformed embryo a human being, but only a potential one ... so our reason cannot recognize as a Christian one who has failed to receive, with regard to the entire mystery, the genuine form of our religion. (*On the Holy Spirit, Against the followers of Macedonius*)

Gregory here is not primarily concerned with the human embryo but is engaged in a polemic against 'Christians' who deny the divinity of the Holy Spirit. He uses the *analogy* of the incomplete or unformed embryo to deny the Macedonians the name of Christian. However, all analogies limp, and the use of the analogy in this context obscures important elements of Gregory's teaching on the embryo as developed in detail in *On the Making of Man*. There he argued that the embryo contains within it the power to develop to maturity, that it already possesses a human spiritual soul and, therefore, that it already contains the future man.

What then was the attitude of those who held that the soul was neither generated by the parents (Tertullian, Gregory) nor pre-existed (Clement), but was specially created by God? One of the first clear exponents of this view was Lactantius. He argued that as the soul was spiritual it could not be generated by the parents but must be specially created by God (*On the Workmanship of God* 19). When he addressed the question of when the soul was created he was most concerned to refute the Stoic claim that the soul was given after birth.

> For [the soul] is not introduced into the body after birth, as it appears to some philosophers, but *immediately after conception*, when the

divine necessity has *formed* the offspring in the womb; for it so lives within the bowels of its mother, that it is increased in growth, and delights to bound with repeated beatings. (*On the Workmanship of God* 17, emphasis added)

Here Lactantius is clear that the foetus possesses a soul while still in the womb. However, he is unclear on the question as to when precisely this happens. There is an apparent contradiction between the assertion that it happens 'immediately after conception' and the assertion that it happens 'when the divine necessity has formed the offspring'. Did Lactantius have in mind the moment when the seed and blood mix to constitute the early embryo, or when the human heart is formed, or when the whole work is complete at 40 days (see *On the Workmanship of God* 12)? Either the word 'immediately' could be taken loosely to mean relatively soon after conception (six weeks), or the phrase 'had formed' could be taken loosely to mean has formed the embryo but has not completed the form. It is possible that Lactantius was unclear himself when during pregnancy ensoulment occurred, as his primary focus was to deny that it happened at or after birth.

It is in the fourth century that we first find Christians voicing the opinion that ensoulment happens between conception and birth and, in particular, that it occurs at the moment that formation is complete. This opinion seems to lie behind a passage in the Apostolic Constitutions: 'You shall not kill a child by abortion, nor kill it after it is born. For everything that is shaped and has received a soul from God, if killed, shall be avenged, as having been unjustly destroyed' (*Apostolic Constitutions* 7.3). It is more clearly expressed in a work written in the fourth century which was for many years attributed to Augustine: 'Moses handed down that if someone strikes a pregnant woman and causes a miscarriage, if it is formed he should give life for life, but if it is unformed he should be punished with a fine, thus proving that there is no soul before form' (*Questions on the Old and New Testament* 23). The anonymous writer seeks further support from Scripture for the view that ensoulment does not occur until the body is formed. He argues that, as God first formed Adam's body and then breathed in the breath of life, so God first forms the body of the embryo and only after this is complete gives the soul. A similar argument would later be used by the fifth-century bishop Theodoret of Cyrus (*Questions on Exodus* 48).

The most influential Latin-speaking theologian of the fourth or fifth century was Augustine of Hippo. He admitted his uncertainty as to when the embryo acquired a soul and began to live: 'And therefore the following question may be very carefully inquired into and discussed by learned men, though I do not know whether it is in man's power to resolve it: At what time the infant begins to live in the womb' (*Enchiridion* 86). Augustine was clear that long before birth the foetus showed signs of life, and argued that, at least from this point, it must possess a human soul. Furthermore, if it possessed a soul, then if it died before birth it would also share in the resurrection: 'If all human souls shall receive again the bodies which they had wherever they lived ... then I do not see how I can say that even those who died in their mother's womb shall have no resurrection' (*City of God* 22:13; see also *Enchiridion* 86). Concerning embryos that are not fully formed, he says: 'who is there that is not rather disposed to think that unformed abortions perish, like seeds that have never fructified?' (*Enchiridion* 85). However, he questions this reaction: 'but who will dare to deny, though he may not dare to affirm, that at the resurrection every defect in the form shall be supplied' (ibid.). What is crucial for Augustine is not form but life. From the moment the embryo can be said to be alive, it possesses a soul. This can certainly be said of the foetus when it moves around, but Augustine also encourages his reader to consider 'whether life exists in a latent form before it manifests itself in the motions of the living being' (*Enchiridion* 86).

Augustine was uncertain whether the soul was generated by the parents (the view put forward by Tertullian and Gregory of Nyssa) or whether it was created immediately by God (as Lactantius and Jerome believed). He never wholly excluded the former view, according to which the soul would have to be present from conception. Indeed, even if the latter view was true, God might still create the soul at the moment of conception. However, his wish to keep open this possibility caused him some difficulties when he came to interpret Exodus 21:22–5. For the text that Augustine received was dependent on the Septuagint and seemed to suggest that only the killing of a 'formed' foetus was homicide.

> If therefore there is an unformed offspring, animated as yet only in an unformed way (since the great question of the soul is not to be rushed into rashly with a thoughtless opinion) then on this account the Law does not pertain to homicide, because it is not yet possible to say that a *living* soul is in this body since it is bereft of sense, if [the soul] be such a kind as to be in flesh that is not yet formed and hence not yet endowed with sense. (*Questions on Exodus* 80)

Based on the Septuagint text, Augustine feels constrained to accept the view that abortion before formation is not homicide. However, he is not willing 'rashly' to draw from this the conclusion that the soul is not present before formation. His proposed solution to this is to say that the soul of the unformed offspring cannot be said to be a living soul (*anima viva*) if it is deprived of sense (*sensu caret*). Early abortion is not counted as homicide because, while the soul may be present, it is in an insensible state. Augustine's solution is less than satisfying, but it bears witness to his unwillingness to accept the argument of his contemporaries that the Law proves that 'there is no soul before form' (*Questions on the Old and New Testament* 23). It is, then, somewhat ironic that this anonymous text was later attributed to Augustine, and, that it, together with the passage of Augustine on Exodus, was seen as a proof that the greatest of the Fathers accepted the theory of delayed ensoulment.

From the fifth century, the doctrine that the soul is specially and individually created by God and is not derived from the parents came to prevail in the Latin West. Within this context, and with the support of passages from Augustine, Pseudo-Augustine and Jerome (ultimately derived from the Septuagint of Exodus 21:22-5) the belief that God gives the soul only after the form is complete likewise prevailed. In the East the picture was quite different, due to the influence of Gregory of Nyssa and Basil, and later of Maximus the Confessor and John Damascene. Neither creationism nor delayed ensoulment attained the level of acceptance in the East that these doctrines enjoyed in the West.

In the Middle Ages, the question of the moment of ensoulment was shaped by another important force: the rediscovery of Aristotle's works and their introduction into the new university culture of the thirteenth century. In this context a potent new synthesis was developed between the (Christianized) philosophy of

Aristotle and Latin theology. The most prominent architect of this synthesis was the theologian and philosopher Thomas Aquinas. Basing his account on that of Aristotle, Thomas argued that there was a succession of souls in the embryo: that it was first merely vegetative (*nutritiva*), then animal (*sensitiva*) then human (*intellectiva*). As the culmination of the process of development, the intellectual soul is given last.

> It is in this way that through many generations and corruptions we arrive at the ultimate substantial form, both in man and other animals … We conclude therefore that the intellectual soul is created by God *at the end* of human generation, and this soul is at the same time sensitive and nutritive, the pre-existing forms being corrupted. (*ST* Ia Q.118 art. 2 ad 2, emphasis added)

According to this view, the embryo is truly alive and its activities of growth and nutrition are expressions of this life. However, the life the embryo has initially is not specifically human life, and the development of the embryo is not an activity of the embryo directed from within, but rather an activity of the generating parent from outside, through the instrumentality of the seed.

> This active force which is in the semen, and which is derived from the soul of the generator, is, as it were, a certain movement of this soul itself … consequently there is no need for this active force to have an actual organ; but it is based on the (vital) spirit in the semen which is frothy … This matter therefore is transmuted by the power which is in the semen of the male, until it is actually informed by the sensitive soul … As to the active power which was in the semen, it ceases to exist, when the semen is dissolved and the (vital) spirit thereof vanishes. (*ST* Ia Q.118 art. 1 ad 3-4)

Gregory of Nyssa had based his evaluation of the embryo on the belief that the process of development was achieved 'not by the importation of any other power from without, but by the power which resides in it transforming it' (*On the Making of Man* 29.4). Thomas Aquinas denies the existence of such an immanent power within the embryo, holding instead that the power of development is located not in the embryo, the one generated, but in the father, the one generating: 'The formation of the body is caused by the generative power, not of that which is generated, but of the father generating from seed, in which the formative power derived from the father's soul has its operation' (*ST* IIIa Q.33 art. 1 ad 4). Thomas interpreted Aristotle as claiming that the intellectual soul comes 'from outside', when formation is complete, which is at 40 days for males and 90 for females (*Commentary on the Sentences* III, D.3, Q.5, art. 2, citing Aristotle *History of Animals* 7.3, 583b 3–5, 15–23). The claim that the soul was created specially by God (not generated by the parents) and that this occurred after the embryo had been fully formed was the common teaching of the medieval scholastic theologians. Thomas's view was, then, far from unique, but it merits special attention as the most influential of the accounts from this period.

In evaluating the contribution of Thomas Aquinas to the question of when the soul is created, it is necessary to examine not only his conclusions but also his arguments and his assumptions, for his philosophy has been invoked in recent theological discussion both by those who wish to argue for delayed ensoulment (Donceel 1970) and by those who favour ensoulment at conception (Heaney 1992).

It is useful to compare the account given by Gregory of Nyssa and that of Thomas Aquinas. Thomas understood the soul to be the substantial *form* that made the living body what it was. Without a soul the body would not be a living body, and would not be a human body, except by analogy. For this reason he did not believe that Adam's body was first formed and afterwards given life. This would not make sense.

> Some have thought that man's body was formed first in priority of time, and that afterwards the soul was infused into the formed body. But it is inconsistent with the perfection of the production of things that God should have made either the body without the soul, or the soul without the body, since each is a part of human nature. This is especially unfitting as regards the body, for the body depends on the soul, and not the soul on the body. (*ST* Ia Q.91 art. 4 ad 3)

Gregory and Thomas both affirmed that body and soul come into being at the same time. However, what Gregory had in mind was the forming body, whereas what Thomas had in mind was the fully formed body. For Gregory there is a human body, of a sort, from the beginning. For Thomas the body of the embryo is not a human body until it is fully formed at 40 days.

Both Gregory and Thomas accepted the principle that an effect cannot be greater than its cause, that is to say, only a human being can make a human being. If the embryo has the inherent power to produce an adult human being, then it already possesses a human nature and is already a human being. For this reason it is imperative for Thomas to deny that development is directed from within and for him to assert that it is caused by the parent through the semen as an instrument. Thomas also felt it necessary to assert that the semen remained present through the 40 days until formation was complete.

Both Gregory and Thomas accepted the Aristotelian claim that everything that is alive possesses soul and that there are different kinds of soul: vegetative (or nutritive), animal (or sensitive) and human (or intellectual). Gregory even claims that Moses in the first chapter of Genesis teaches that 'the power of life and soul may be considered in three divisions' (*On the Making of Man* 8.4).

Where Gregory and Thomas differ is that Gregory does not see human development as involving a succession of souls but just one specific soul guiding development and gradually acquiring the use of its own powers. Thomas, as seen above, held that development occurred through a succession of generations and corruptions.

Gregory and Thomas differed on their account of the origin of the soul. Gregory held that the soul was passed on from the parents, whereas Thomas held this to be heretical (*ST* Ia Q.118 art. 2), as incompatible with the spiritual character of the soul. The standard Western medieval doctrine, that souls were specially created by God, had by that time been taken out of the context of divine foreknowledge (and the pre-existence of all creatures in the mind of God). The creation of the soul by God was thus contrasted with the action of the parents in procreation. The *infusion* of the rational soul, as it was termed, was understood as a divine intervention that took place upon completion of a natural process – the formation of the body. The danger with this doctrine is that the embryo could be seen neither as human nor as spiritual, but as a sort of biological preamble to the work of God. This isolation of the biological from the human and the spiritual is at odds with the insistence seen elsewhere throughout Thomas's work that the spiritual soul is at one and the same time the form of a living body.

Thomas claimed to be following Aristotle on the subject of

human generation. However, there are some significant differences between their accounts. Aristotle was not a Christian and did not have a doctrine of creation. Clearly then, when he said that the rational principle came from outside he did not mean that it was created by God and infused into the embryo. This draws our attention to another significant point. As highlighted in Chapter 2, Aristotle clearly stated that the rational soul-principle was given with the male seed (*Generation of Animals* 136b 28-9, 137a 8-12), thus at or before conception. There are no grounds in Aristotle for the identification of completion of form at 40 days with the acquisition of a rational soul. Furthermore, Aristotle did not say that the development of the embryo was due to an external power, but that the cause of generation was in a way from the parent and in a way inherent in the embryo. These differences from Aristotle are significant not primarily because Thomas has failed to present an accurate account of someone else's thought, but because Aristotle's own account seems in certain respects superior to that of Thomas, and certainly more integrated with the biology.

In summary:

- There were a number of different views about ensoulment both in the ancient world and within Judaism. Christians were unified in rejecting the view that the soul was given at birth. The earliest Christian texts placed ensoulment at conception.
- This view seems to have prevailed until the fourth century when, under the influence of the Septuagint version of Exodus 21:22-5, Christians increasingly came to identify ensoulment with formation, generally set at around 40 days. However, this view was much less prevalent in the East and it is not unquestioned in the West. Augustine remained uncertain as to the moment of conception and kept open the possibility that the soul might be present from conception.
- It was in the Middle Ages in the West that the identification of formation with the time of ensoulment became dominant. This was due to a number of factors, not least the triumph of the theory of direct creation by God as the origin of the soul, and the philosophical influence of the writings of Aristotle in the new universities.

● Thomas Aquinas presents a coherent and powerful argument for
  delayed ensoulment. However, his arguments were premised on a
  number of assumptions which now seem questionable, not only
  in the area of biology but also in the interpretation of Aristotle.

The views of Thomas Aquinas and other scholastic theologians
remained dominant throughout the Middle Ages (see for example,
Dante, *Purgatorio* canto 25). While the Middle Ages saw debates
over many theological and philosophical issues, the overall shape of
medieval embryology remained unaltered. There was a consensus
in the West that the human soul was directly created by God and
that it was infused into the embryo when the form of the body was
complete, generally held to be 40 days or thereabouts. It took a
major intellectual upheaval to provoke Western theologians to
question the basis of these received ideas. This upheaval had two
aspects: religious and scientific.

The sixteenth-century Protestant Reformation involved a radical
reappraisal of the whole of the Western theological tradition. As a
movement it left no area of theology untouched and so, in its turn,
it left its mark on the understanding of the embryo.

The seventeenth century witnessed a scientific revolution which
reshaped embryology as it did the other natural sciences. It
vindicated Galen's view that both male and female supply seed and
that the ovaries of a woman are the functional equivalent of the
man's testes. Subsequent centuries have brought further scientific
developments, not least in the area of genetics. These discoveries
clearly have implications for the timing of ensoulment and the
theological status of the embryo.

However, before turning to these areas there is a further piece of
the theological context for medieval embryology that needs to be
explored. From the patristic period, theologians had reflected on
the embryonic life of Christ. This had theological significance
because of the doctrine of the incarnation: that the Word was made
flesh in the womb of the Virgin Mary. Medieval Christians, both in
the Greek East and the Latin West, held it to be dogma that Jesus
was fully human, and thus possessed a rational soul, from the first
moment of his existence. How this affected their understanding of
the human embryo is the topic of the next chapter.

9

The Embryonic Christ

In reality it is only in the mystery of the Word made flesh that the
mystery of the human being truly becomes clear.

(Vatican II, *Pastoral Constitution on the Church in
the Modern World*)

When Jesus was poorly received in his own village, he said of
himself, 'prophets are not without honour except in their own
country and in their own house' (Matthew 13:57). Whatever else
may be said of Jesus, in his own time he was widely recognized as a
prophet (Matthew 21:11; Luke 7:16; John 6:14 and elsewhere).
Christians understand Jesus to be 'the one who is to come'
(Matthew 11:3), the archetypal prophet, the fulfilment of the whole
of the Law and the prophets. Thus, what was true of the prophets
will be still more true of Jesus.

This has implications when we come to consider the conception
of Jesus and his life as an embryo. For, as the prophets Isaiah and
Jeremiah were called and set apart while they were in the womb
(Isaiah 49:1; Jeremiah 1:5), so Jesus was set apart from the first
moment of his existence (Matthew 1:20-23; Luke 1:31-5). In the
plan of God, the call of the prophets preceded their conception.
Much more so must the sending of the Chosen One have been
ordained by God from the beginning.

In the gospel accounts of Matthew and Luke, the identity of
Jesus is expressed, amongst other ways, through narratives of his
conception, birth and early infancy (Matthew 1:18-2:23; Luke 1:5-
2:40) just as, in the Hebrew Scriptures, the identity of Isaac as the
child of the promise had been expressed in the story of his
conception by Sarah (Genesis 17:15-18:15, 21:1-7). The pattern
established in Sarah, a barren woman who is blessed by the Lord
with a child, is repeated in Rachel (Genesis 29:31), in the wife of

Manoah (Judges 13:2), in Hannah (1 Samuel 1:5-6) and, in the New Testament, in Elizabeth (Luke 1:7). In each case the miraculous conception is a sign that God has a special role in store for the child. For this reason the events surrounding the naming of John (the Baptist) led people to say 'What then will this child become?' (Luke 1:66).

Luke juxtaposes the story of the conception of John the Baptist with that of Jesus to bring out both the continuity and the newness of the coming of Christ. The births of John and Jesus are both announced by the message of an angel (as those of Isaac and Samson had been). Both pregnancies are miraculous and come as a sign of the surprising and life-giving power of God. The conception of John in Elizabeth fits into the pattern of Isaac and Sarah, of a barren woman, who had given up all hope of becoming a mother, being granted a child in her old age. However, the conception of Jesus is something utterly new. Mary is not an old woman but a young woman. The new miracle is not only to make the barren fruitful, but to bring life by the power of the Holy Spirit without the need of a human father. It is an event without precedent in the history of the Jewish people. Nevertheless, the very newness of the action is in continuity with the Hebrew understanding of the Lord who 'creates something new' (Numbers 16:30; see also Isaiah 42:9, 43:19, 48:6 and Jeremiah 31:22). The conception of a child in the womb of a virgin is a radical demonstration of the power and the presence of God who comes to visit his people (Genesis 21:1; 1 Samuel 2:21; see also Genesis 50:24; Exodus 4:31; Jeremiah 29:10). Hence, the child to be born of the virgin is called Emmanuel, which means God with us (Matthew 1:23; Isaiah 7:14).

In the Hebrew Scriptures the presence of God with his people is expressed in a number of ways. God spoke his word (*dabar*) to the people, gave them a share in his wisdom (*hochmah*) and gave them his law (*torah*). The ten commandments, written on two slabs of stone and symbolizing the whole of the law, were placed in a box called the ark of the covenant. The ark was carried from place to place and was housed in a tent until David brought it to Jerusalem and Solomon built the temple to accommodate it. When Moses received the law on Mount Sinai, the glory of God was said to settle on the mountain and to cover it like a cloud. After the law had been given, the glory of God overshadowed the tent and filled the inner tent. Later it came to fill the temple.

For Christians, Jesus not only speaks the word of God but embodies the word. He is the word made flesh who has set his tent among us (John 1:14), a reflection of the glory of God (Hebrews 1:3). Therefore, when Mary carries Jesus in her womb she becomes the ark of the new covenant. The announcement of the angel to Mary that the power of the Most High would 'overshadow' (*episkiasei*) her (Luke 1:35) immediately brings to mind the glory of God that overshadowed (the same word in the Septuagint: *epeskiadzen*) the tent where the ark rested (Exodus 40:35). Luke then tells the story of Mary visiting her cousin Elizabeth in such a way as deliberately to echo the story of David bringing the ark to Jerusalem. As he brings the ark of the covenant into the city, David acknowledges the presence of the Lord by leaping and dancing before it (2 Samuel 6:16), and by his question 'How can the ark of the Lord come into my care?' (2 Samuel 6:9). As the pregnant Mary enters the house, John, the unborn prophet, leaps for joy (Luke 1:41) and Elizabeth greets Mary with the words 'And why has this happened to me, that the mother of my Lord comes to me?' (Luke 1:43). The hidden domestic scene of two pregnant women greeting one another thus takes on great theological importance. By greeting Mary as 'mother of my Lord', Elizabeth not only bears witness to Mary's status as the ark of the new covenant, but also acknowledges both the presence of Jesus and his identity as her Lord.

From the first generation, Christians have struggled to find an adequate theological formula to express the true identity of Jesus. Some early followers of Jesus regarded him as a great prophet, but not as divine (Ebionites). Others regarded him as a semi-divine figure, but not as a true flesh-and-blood human being (Docetists). To mention these opinions in such a cursory way is, of course, to take one point of doctrine out of context in order to construct a simplified schematic picture. It gives us little understanding of who the Ebionites and the Docetists were, or what reasons they had for holding the beliefs they held. Nevertheless, the rejection of these two notional extremes was important for the Christians in the first and second centuries CE. In this way Christian orthodoxy came to be defined by the simultaneous proclamation of both the divinity and the humanity of Jesus.

The focus for much Christian reflection on the human and the divine in Jesus was provided by the verse, 'the word was made flesh' (John 1:14). If the word was made flesh then it followed that Jesus was both 'the word' and 'made flesh'. For Jesus to be acknowledged as 'the word' was for him to be recognized as divine, as Lord and Saviour, as Son of God. For Jesus to be acknowledged as 'made flesh' was for him to be recognized as truly human, as son of Mary, as son of man. Only if Jesus were both word and made flesh could he both bring salvation and be the firstborn of a new and restored humanity. This understanding was expressed by Irenaeus of Lyons in the late second century by saying that the word of God became human so that human beings could become divine: 'For it was for this end that the word of God was made man, and He who was the son of God became the son of man, that man, having been taken into the word, and receiving the adoption, might become the son of God' (*Against Heresies* III.19).

From the third century most Christians explicitly upheld the doctrine that Jesus was both divine and human, was both son of God and son of man. However, rather than settling the issue this gave rise to many highly contentious questions. If the son of God was begotten by God the Father, was there a time when he had not yet been begotten? Or, if the son of God was co-equal and co-eternal with God the Father, was he then a second 'unbegotten'? Could any son be said to be the same age as his father? On the other hand, did any son have a different nature from his father? And what of the humanity of Christ? Did Jesus possess a rational soul independent of, or in addition to, embodying the word? If so, were the divine word and the human Jesus really one Christ or two Christs?

In the course of such controversies, which continued to rage from the third to fifth century and even later, the doctrine that Jesus Christ was both divine and human was subject to further clarification. The word who was made flesh in Jesus was *fully* divine: 'God from God, Light from Light, true God from true God, begotten not made, of one Being (*homoousios*) with the Father'

(Creed of Nicea, CE 325). Similarly, the flesh taken by the word was *fully* human, possessing a rational soul and body, lacking nothing in human nature, like us in all things but sin (Hebrews 4:15). Moreover, the divine and human in Jesus were also fully united in *one person* but *without confusion* between what was divine and what was human. The Council of Chalcedon in CE 451 thus defined Christ as 'at once complete in divinity and complete in humanity, truly God and truly man ... recognized in two natures, without confusion, without change, without division, without separation'.

The teaching of Chalcedon had been anticipated in great part by the *formula of reunion* a statement drawn up by Cyril of Alexandria for John of Antioch and the basis for a reconciliation between the churches of Alexandria and Antioch in CE 433. Chalcedon therefore received and reaffirmed the letter containing this formula. This document is important for our purposes because it states explicitly when the word became incarnate: at the moment of Jesus's conception. 'According to this understanding of the unconfused union, we confess the holy virgin to be the mother of God because God the word took flesh and became man and *from his very conception* united to himself the temple he took from her' (*Letter of Cyril to John of Antioch*, emphasis added). The formula begins by reiterating the dogma of Ephesus (a council held in CE 431) that Mary is 'the mother of God' (*theotokos*). By giving this title to Mary, Cyril defended the unity of the divine and human Jesus as one Christ, one son. Mary was not merely the mother of a man who was then united to God, but she was the mother of God-become-man. Cyril then identified the conception of Christ as the moment of the incarnation, again to exclude the idea the that the human Jesus existed independently prior to being united to the word. For Cyril, it was essential to say that Jesus was God incarnate from the very first moment of his existence, that is, from the moment of his conception. Otherwise the human Jesus would be, in himself, separate and independent of the divine son. 'From his very conception' meant from the very beginning, that is, in his totality.

The doctrinal concern to define Jesus's conception as the moment of the incarnation gave yet greater significance to the meeting of Mary and Elizabeth. Mary set off to visit Elizabeth 'with haste' (Luke 1:39) as soon as she heard the news of Elizabeth's pregnancy. When she arrived she was greeted as 'the mother of my Lord' (Luke 1:43). Thus, at that point, God was already incarnate in her womb. It is noteworthy that the Feast of the Annunciation (commemorating the moment when the angel appearing to Mary to announce that she was to be the virgin mother of Christ), celebrated on 25 March both in the Orthodox East and Catholic West, is regarded in both traditions as a Feast of the Incarnation. For example, on that day, the Catholic faithful are invited to kneel during the words of the Nicene Creed 'he became incarnate from the Virgin Mary, and was made man'. In the Eastern liturgy the faithful sing, 'God empties himself, takes flesh, and is fashioned as a creature when the angel tells the pure virgin of her conception' (Great Compline for the Feast of the Annunciation, Byzantine rite; see Saward 1993, p. 7).

Defining the conception of Jesus as the moment of the incarnation also has implications for when and how Jesus acquired his soul. This is shown, for example, in the condemnations of Origenism drawn up by the Emperor Justinian which concerned not only the doctrine of the pre-existence of souls but also the implications of this doctrine for the soul of Christ. If Christ's soul had pre-existed, then the union of human and divine would not have occurred when 'the word was made flesh' but long before that, when the soul was united to the word. According to Origen, this happened gradually.

> [T]he soul which belonged to Christ elected to love righteousness, so that in proportion to the immensity of its love it clung to it unchangeably and ... destroyed all susceptibility for alteration and change; and that [union] which formerly depended upon the will was changed by the power of long custom into nature. (*On First Principles* II 6.5)

Origen's doctrine not only strained the words of Scripture but also portrayed the pre-existent soul of Christ as an 'intermediary between God and the flesh' (*On First Principles* II 6.3) insulating God from the flesh and thus threatening the radical and paradoxical truth of the incarnation: that God has indeed become a human being. The condemnations of Origen explicitly concerned the relation of body and soul in the conception of Jesus. The first condemned the view that the soul of Christ existed before the body. The second condemned the view that the body exists before being united to the (pre-existent) soul.

> II If anyone says or thinks that the soul of the Lord pre-existed and was united with God the Word before the incarnation and conception of the virgin, let him be anathema.
>
> III If anyone says or thinks that the body of our Lord Jesus Christ was first formed in the womb of the holy Virgin and that afterwards there was united with it God the Word and the pre-existing soul, let him be anathema. (*Anathemas of the Justinian against Origen*)

A still clearer presentation of this doctrine is found in the synodal letter of Sophronius of Jerusalem which was 'received as orthodox and as salutary' at the Third Council of Constantinople (CE 680).

> [He] assumed the whole mass [of our nature], flesh consubstantial with us, a rational soul of the same kind as ours, a mind like ours. For man is and is known to be all these things; and he was made man in truth at the very instant of his conception in the all-holy Virgin. (Sophronius, *Synodal Letter*, see Saward 1993, pp. 4-5)

This statement of Sophronius can be seen to be but the working-out of the definition of Chalcedon that Jesus is 'at once complete in divinity and complete in humanity' together with the belief that the incarnation occurred the moment that Jesus was conceived in the womb of the virgin. It was a doctrine reiterated by many of the Fathers of the Church, including John Damascene (*On the Orthodox Faith* 3.2) and shaped the theology of both the Latin West and the Greek East.

The logic of the argument can be summarized as follows:

- Jesus was fully divine and fully human from his conception,
  → therefore he was fully human from conception.
- Jesus was fully human from conception,
- but he would not be fully human if he lacked a human soul,
  → therefore Jesus possessed a human soul from conception.

At least in the case of Jesus, then, the soul was created and united with the body at the moment of conception. The question then immediately arises: does what is revealed about the soul of Christ have implications for the Christian understanding of the soul of the human embryo in general? One influential theologian who argued that it did have such implications was Maximus the Confessor. Maximus was a follower of Sophronius of Jerusalem and an important defender of the incarnation at a time of 'monothelite' controversy (a theological dispute which engulfed the Church during the seventh century). Maximus argued that if Jesus acquired a rational soul at the moment of conception, and Jesus shares the same human nature as all other human beings, then everyone acquires a rational soul at conception. According to Maximus, the doctrine that the soul is present in the embryo from conception was implied by the incarnation: 'I consider nature's very maker, by the mystery of his incarnation, to be the champion and infallible teacher of this doctrine' (*Ambigua* 2, 42). An obvious rejoinder to this line of reasoning is to say that that the conception of Jesus was an *exceptional* event, unique in at least two ways. First, the conception of Jesus occurred by a miracle, conceived in a virgin by the power of the Holy Spirit. It was a conception without human (male) seed and therefore cannot provide the pattern for conception that is the result of the union of male and female. Secondly, the conception of Jesus was the moment of the incarnation. This Christian doctrine, which provides the premise for Maximus's argument, is equally a reason to distinguish the conception of Jesus from human conception in general.

Maximus anticipated such objections. In response he distinguished the way something comes to be from the nature it possesses. Jesus came to be in a different way from us, in a conception without seed. Nevertheless, his nature is the same as ours. Indeed, this communality of nature is required by the doctrine of the incarnation. In the words of Chalcedon, he is, 'of one substance with the Father as regards his divinity, of one substance with us as regards his humanity'. Jesus was conceived of a virgin, but in his humanity he is no different to those conceived by ordinary human generation. Thus, if Jesus possessed a human soul from the first moment of his conception, then the same must surely be true of all human beings.

The premise of this argument, that Jesus received his soul at conception, is implied in the scriptural scene of the visitation (Luke

1: 39–56) and, more fundamentally, in the doctrine of the incarnation. It was accepted by all orthodox Fathers of East and West, and is either implicit or explicit in the teaching of several ecumenical councils (most notable at Chalcedon). Thus, if a Christian wishes to deny that all human beings receive their soul at conception, this can only be done by suggesting that the humanity of the embryonic Christ was in some way *exceptional*. However, this alternative is highly problematic, as we can see when we turn from Maximus the Confessor to Thomas Aquinas. For the prevalent approach in the Latin West in the thirteenth century was to embrace just such an 'exceptional' account of the embryonic Christ.

In line with all other Catholic theologians of the period, Thomas Aquinas accepted the doctrine that incarnation occurred the moment that Jesus was conceived. He explicitly rejected the view that the flesh of Jesus was first formed and then afterwards united to God.

> We may say properly that 'God was made man', but not that 'man was made God': because God took on what is human – and what is human did not pre-exist, as subsisting in itself, before being assumed by the word. But if Christ's flesh had been conceived before being assumed by the word, it would have had at some time its own existence (*hypostasis*) other than that of the word of God. (*ST* IIIa Q. 33 art. 3)

Here Thomas expressed succinctly the same point that had been made long before by Cyril of Alexandria: if God truly became a human being, then that human being could never have been other than God incarnate. Thus, Jesus was 'the word made flesh' from the very beginning of his human existence, that is, from his conception. To think that the flesh had an existence prior to being assumed is to think of the son of man and the son of God as two beings, two Christs. This was the error of Nestorius so acutely identified by Cyril. It may seem a technical point, but it goes to the very heart of the incarnation, that claim so central to Christian faith, that Jesus is truly divine and truly human, the word of God made flesh.

Thomas also accepted the corollary that Jesus possessed a human soul from the first moment of his conception. For what makes human flesh human is that it is informed by a human soul.

The soul is not only the principle of reason and action, it is the life principle of the physical body. In the terminology of Aquinas, the soul is the *form* of the living body (*forma corporis*). To say that 'the word was made flesh' was thus to say that the word assumed human flesh endowed with a human rational soul. Furthermore, according to Thomas, the flesh of Christ was assumed 'through the medium of the soul' (*ST* IIIa Q.6 art. 1). This was an expression of his general view that matter exists for the sake of form and not vice versa (see for example *ST* Ia Q.89 art. 1). Thomas thus argued that from the moment the word was made flesh, the flesh was animated by a human soul (*ST* IIIa Q.6 art. 4 and again *ST* IIIa Q.33 art. 2). In defence of this he also quoted John Damascene: 'At the very instant that there was flesh, it was the flesh of the word of God, [and] it was animated with a rational and intellectual soul' (John Damascene, *On the Orthodox Faith*, 3.2, quoted *ST* IIIa Q.33 art. 2).

Thomas was then a strong defender of the traditional Christian doctrine that Christ was fully divine and fully human, possessing human flesh and a human rational soul, from conception. However, with regard to human beings in general, he held that the soul was not infused until the body was perfectly formed, which, according to Aristotle, was 40 days (for males) or 90 days (for females) after conception, or according to Augustine, was 46 days after conception (*Commentary on the Sentences* III, D.3, Q.5, art. 2). This delay was because 'in everything generated, that which is imperfect precedes in time that which is perfect' (*ST* IIIa Q.33 art. 3 obj. 3). According to Thomas Aquinas, human beings ordinarily come to be not instantaneously but through a succession of changes culminating in the perfected foetus, into which God infuses a rational soul (*ST* Ia Q.118).

The embryonic phase of human development was thus seen as a preamble to human nature rather than a part of human nature. However, as the flesh of Christ was generated by an infinite power, the power of the Holy Spirit, there was no need for an imperfect preamble to Christ's humanity. Therefore, according to Thomas, Jesus was never an embryo. He was conceived as a perfected foetus, 'already fashioned and endowed with organs of sense' (*ST* IIIa Q.33 art. 2 ad 3). Moreover, not only was Jesus conceived with a fully formed body, he was also conceived as a comprehensor, possessing the vision of God through his human understanding. In addition to this, from the first instant of his conception Jesus also possessed perfect conceptual knowledge of all things and had the use of his understanding and free will (*ST* IIIa Q.34, art. 1–4)!

One evident difficulty with this account of Jesus is that it seems to leave no room for change or development. If Jesus knew everything from the first moment of his conception, how could he learn anything for himself? And if he never learned or discovered anything for himself, how could he be said to be human? By the time Thomas came to write the *Summa Theologiae* he was aware that this was problematic. In response, he attributed a further kind of knowledge to Christ over and above any infused knowledge that he also possessed: empirical or acquired knowledge.

> And hence, although I wrote differently (*Commentary on the Sentences* III, D.4, Q.14, art. 3), it must be said that in Christ there was acquired knowledge, which is properly knowledge in a human fashion, both as regards the subject receiving and as regards the active cause. For such knowledge springs from Christ's active intellect, which is natural to the human soul. (*ST* IIIa Q.9, art. 4)

Nevertheless, by continuing the assertion that Jesus knew all things with his human mind by infused knowledge and prior to learning anything for himself, Thomas seems to leave Jesus with nothing to learn. It is not clear Thomas's later acknowledgement of the importance of active learning in human life is reconcilable with his account of an all-knowing human Jesus.

A similar pattern can be seen in Thomas's description of the first human being, Adam. Adam is also created fully formed (from dust) and with perfect infused knowledge, so that he could name all the animals (*ST* Ia Q.94 art. 3). On the other hand, Adam's offspring, had they been born in the Garden of Eden, would not have been born with any infused knowledge (*ST* Ia Q.101 art. 1), neither would they have been born with the perfect use of reason. The explanation Thomas gives for this is telling: 'In all things that produced by generation, nature proceeds from the imperfect to the perfect, therefore children would not have had the perfect use of reason from the very outset' (*ST* Ia Q.101, art. 2). Here the imperfect/perfect distinction relates to infants who are clearly human but who have not developed their rational powers (in part because of the wetness of their brains which need to dry out see *ST* Ia Q.99 art. 1). In the case of the possible children born into the state of innocence, Thomas has no hesitation in attributing to them the imperfections of immaturity. However, in relation to the infant Jesus, he shows a consistent unwillingness to accept the implications of human immaturity. Rather than growing in wisdom and stature (Luke 2:39, 52) Jesus is conceived fully formed, with the use of free will from the first moment of his conception, even though, in other children, this power does not develop until much later (see for example *ST* IIaIIae Q.189 art. 3; *ST* IIIa Q.80 art. 9 ad 3): 'As was stated above, spiritual perfection was becoming to the human nature which Christ took, which perfection he attained not by making progress but by receiving it from the very first' (*ST* IIIa Q.34 art. 2).

The claim that Jesus was never an embryo makes sense in a context where Jesus is thought not to share in the imperfections of immaturity, a context in which he is held to be conceived perfect in the sense of mature and fully formed. However, this whole approach seems to undervalue the developmental aspect of human nature. From the perspective of modern Catholic theology, the medieval picture of Jesus's perfect humanity is very difficult to sustain. So strong is the contemporary emphasis on change and transition, that a human nature which did not pass from immaturity to maturity would not be recognizably human. For the same reason, it seems incredible to assert that Jesus was never a human embryo and was conceived at the stage that the other human beings reach at 40 or 90 days (and yet, despite this, to say that he remained within the womb for a full nine months). Yet if the medieval account of Jesus in the womb is no longer sustainable, then it is much more difficult to argue that Jesus was an *exception* in receiving his soul at conception. Catholic theologians therefore need to re-examine the argument of Maximus that if Jesus received his soul at conception then all human beings receive their souls at that point. One theologian who has led the way in this regard is John Saward. His work *Redeemer in the Womb* (1993) has strongly influenced the present chapter.

We can say with some confidence then that contemporary Catholic theology has little sympathy for the perfectionist account of the infant Jesus. However, modern theologians might have reservations about Maximus's argument for other reasons. Since the rise of the historical-critical approach to the Scriptures, there has been increasing hesitancy among scholars about taking the infancy narratives as a reliable guide to the identity of Jesus. This is for a number of reasons, not least the privileged place given to the Gospel according to Mark as, by common, though not universal, consent, the earliest of the four gospels. Mark contains no infancy narrative and if Mark is held to be the original or archetypal gospel, it is easy to see the infancy narratives as secondary additions. Furthermore, from a historical perspective, the events of the public life of any figure are generally much more accessible than the story of his or her early life. The Catholic exegete Joseph Fitzmyer is by no means alone in seeing these narratives as theological constructions by later Christians reading back from 'what Jesus was recognized to be after the resurrection [to what] he must have been still earlier' (Fitzmyer 1981, p. 340). But before addressing the issue of scriptural interpretation, it is necessary to highlight other significant theological developments which shape the modern context.

Several strands of theology arising after the Second Vatican Council (1962–5) expressed a dissatisfaction with the style of thinking about Jesus that started with definitions such as the Nicene Creed or the definition of Chalcedon. In the view of many, such an approach threatened to undermine a true grasp of the reality of Christ by replacing Jesus with an abstraction. In contrast to this formulaic 'Christology from above' theologians such as Karl Rahner and Eduard Schillebeeckx urged the development of a 'Christology from below' which started by an engagement with the historical Jesus (that is, Jesus as discovered through historical-critical methods) and even more, by reflection on the contemporary experience of being human. Such an approach has also informed liberation theologians and feminist theologians seeking to reread the texts of the tradition in the context of those who suffer or whose voices have hitherto been marginalized.

Finally, many contemporary Christians are uneasy about using arguments from Scripture or tradition to adjudicate on matters that belong to or border on the natural sciences. In this they are moved by the spectre of Galileo and the fear of discrediting the faith by making rash assertions that may later be disproved. To be sure, the creation of the soul is not itself a subject for scientific investigation. Nevertheless, theological statements about the soul of the embryo have to be made in the context of a scientific embryology and must be compatible with what is known from biology. It is a brave theologian who will second-guess the results of future embryology on the basis of arguments taken from Scripture and tradition.

The development of the historical-critical method, the emergence of Christologies 'from below' and hesitancy over the relationship of science and religion combine to make the argument of Maximus unfashionable, even quaint, in a modern theological context. However, they do not touch upon its validity. Even if the analysis of Fitzmyer is allowed to pass without further comment (and it would be fair to say that there is much debate about the use, application and limits of the historical-critical approach to the Scriptures) this does not undermine the theological significance of the infancy narratives. Indeed, the precise point of scholars such as Fitzmyer has been that these passages should be read primarily as theological rather than historical texts. As we have seen, the argument of Maximus rests centrally on the theology of the incarnation as expressed, among other ways, through the infancy narratives. The theological claim that Jesus is 'God with us' (Matthew 1:23) and 'son of God' (Luke 1:35) from the first moment of his conception has in no way been undermined by recent scriptural scholarship.

For those who are developing a Christology from below, it remains important to ask not just what Jesus did and said, but who he was, who he is. In emphasizing the communality of Jesus's nature with our nature and his life in the womb with our life in the womb, Maximus is stressing the very humanity of Jesus so dear to these new theological approaches. What modern theologian would object to the words of Leo the Great on the humanity of the infant Jesus? 'Christ's flesh was not of another nature to ours: nor was the soul breathed into him from another source to that of all other men' (Letter 35 to Julian). Whatever must be said of the soul of the human embryo must be said of the soul of the embryonic Jesus, and vice versa. The infancy narratives remind us that to be human is to be born of woman. In this way the life of Jesus in the womb sanctifies the earliest phase of human life. Simply by adverting to the fact that Jesus was an embryo we imply a new status for the embryo, whether or not we do so by using the language of the creation of a human soul.

This also goes some way to addressing the third element in the modern context, concern over the proper relationship of science and religion. In saying that Jesus was son of God and son of man from the first moment of his conception, we are expressing a truth about the identity and significance of the embryonic Christ.

We are not asserting anything about the shape or form or powers of the embryo, except to say that he was as all human embryos are. This identity of Christ with human beings from the very beginning of our existence is captured by the seventeenth-century Anglican theologian Lancelot Andrewes: 'For our conception being the root as it were, the very groundsill of our nature; that he might go to the root and repair our nature from the very foundation, thither he went' (Sermon IX on the Nativity, in Saward 1993, p. 100). This may well have ethical implications in relation to the treatment of human embryos by scientists, but it does not circumscribe what may be discovered about the nature of the embryo. It does not imply particular scientific claims about the embryo, nor does it absolve us from the need to relate the scientific story and the theological story through a common narrative. The aim in arguing from the embryonic Christ to the embryonic human being is not to anticipate the biological investigation of the embryo but to illuminate the embryo's theological significance, and hence its ethical significance.

In summary:

- Reflection on the infancy narratives and on the doctrine of the incarnation led Christians to affirm that Jesus was both divine and human from the first moment of his conception. One of the implications of this affirmation is that Jesus had to have been fully human from the first, and thus had to have possessed a human soul from conception.
- Maximus the Confessor argued that as Christ had a rational soul from conception and as his nature is like ours in all things except sin, then every human being has a rational soul from conception.

- The claim of Thomas Aquinas that Jesus was exceptional in receiving his soul at conception is plausible only to the extent that other claims about his humanity are plausible: that he was never an embryo, that he was conceived as a foetus, that he attained human perfection 'not by making progress but by possessing it from the very first'.
- From a modern perspective the account of Jesus in the womb outlined by Maximus the Confessor is far more satisfactory than that given by Thomas Aquinas and other medievals. Thus, in so far as we accept this perspective, Maximus provides a very strong argument for saying that the human soul is present from conception.

In the Middle Ages, while theologians defended the doctrine that Jesus possessed a soul from the first moment of his conception, they did not infer from this that human embryos generally acquire their souls at conception. It was in the sixteenth century that the West saw a revival of the idea that ensoulment occurs at conception. This was influenced not by reflection on the embryonic life of Christ but by a number of other theological themes.

10

Imputed Dignity

All creatures are pure nothingness. I do not say that they are little or
that they are anything, but they are pure nothingness.

(Meister Eckhart, *Sermons*)

The Reformation altered the theological landscape and reshaped
the context, the bases and thus the method of Christian theology. In
this way it could not but have an impact on the understanding of
human life and human origins.

The term 'Reformation' covers a complex movement having a
social and political dimension as well as doctrinal and liturgical
aspects. It involved great numbers of people in different countries
and it took different forms in different countries. Among the most
influential was that 'associated with the German territories and with
the pervasive personal influence of one charismatic individual –
Martin Luther' (McGrath 1993, p. 6). Luther had been troubled by
the question of how a human being could ever be justified before
God. He had felt oppressed by the belief that justification was
something that had to be earned by good deeds, for these never
seemed sufficient to give confidence that someone was destined for
heaven rather than for hell. Trapped within this mindset, even the
religious rituals of forgiveness – the confession of sins to a priest
and the offering of the Mass – could appear as good deeds. Luther
finally found a way out of his distress through reading the letters of
Paul. These he understood as teaching that justification came not
by good deeds but as a wholly gratuitously gift of God. The phrase
'the righteousness of God' that had once so troubled him now
connoted the quality by which the merciful God gave justification to
the believer, through faith.

> [T]he righteousness of God is revealed by the gospel, namely, the
> passive righteousness with which merciful God justifies us by faith, as

> it is written 'He who through faith is righteous shall live.' Here I felt
> that I was altogether born again and had entered paradise itself
> through open gates. (Luther, *Preface to Luther's Latin Writings*, from
> Dillenberger 1961, p. 11)

The centrality of this experience for Luther's understanding of the
gospel is often summarized by the tag '*sola fide*' – by faith alone.
The gift of justification is not deserved or merited but was won by
Christ on the cross and is received passively by the believer. Luther
later saw confirmation of this doctrine in his reading of Augustine's
On the Letter and the Spirit.

A consequence of Luther's emphasis on the wholly unmerited
character of justification, the flip-side of the coin, as it were, is that
human beings are themselves utterly unable to do anything to earn
salvation. Without the grace of God all human beings are in a
hopeless situation. Luther understood sin not just as the occasional
acts of people who had the power to act well or badly. Since the
Fall, human beings were effectively incapable of acting well and
condemned always and inevitably to act according to the sinful
nature they had inherited, a theme Luther developed in 1525 in
The Bondage of the Will. He thus reiterated Augustine's understanding of original sin, that is, the doctrine that all human beings
were conceived in sin, a sinfulness inherited ultimately from Adam.

> Nor should we sin or be damned by that one sin of Adam, if the sin
> were not our own: for who could be damned for the sin of another,
> especially in the sight of God? Nor is the sin ours by imitation, or by
> working; for this would not be the one sin of Adam; because, then, it
> would not be the sin which he committed, but which we committed
> ourselves; – it becomes our sin by generation. (*The Bondage of the
> Will* sect. 152)

This sin was present in human beings from the first moment of
their existence and was passed on from generation to generation by
'sinful seed' – a term used by Luther in his *Confession of Faith*
(1528) and taken up in the *Solid Declaration of the Formula of
Concord* of 1577.

This emphasis on the inheritance of sin and the presence of sin
from conception inclined Luther to accept a traducianist account of
the origin of the soul, just as it had inclined Augustine not to
exclude traducianism. If the soul were not inherited from the

parents then it seemed that God would be unjust, for he would be creating new souls in a state of sin. In 1527 Luther still seems to have accepted the common medieval view of ensoulment: that 'man's conception is twofold: that the one is from the parents, but that the other takes place when the little body is prepared, and the soul infused by God, its Creator' (*Sermon on the Day of the Conception of the Mother of God*). However, by 1545 Luther was clearly more inclined to traducianism.

> We are inclined with him [Augustine] to the view that the whole man with body and soul is by traduction. For to God it is not impossible to make an immortal soul from human seed. Since he from the flux of nature makes a mortal body, ought he not then to be able to make from the seed also a soul? (*Disputation of Peter Herzog 'de homine'*, quoted in Williams 1970, p. 33)

On several occasions Luther expressed his preference for this account of the origin of the soul (See Althaus 1981, p. 160 n. 91), however, this view was not shared by all Lutherans. For example, in 1540, Melanchthon maintained the received medieval view that the soul was directly created by God and infused at 40 days, after the body was fully formed (*De Anima*, see Nutton 1990, p. 147; Williams 1970, p. 35). Nevertheless, it was Luther's view which was to predominate in the Lutheran tradition. While neither traducianism nor its apparent consequence, the presence of the soul from conception, were regarded as dogma, these conclusions seemed to flow naturally from central themes in Luther's thought. It is not surprising, then, to find them defended strongly by later generations of Lutherans, even up to the twentieth century.

> The theory of Traducianism, on the other hand, lies under none of the objections that may be raised against the theory of Creationism. It places the seat of sin in the soul, the immaterial part of man, where it properly belongs. It relieves God from the charge of being the author of sin or responsible for its continuance. It makes parents real parents as being parents of the whole child. It affords a clearer foundation for the propagation of original sin on the acknowledged principle that like begets like. (Little 1933)

The tendency of Luther and later Lutherans to accept traducianism was also supported by other more general features of the Reformation. The great methodological principle of the Reformation was *sola scriptura*. This did not mean that only what was in the Bible was true or useful, but it did mean that doctrines that were not explicit in Scripture were not to be imposed as dogma. This principle had the effect of freeing theologians from much of received Christian tradition and of inspiring them to return to the sources afresh. There was a greater willingness to criticize aspects of the tradition which were dominant in the Middle Ages but which had not been dominant in the early centuries of the Church. There was a renewed interest in the Fathers, particularly Augustine, and patristic texts were no longer seen mainly through the lens of legal or theological selections such as those of Gratian and Peter Lombard. It was thus relatively easy for Luther to revive a strand of thought from Augustine that had been rejected in the Middle Ages.

These general features of the Reformation – *sola fide* and the emphasis on the unmerited character of justification, *sola scriptura* and the radical questioning of received medieval tradition – were common to all the mainstream Reformers. However, there were also important differences between the Reformers which created divisions that endure to the present day. In style, Luther was primarily a preacher and a commentator on Scripture. He returned to certain themes throughout his writings, but did not construct a systematic theology. Indeed, in some ways his approach was strongly antithetical to such systemization. He proclaimed a theology of the cross which was built upon the experience of human need, a theology he distinguished sharply from the confident scholastic theology of the Middle Ages in which theologians drew upon Aristotle to understand the visible things of creation. 'That person does not deserve to be called a theologian who looks upon the invisible things of God as though they were clearly perceptible in those things which have actually happened' (*Heidelberg Disputation* of 1518, thesis 19). As a result, Luther rejected the authority of reason.

> Reason ... is the fountain and head of all mischiefs. For reason feareth not God, it loveth not God, it trusteth not God, but proudly contemneth him. It is not delighted with his words or works, but it murmureth against him, it is angry with him, judgeth and hateth him:

to be short 'it is an enemy to God' (Romans 8:7), not giving him his glory. This pestilent beast (reason I say) being once slain, all outward and gross sins should be nothing. (*Commentary on Galatians*, from Dillenberger 1961, p. 128)

In comparison, Calvin was a more systematic thinker, careful to make distinctions, happy to make use of reason within the context of faith. In many areas of doctrine, with respect to the Eucharist, the incarnation of Christ and the origin of the soul, Calvin criticized Lutherans for failing to make the proper distinctions. With regard to the Eucharist, Luther did not distinguish adequately between a bodily presence and the sacramental presence of a body. This led some Lutherans to attribute Christ's presence in the Eucharist to the ubiquity of Christ's glorified body. This, in turn, exposed a more fundamental confusion: of the divine and human natures of Christ.

And, indeed, some, to their great disgrace, choose rather to betray their ignorance than give up one iota of their error. I speak not of Papists, whose doctrine is more tolerable, or at least more modest; but some are so hurried away by contention as to say, that on account of the union of natures in Christ, wherever his divinity is, there his flesh, which cannot be separated from it, is also; as if that union formed a kind of medium of the two natures, making him to be neither God nor man. (Calvin, *Institutes of the Christian Religion* [1559], IV.17.30)

A failure to make the proper distinctions in regard to the Eucharist led to confusion in regard to the incarnation. In a similar fashion, Calvin differed from Luther in his account of the soul. In contrast to Luther (*Assertion of all the Articles of M. Luther Condemned by the Latest Bull of Leo X*, article 27) Calvin assented to the natural immortality of the soul as taught by Plato (*Institutes* I.15.6). Calvin also did not believe that the inheritance of original sin necessarily implied that the soul was generated by the parents (*Institutes* II.1.7). His position was followed by several later Reformed theologians, for example Francis Turretin (1623–87).

Since, therefore, the opinion of propagation [i.e. traducianism] labours under inextricable difficulties, and no reason drawn from any other source forces us to admit it, we deservedly embrace the option of creation as more consistent with Scripture and right reason. (Francis Turretin, *Institutes of Electic Theology* IX.13.10)

Like Jerome and Thomas Aquinas, Calvin was inclined to a creationist view of the origin of the soul. However, in line with many post-renaissance Christians he was critical of Aristotle's account of human reproduction, preferring Galen's view that both male and female produced seed. This led Calvin to differ from Aquinas and the later Latin tradition on the timing of ensoulment. Being more favourable to Plato than Aristotle in philosophy and more favourable to Galen than Aristotle in biology, Calvin saw no reason to follow the Aristotelian view that the soul was infused at 40 days or thereabouts. He held rather that the soul was created and infused at the moment of conception (Sermons on Job, 12, in Bouwsma 1988, p. 78). Thus, while Luther and Calvin were led to opposite conclusions concerning the origin of the soul (traducianist and creationist respectively) both moved away from the received medieval account and both tended to support the view that the soul was present from conception.

Another element in the theological context of the Reformation relevant to the understanding of the human embryo is the question of predestination. Calvin agreed with Luther in emphasizing justification through the unmerited grace of God, but he pushed this back, prior to any response by the believer (even the response of faith) into the elective will of God. In this way he took up another strand in the later thought of Augustine and renewed theological interest in the doctrine of predestination. Calvin's account of the doctrine divided Reformed Christians and caused fierce controversy between Calvinists and Roman Catholics. To many, the doctrine undermined the reality of human freedom and made God appear unjust and arbitrary in his judgements. Nevertheless, the Catholic Church did not condemn the doctrine of predestination to eternal life. The Council of Trent condemned only the view that God is the author of sin such that sinners are 'predestined to evil by divine power' (Trent: *Decree on Justification*, canons 6, 17). There is, on the contrary, a version of the doctrine of predestination that is fully consonant with the Catholic faith (see, for example, Thomas Aquinas, *ST* Ia Q.23). It is the faith of all orthodox Jews and Christians that God foreknows human actions and that he is the source of all that is good, including good deeds. However, because of the subtlety of this doctrine and the difficulty of expressing it clearly in a way that is compatible with belief in human free will, it was deliberately de-emphasized in the Catholic tradition subsequent to the Reformation. This is shown, for example, in the advice of Ignatius of Loyola, 'Although there is much truth in the assertion that no one can save himself without being predestined ... we ought not, by way of custom, to speak much of predestination' (*Spiritual Exercises: Rules to Have the True Sentiment in the Church* 14–15).

The Calvinist emphasis on predestination provided a context within which it was easier to see in the human embryo the future deeds that he or she was to do. This is exactly the context of Psalm 139, in which God beholds the unformed embryo and sees his or her future deeds before any of them have come to be. In this perspective, the embryonic human being is called to a future that God has already prepared. The doctrine of predestination encourages us to trace future human significance back to the very beginning of human existence. This does not necessarily imply that the soul is given at the moment of conception. Nevertheless, it seems to favour immediate ensoulment as theologically fitting or appropriate and has therefore been suggested as one reason why Calvin 'tended to make conception and the creation of the soul coincident' (Williams 1970, p. 37).

It has been argued that the human embryo has significance for us only in retrospect, that adults can look back to the moment of their conception but that the human embryo does not necessarily have a future to look forward to (Berry 1996, p. 96). Even in nature, many embryos die before they can be born. In the case of abortion or in vitro fertilization, the fate of the embryo depends in part on human decisions. However, the idea that an embryo has human significance only in retrospect seems at odds with the fact that the embryo is already a living being given life by God and being formed by God. The embryo is not only a potential human adult but is an actual human creature. It is for this reason that Dietrich Bonhoeffer could say:

> Destruction in the mother's womb is a violation of the right to live which God has bestowed upon this nascent life. To raise the question whether we are here concerned already with a human being or not is merely to confuse the issue. The simple fact is that God certainly intended to create a human being and that this nascent human being

has been deliberately deprived of his life. And that is nothing but murder. (Bonhoeffer 1955, p. 131)

The conception of the human embryo, like the birth of a child, is a sign of hope. It naturally evokes the response, 'What then will this child become?' (Luke 1:66). To reflect theologically on the embryo or on the new-born infant is, therefore, to consider the destiny of each person that is hidden in God. This is not altered by the fact that tragically, even in the developed world, some babies die before their first birthday. The days of the embryo, whether they are to be many or few, whether accomplishing great deeds or cut short before ever seeing the light of day, are already written in the book of God. Where the destiny of the embryo lies in the hands of others this gives them a responsibility to respect the life that has been given and to work with, rather than against, the plan of God.

At the centre of Reformed theology and closely associated with the doctrines of original sin and predestination is the doctrine of imputed righteousness. Luther thought it was essential to say that justification did not really belong to the sinner but was imputed to him or her as something extrinsic. In a sermon preached in 1519, 'Two Kinds of Righteousness', Luther argued that the believer's sins were covered up by an 'alien righteousness': the righteousness of Christ. This language was fully endorsed by Calvin, 'it is entirely by the intervention of Christ's righteousness that we obtain justification before God. This is equivalent to saying that man is not just in himself, but that the righteousness of Christ is communicated to him by imputation, while he is strictly deserving of punishment' (*Institutes* III.11.23). Thus both Luther and Calvin emphasized the unmerited character of divine justification. The sinner does not deserve to be justified but justification is imputed to him. The sinner is acquitted by God, but from a subjective point of view he or she is still guilty of sin. The justification comes from outside, not from within as something achieved by or belonging to the person. In this way Luther can be seen as taking up and recasting the earlier doctrine of the Rhineland mystics that 'all creatures are pure nothingness'. What gives the creature worth or status and rescues it from nothingness and from the vanity and emptiness of sin is the free action of God. The creature has status not on its own account but only in relation to God the Creator and Redeemer.

From a Catholic perspective it is not possible to say that the creature has no status on its own account, for that would seem to negate the truth of creation: God looked upon all he had made and found it to be very good (Genesis 1:31). It is also Catholic dogma that human beings retain a certain degree of free will despite the Fall (*Council of Trent: Decree on Justification*, canon 5). Nevertheless, it is also Catholic dogma that no one can be justified 'without divine grace through Jesus Christ' (ibid., canons 1-2; see also *Council of Orange*, canons 1-25). The emphasis of the Reformers on the weakness of human beings without God and the worth of human beings in relation to God reflects a fundamental theme in the gospel that is accepted by all Christian traditions. 'God chose what is foolish in the world to shame the wise; God chose what is weak in the world to shame the strong; God chose what is low and despised in the world, things that are not, to reduce to nothing the things that are' (1 Corinthians 1:27-8). God saves those who are weak and are as nothing, and opposes the strong and the proud, therefore the weakness and apparent insignificance of the human embryo is reason to suppose that the embryo is more valued by God and not less. On this basis Andrew Linzey complains that 'so little are unborn humans regarded, that their very "leastness" has been turned into an argument against respecting them' (Clarke and Linzey 1988, p. 41).

The same theological attitude expressed in the doctrine of imputed righteousness shows itself again in relation to the doctrine that human beings are made in the image of God. Luther understood the presence of the image of God in Adam not in terms of certain attributes he had (free will, reason, an immortal soul, dominion over the animals) but in terms of his relationship with God. The image of God referred to the godliness which Adam possessed and which was lost by the Fall. For Luther, the image of God was not something actual in fallen human beings. It was something that has been lost and that had to be restored by Christ. Calvin also sometimes spoke as though the image of God was wholly destroyed, cancelled or obliterated by the Fall (Hoekema 1994, p. 43). However, he qualified his remarks by saying that while the glory of God that shone in Adam had certainly been diminished and obscured by the Fall it was not wholly destroyed, for 'the image of God extends to everything in which the nature of man surpasses that of all other species of animals' (*Institutes* I. 15.3). Calvin follows Augustine in placing the image of God in the soul and the spiritual powers. Nevertheless, this image is best seen in Christ and in the saints and achieves its full lustre only in heaven. Thus Calvin followed Luther in relating the image of God to the narrative of Fall, redemption and glorious resurrection. The idea of placing the image of God in the context of redemption and salvation had already been anticipated by Augustine (see especially the later books of *On the Trinity*), though this aspect of his thought was largely neglected by the medieval theologians.

A further twist in this tradition is reflected in the work of the twentieth-century Reformed theologian Karl Barth. Taking up a theme from the Jewish philosopher Martin Buber, Barth argued that the image of God consisted principally in being in a relationship with another person. The human being was not to be thought of as an individual possessing a special quality – reason or the soul – but as a person who confronted another. What it was to be a person was constituted by such an 'I–thou' relationship. It was for this reason, according to Barth, that the human being made in the image of God was immediately described relationally as 'male and female' (Genesis 1:27). This constitutes the image of God because in God too there is a relationship of I and thou, in the Trinity. Also, human beings are created to be in relationship with God 'created as a Thou that can be addressed by God but also an I responsible to God' (*Church Dogmatics* III, 1, quoted in Hoekema 1994, p. 50). Barth can be seen as developing the dynamic and relational account of the image of God found in Luther and Calvin, placing human worth not in some intrinsic quality of the person as an individual, but relative to the person's creation and redemption by God and relative to other human beings through whom the person is constituted as a person. This emphasis moves the focus away from what the embryo has already achieved (in terms of powers or abilities) and on to the relationship the embryo has to the Creator and its relationship to its mother and father. It is in this context that Barth asserts that 'the unborn child is from the very first a child. It is still developing and has no independent life. But it is a man and not a thing, nor a mere part of the mother's body' (Barth 1961, p. 415).

This relational view of the human person has been invoked on both sides of the debate about the status of the embryo. Dr Caroline Berry has noted that the mother is not generally aware of the embryo until implantation, and sees in this lack of experienced relationship between mother and embryo a lack of human status.

> In his wisdom, God seems to have arranged the natural order so that the mother only becomes aware of her fetus and able to value it after implantation has taken place. Is there any suggestion here that God himself values the embryo more after implantation? (Berry 1993, p. 28)

Berry's argument has validity, not inasmuch as it relates to what we happen to value, but inasmuch as it relates to what we are 'able to value'. If it were true that we could not be aware of the human embryo then it is difficult to see how we could regard it as having human status or significance. However, the claim that a mother is unable to value her embryo before implantation is untrue. One of the ironies of in vitro fertilization is that, while it has resulted in the deliberate destruction of thousands of embryos, it has also allowed parents to feel hope and wonder at the sight of the newly conceived embryo.

> I just sat in the sitting room staring at the photo, thinking that this could be the first photo in an album of our children's lives ... the more I looked at that photo, the more real those two little translucent splodges became. They are, after all, already embryos. They've already passed the beginning of life. (Elton 2000, p. 333)

At least in the setting of IVF, parents can relate to and value, or fail to value, their embryos. The concern of those parents who value and protect each of their embryos, as best they can, provides us with an image, however imperfect, of God's concern for each human embryo. From the first moment of its existence, even when its existence is known to God alone, the embryo exists in relation to a mother and a father and in relation to God.

An important sociological and spiritual shift that occurs in parallel to these theological developments is seen in the Reformers' criticisms of Christian monasticism and its promotion of a new ideal of the Christian family. From its beginnings in the preaching of Jesus and the practice of the Early Church, Christianity had shown evidence of ambivalence about marriage and family. On the one hand Jesus criticized those who were failing to honour their father and mother, by giving to the Temple what should be spent caring for their parents (Matthew 15:4-6) and emphasized the significance of the marriage bond as set out in the first chapters of the book of Genesis (Matthew 19:4-6). On the other, he told his disciples that some had made themselves 'eunuchs' for the sake of the kingdom (Matthew 19:10-12) and that they had to 'hate' their own families: 'father and mother and wife and children and brothers and sisters' (Luke 14:26-7) if they were to be his disciples. Jesus himself was not married, nor was the great apostle Paul. From very early in the Christian tradition men and women renounced marriage and family and led lives of consecrated celibacy (see for example Ambrose, *Concerning Virgins* or Gregory of Nyssa, *On Virginity*). Some insight into the motivation of this renunciation is given by Brown (1988). Very soon this form of life came to be viewed as the perfection of the Christian life and married lay people lived in the light or rather the shadow of this ideal.

It was against such claims to perfection, and the idea of merit it seemed to embody, that the Reformers reacted. In its place they promoted the family as the primary locus of the Christian life. 'The Reformation movements made the sexually monogamous, procreation-centered family both the center of their basic community and their strongest metaphor of divine blessing' (Harrison 1995, p. 35). The primary resource for this shift in emphasis was the account of marriage, family and fertility provided by the Hebrew Scriptures. This again illustrates the way in which different aspects of Reformation thought reinforced one another in a new religious matrix. *Sola scriptura* provided the source for a renewed theology of the family. The effects of this upon consideration of the embryo was further to favour its protection, not only for what it was in itself, a child in the womb, but as a gift of God understood in the context of the duties of procreation, the blessing of children and the goods of marriage and family life.

> In general, pietism dealt extensively with married love. For the conjugal life and specifically the procreative act and for the growing fetus appropriate prayers were formulated. In his *Evangelische Glaubens-lehre* in connection with the article on faith, Spener asserted

that even infants dying within the mother's womb had light and faith
poured into them by God. (Williams 1970, p. 43)

In the twentieth century, and especially since the Second Vatican
Council, Catholic theology also came to emphasize the role of the
laity in the Church and the vocation of marriage as a means of
finding holiness in the world (for example John Paul II 1981).

The theological factors mentioned above shaped the views of the
churches that emerged from the Reformation, and to varying
degrees they continue to influence contemporary Protestantism,
particularly the more conservative or evangelical branches of this
tradition. However, in the eighteenth century some of the same
forces that shaped the Reformation would give rise to a
reconfiguration of Christianity certainly as radical as the classical
Reformation. This second Reformation, sometimes termed the
'Enlightenment', took as its basis the power of human reason and
the liberty of the individual, and rejected not only the tradition and
the authority of the Church but even the very concept of revelation
and the idea of miraculous intervention. The movement which
began with Luther's polemic against human reason led, in two short
centuries, to Kant's *Religion within the Limits of Reason Alone*. The
strand of the Christian tradition which emerged from the
Enlightenment is generally termed Liberal Protestantism (McGrath
1994, pp. 92-4) and includes such figures as Schleiermacher
(1768-1834), Harnack (1851-1930) and Tillich (1886-1965). This
far from homogeneous post-Enlightenment Christian tradition had
little immediate impact on Christian attitudes toward the human
embryo. However, in the mid twentieth century this movement
would provide the context within which some Christians would
come to see abortion as ethically acceptable in a wide variety of
circumstances. This view will be explored in Chapter 13 in the
context of examining the causes behind the changes in abortion law
in Britain and the USA in the nineteenth and twentieth centuries.

The purpose of the present chapter has been to examine the
theological matrix produced by the sixteenth-century Reformation
in terms of its impact for the Christian understanding of the
embryo. From this investigation a number of significant themes
have emerged.

- The context of the Reformation allowed for the re-examination of theological issues thought settled in the Middle Ages. The Reformers were not bound by the tradition of medieval Aristotelianism (represented *par excellence* by Thomas Aquinas) or by standard legal and theological collections such as those of Gratian or Peter Lombard.
- As might be expected, the results of this freedom were not uniform. Some Reformers, such as Melanchthon, maintained the standard medieval view that the soul was created by God and infused into the child 40 days after conception. Others held that the soul was generated by the parents (Luther) or that it was created at the moment of conception (Calvin).
- Luther's belief that the soul was generated by the parents (or more specifically, by the father) stemmed from his wish to defend the doctrine of original sin as inherited from Adam and present in each human being from conception. This argument is not dogma for Lutherans, but it has remained influential within the Lutheran tradition.
- Calvin's emphasis on the predestination of the elect provided a context within which it was easier to attribute great significance to the human embryo. Predestination does not necessarily imply that the soul is present from conception but it coheres naturally with this belief and Calvin himself seems to have identified conception as the moment the soul was created.
- Both Luther and Calvin emphasized that justification before God was not an achievement of the Christian but was due to the righteousness of Christ imputed to him or her. In an analogous way, a relational view of human worth would see the value of the embryo not in terms of its present powers or activities but in terms of its relationship with God its creator.

The Reformers sought to understand the human embryo in a new theological context. The doctrines of original sin, predestination and imputed righteousness, and just as significantly, the freedom Christians felt to set aside received medieval opinions, led to a revival of the early Christian view that the soul was present from conception. Many of the theological considerations that shaped the Reformers' attitudes to the embryo have weight also for Catholics and Orthodox Christians. The Reformation was a time of controversy and confusion, and many points of doctrine are still disputed among Reformed Christians and between these traditions and the Catholic tradition. Yet it also represented a period of great theological creativity. The Reformation provided some enduring insights that can deepen the contemporary Christian's appreciation of the human embryo.

To these theological influences there were soon added the effects of changes within the natural sciences. It was in the seventeenth century that the foundations were laid for modern embryology, but not before some false starts and several curious detours. The task of the next chapter is to map out the history of these scientific developments and to assess the way that theological implications were drawn from them.

11

Embryology through the Looking-glass

The Cartesian system is the romance of Nature, something like the story of Don Quixote.

(Attributed to Blaise Pascal)

It would be no exaggeration to say that embryology between the fourth century BCE and the seventeenth century CE was dominated by the work of Hippocrates and Aristotle (see Chapter 2). Nevertheless, this span of two millennia saw some dissent and development particularly in the Hellenistic period (third century BCE to second century CE), the high Middle Ages (eleventh to thirteenth century CE) and the Renaissance (fifteenth to sixteenth century CE). Therefore these periods will be examined in turn before considering William Harvey, René Descartes, and the great revolution in embryology in the seventeenth century.

One dissenting view in the ancient world, according to Plutarch, was that of the Stoics. They denied that the embryo had life or soul independently of the mother, attributing to the embryo a vegetative existence prior to birth. Among these Seneca (4 BCE–CE 65) is worthy of note for claiming that the seed enclosed 'all the lineaments of the bodie and all that Posterity shall discover in him' (quoted in Needham 1959, p. 66). This speculation seems to anticipate what was to be become a dominant theme in the embryology of the seventeenth and eighteenth centuries: the preformation of the embryo in the seed. However, in the context of the ancient world, Seneca's suggestion appears only as an obscure and isolated opinion.

In the third century BCE, the rise of anatomy represented an important development in the understanding of human biology.

Herophilus of Chalcedon pioneered human dissections, including the vivisection of criminals (according to Celsus, *On Medicine*, Preamble). The anatomical treatises of Herophilus have been lost, but they were widely read by later physicians such as Soranus and Galen in the second century CE. It is probably to Herophilus that we should attribute the discovery of 'female testes' connected to the uterus. This anatomical discovery, recounted by Galen, greatly strengthened the case for Hippocrates' two-seed account of generation, effectively undermining, at least among physicians, Aristotle's account of male seed concocting female blood.

Galen also departed from Aristotle in denying the priority of the heart in nutrition and in sensation. According to Galen there were three principle organs: the heart, the liver and the brain, responsible for vitality, nutrition and sensation respectively. Whereas Aristotle thought that arteries, veins and nerves all proceeded from the heart, Galen thought that the arteries proceeded from the heart, the nerves from the brain and the veins from the liver. Nevertheless, in regard to philosophy, Galen was much closer to Aristotle than he was to Hippocrates, giving explanations in terms of powers and faculties rather than material or mechanical causes. Aristotle's thesis that 'Nature does nothing in vain' (*Politics* I.2), is evident throughout Galen's work. For example, *On the Use of Parts* attempts to give a functional account of all the various parts of the human body.

With Galen, the classical period of embryology comes to an end. It would exercise influence upon the Talmud (second to fourth century CE), upon the theologians of the Early Church such as Tertullian, Augustine and Jerome (second to fifth century CE) and also leave its mark in the Koran and the *Haddith* (seventh century CE). But in each of these traditions, Jewish, Christian and Islamic, the interest was, at least initially, more theological than it was medical or scientific.

It was not until the Middle Ages, in the eleventh century CE that there was a return to the scientific study of embryology. In this endeavour first place goes to Ibn Sina (980–1037) better known to the Latin-speaking world as Avicenna. He was a philosopher and physician who was born and flourished in Persia at the time of the Samanid dynasty. Avicenna inherited a Greek classic tradition in which natural philosophy and medicine were dominated by the writings of Aristotle, Galen and Hippocrates. Where these authorities differed, philosophers tended to follow Aristotle and physicians tended to follow Galen and Hippocrates. Having a foot in both camps, Avicenna sought to reconcile Aristotle and Galen (Musallam 1990, pp. 32ff.). He agreed with Galen that females produced seed from the 'female testes' and that this combined with the male seed in the act of generation. However, he agreed with Aristotle in giving to the female seed the same passive role that Aristotle had assigned to the menstrual blood. The male seed was formative; the female seed provided the matter. In relation to the organs of the body Avicenna followed Galen in giving equal weight physiologically to heart, liver and brain, but he followed Aristotle in making the heart the first organ to appear in the embryo. The significance of Avicenna lies first in presenting classical Greek thought, particularly Aristotle and Galen, to an Arabic and thence a Latin world, but also in his willingness to engage with and criticize both Aristotle and Galen in an effort to establish the best available account.

During the twelfth and thirteenth centuries the writing of Avicenna and other Muslim scholars, and with them the works of Aristotle, Hippocrates and Galen, were translated from Arabic into Latin. Thus it was through Muslim learning that medieval Christians rediscovered the Greek scientific heritage. Nevertheless, in the context of the new European universities, scholars such as Albert of Cologne (1200–80) elaborated on the works of Galen or Aristotle. Albert undertook investigations of his own, writing new works on plants, minerals and natural history. Like Avicenna, Albert preferred Galen to Aristotle on physiology and accepted the two-seed account of generation. However, he also supplemented both Galen and Aristotle with his own observations. He repeated for himself Hippocrates' experiment of opening hens' eggs at different stages of development and observing the results. He also dissected fish and other animals. In this way he opened a new chapter for embryology.

> The importance of Albert in the history of embryology is clear. With him the new spirit of investigation leapt up into being, and, though there were many years yet to pass before Harvey, the modern as

opposed to the ancient period of embryology had begun. (Needham 1959, p. 91)

While Albert was fascinated by questions of natural history, his pupil Thomas Aquinas (1226-74) was primarily interested in metaphysics, ethics and theology. Albert and Thomas together championed the importance for Christians of critically engaging with the thought of Aristotle, but Thomas tended to focus on those areas furthest from empirical science and differed from Albert in some respects. For example, he reverted to a more purely Aristotelian account of generation, denying the two-seed doctrine of Hippocrates and Galen, arguing explicitly for the view that it was the blood of the woman that was the equivalent of the male seed (*ST* IIIa Q.31 art. 5). In the years immediately after Thomas's death, the interpretation of Aristotle and his acceptability for Christian theology were to become the subject of intense debate. In 1277 a series of Aristotelian propositions was condemned at Paris University and condemnations followed in Oxford the same year (Tugwell 1988, pp. 236-43). In the wake of these events, writers such as Giles of Rome, who was in Paris at this time, became interested in the embryo precisely as the context for interpreting Aristotle's philosophy (Hewson 1975, pp. 44-5). However, Giles and later medieval writers who discussed the embryo (such as Dante) tended to be concerned with the philosophical and theological matters and failed to build upon Albert's empirical work in biology.

The scientific story is taken up by the great individual genius of Leonardo da Vinci (1452-1519). Leonardo was a product of the Renaissance: a great revival of interest in Greek and Roman eloquence and architecture, and the subsequent availability of a much greater range of classical thinkers than were known of in the Middle Ages. These rediscovered writers included atomists, sceptics, Stoics and Platonists, alongside Aristotle and Galen. In such a context, Leonardo readily abandoned the Aristotelian account of embryology found in different forms in Avicenna, Albert, Thomas, Giles of Rome and Dante. In what seems to be a return to Stoic speculations, he argued that the soul of the mother gave life to the body of the foetus. He even went so far as to claim that the heart of the foetus did not beat until after it was born – a retrograde suggestion that later was corrected by Harvey. Leonardo's major contribution to embryology lies in his detailed anatomical drawings, including one famous sketch of a dissected pregnant uterus. In this way he anticipated the rise of anatomy of the sixteenth century. In 1514 Andreas Vesalius was born: 'the greatest anatomist of any age' (Needham 1959, p. 100). While Vesalius did not make a direct contribution to embryology, a younger contemporary, Ulysses Aldrovandus (1522-1605), applied the same techniques of accurate anatomical drawing to the development of the chick embryo. The microscope had not yet been invented, but by the mid sixteenth century there was already a realization of the need to return to observation if the formation of the embryo was to be understood.

Another significant feature of the age, already apparent in Leonardo's drawings, was an interest in mechanics. Leonardo stands at the forefront of an era that was fascinated by the idea that living things could be analysed as complex machines. The 'mechanical philosophy', as it came to be known, was later exemplified by Francis Bacon (1561-1626), Galileo Galilei (1564-1642), Thomas Hobbes (1588-1679), Pierre Gassendi (1592-1655) and René Descartes (1596-1650) among others (see Hankins 1985, pp. 114-19; Henry 1997, pp. 56-72). Their views were not identical. In particular there was an important distinction between those (such as Gassendi) who thought that matter consisted of tiny indivisible atoms and those (such as Descartes) who thought that matter was infinitely divisible. Nevertheless, all regarded physical processes as explicable in terms of push and pull, of matter moving predictably according to necessary mathematical laws. The new philosophers were thus united in rejecting vital powers, faculties, formal and final causes and other categories invoked by Aristotle and Galen.

William Harvey (1578-1657) was an anatomist in the tradition of Vesalius and Aldrovandus. He was also interested in accounting for biological phenomena in causal and functional terms. His most renowned work was *On the Motion of the Heart and Blood in Animals*, in which he demonstrated that blood circulated around the body. He showed that the amount of blood pumped by the heart was far greater than could be produced by the body and that therefore the arteries (taking blood away from the heart) and the veins (taking blood to the heart) were somehow connected. This was confirmed four years after his death by Marcello Malpighi (1628–94) who observed the microscopic capillaries that connect arteries to veins. The discovery of the circulation of the blood marked a major advance on ancient physiology, whether Aristotelian or Galenic. Harvey takes his place besides Galileo or Newton at the forefront of a new era in scientific thought. Nevertheless, unlike many scientists of his day, Harvey was not an advocate of the mechanical philosophy. He remained broadly Aristotelian in his understanding of living things and viewed as mistaken the attempt to explain living things by reference only to the diversity of matter, to hardness or softness, to elements or to atoms. In short, 'there can be no doubt that Harvey's leanings were vitalistic' (Needham 1959, p. 141).

After his work on the circulation of the blood, Harvey set himself the task of unravelling the process of generation. He was convinced that there was a basic pattern common to the generation of all animals and that, in particular, all animals began as an egg: *omne vivum ex ovo*. For this reason he thought that maggots came from eggs too small to be seen and not from 'spontaneous generation' out of rotting meat, as Aristotle had thought. He also regarded the first stage of the human embryo as an egg. In the tradition going back to Hippocrates, Harvey thought that there was a close analogy between the growth of a chick embryo and the growth of a human embryo. It is not clear whether he also believed that the human egg was first produced by the female and only afterwards fertilized by the male (as in birds and fish) but his thought certainly tended in this direction. Harvey's saying 'all living things begin as an egg' seems to have encouraged others after him to look for the human ovum.

Prior to Harvey, the two most prominent theories of human generation had assumed that the embryo was produced from a coagulation of fluids: either seed and blood (Aristotle) or seed and seed (Hippocrates, Galen). In either case soon after fertile intercourse the womb should have been filled with a fluid mixture surrounded by a membrane. To test this Harvey carried out a series of experiments, separating deer after rutting and dissecting the does at various stages. To his great surprise he saw no fluid in the wombs of the deer immediately after intercourse, indeed no sign of the embryo in any deer until several weeks after intercourse. Harvey was at a loss to understand how the process of fertilization worked. He gave the analogy of the way in which contagious diseases were passed on, but this was unsatisfactory because it was explaining one unknown cause by reference to another unknown cause. Before the invention of the microscope that was probably as far as he could go.

On Generation of Animals, published in 1651, was not as successful or as well known as his earlier work on the heart, but it nevertheless represented an important advance on ancient biology. Harvey demonstrated once and for all that the embryo was not formed in the way Hippocrates, Aristotle and Galen had supposed, by the mixing of fluids to produce a structure like a raw egg without the shell (Hippocrates, *On the Nature of the Child* 13; Aristotle, *Generation of Animals* 3.9, 758b 5). Harvey also criticized the doctrine of the spontaneous generation and hypothesized the existence of invisible microscopic eggs both in insects and in mammals. In other ways Harvey defended Aristotle and Galen. Against Leonardo and other Renaissance thinkers, he affirmed that the organs of the embryo were active. He was also explicit in his affirmation of epigenesis: 'the idea that morphological complexity develops gradually during embryology from simple beginnings in an essentially formless egg' (Gould 1977, p. 481). Harvey can still be thought of as Aristotelian, but he rendered the old embryology untenable and encouraged later biologists to turn to the microscope to get a better understanding of the process of generation.

Contemporary with William Harvey, but writing some years earlier, was the Flemish physician and professor of medicine at the University of Louvain, Thomas Fienus (1567–1631). He is significant for reviving the theory of immediate ensoulment within the Catholic tradition. His starting point in *On the Formation of the Foetus* (published in 1620) was an Aristotelian account in the tradition of Thomas Aquinas. However, Fienus considered the received view to be flawed in that it failed to identify adequately the efficient cause of embryonic development. Fienus resisted the suggestion that the cause of formation was simply God. This must be true remotely, but we should still look for an immediate and natural cause. He asked whether formation was due to the womb acting as a mould, or to the seed. He argued that it was due to the seed. There was a problem with this idea, however, in that the seed was no longer present after the first few days and could not be active after that point. The vital spirit within the seed could not therefore function as the instrumental cause as Thomas Aquinas suggested (*ST* Ia Q.118 art. 1 ad 3). After ruling out other possibilities, Fienus concluded that formation was directed by the rational soul which was received immediately after conception ('*post conceptum adveniens*': see Needham 1959, p. 120).

In 1621 another physician, Paolo Zacchia (1584-1659), published a book on *Medico-Legal Questions* in which he also defended the opinion that the soul was given at conception. Like Fienus, Zacchia was also critical of the idea of a succession of different souls in the embryo. While the embryo would not exercise certain of its powers until a later stage of development, there was no reason to deny that it possessed a human soul from the beginning. Zacchia did not argue that all the organs were actually present at conception, but rather that the soul was present from the beginning and that this human soul informed the development of the organs. Fienus and Zacchia had to contend with a received tradition which understood all ancient authorities: Hippocrates, Aristotle, Galen, the Septuagint version of Exodus 21:22-5, Jerome and Augustine, as supporting delayed ensoulment. In response, both point out that these sources did not generally talk of a distinction between unensouled and ensouled, but only of a distinction between unformed and formed. Furthermore, the Septuagint was not the authoritative version of the Old Testament and, in this passage, it differed from the official Latin text (see Chapter 4). They also pointed out that both Augustine and Jerome were explicitly agnostic on the timing of ensoulment. Zacchia admitted that delayed ensoulment was the view of Aristotle, but he followed Hippocrates and Galen, against Aristotle, in holding a two-seed view of generation, a view that seems to strengthen the significance of conception. There is an interesting parallel here between the opinions of Zacchia and those of Calvin.

Fienus was a friend of Gassendi, but he did not follow Gassendi in his approach to natural science. Both Fienus and Zacchia inhabited the same conceptual world as Harvey and did not accept the new mechanistic philosophy. Indeed, Fienus's fundamental argument is very similar to one put forward many centuries before by Gregory of Nyssa. If the embryo was formed 'not by the importation of any other power from without, but by the power which resides in it transforming it' (*On the Making of Man* 29.4) then development was a vital activity of embryo. The process of development was therefore due to (the soul of) the embryo, and not directly due to (the soul of) the parent. Thus the embryo must be human, with a human soul, from conception. 'Zacchia and Fienus developed their alternative views within the biological and philosophical framework of both Aristotle and Aquinas' (Ford 1988, p. 48). The defence by Fienus and Zacchia of the view that ensoulment occurs at conception represented a minority opinion for Catholics at the time, but their view began to gain weight when Zacchia was appointed physician-general to the Vatican State in 1644.

The years following Harvey's death saw three influential themes in scientific treatments of embryology. The first was the increasing application of mechanistic ideas to the embryo. In 1658 Gassendi's complete works were published. Four years later Descartes' work on the formation of the foetus was published. Descartes and Gassendi defended the existence of a soul in the sense of a principle of *mind* but rejected the idea of the soul as a principle of *life*. Rather, they understood the organic functions of living things purely in terms of mechanical causes. Both thinkers therefore attempted to explain the formation of the embryo in terms of the interaction of simple physical processes.

The second theme was the supposed discovery of the human ovum. In 1667 Niels Stensen, anatomist, and later Catholic bishop in Munster, described the internal organs of dogfish and suggested that the 'female testes' of Galen were in fact the equivalent of the egg-producing organs of fish. He thus named them 'ovaries'. This suggestion seemed to be confirmed in 1672 by Regnier de Graaf (1641–73) and Jan Swammerdam (1637–80) when they described what they took to be eggs in the ovary of a mammal. The structures they observed were in fact Graafian follicles, small round cavities inside the ovaries in which the much smaller ovum develops and which burst to release the ovum during ovulation. Nevertheless, though the correct identification of the ovum would not take place until von Baer in the early nineteenth century, from the late seventeenth century most biologists became convinced that mammals produced eggs. This seemed to be a vindication of Harvey's view that all animals begin from an egg, and it marked the second great break from ancient embryology. The female element in generation was no longer thought of as a fluid (menstrual blood or female seed) but as an already formed egg.

The third, and in many ways most extraordinary, theme of embryology in the late seventeenth century was the rise of preformationism. The first generation of scientists to make use of the microscope discovered more complexity much earlier in development than they had expected. In 1672 Malpighi investigated chick embryos with the microscope and found that, though it changed shape over time, there was never a time when the embryo was without observable structure. This result was due to the fact that he neglected the development that had already occurred before the egg was laid. Nevertheless, the discovery of an impressive degree of structure at an earlier stage than had previously been imagined, and on a microscopic scale, was enough to convince him that all the structures of the embryo pre-existed inside the egg. What seemed to be development was therefore only differential growth and the unfolding of a structure that was possessed from the beginning. Around the same time, Jan Swammerdam was hardening the chrysalides of butterflies with alcohol and then dissecting them. What he saw was the complete butterfly folded up. He came to the same conclusion as Malpighi, that 'in nature there is no generation but only propagation' (Needham 1959, p. 170). This idea was immediately taken up by Malebranche, a philosophical disciple of Descartes.

> We must suppose that all the bodies of men and animals which will be born until the consummation of time will have been direct products of the original creation, in other words, that the first females were created with the subsequent individuals of their own species within them. (*The Search after Truth*, quoted in Needham 1959, p. 169)

The act of generation was thus imagined as something like the opening of a series of Russian dolls each of which had existed from the beginning, one encased in its mother, which was encased in its mother, and so on: an idea that was termed *emboîtement*. From the perspective of hindsight, it is difficult to take this idea seriously, but the microscope had revealed to people worlds previously unknown. If a whale is compared to a mouse, and a mouse to a flea, and a flea to an animal only observable through the microscope, it is clear that the range of size of the animals spans many orders of magnitude. Why then suppose that what could be seen at the time represented the smallest living forms? Why indeed suppose there was any limit to how small something could be? Charles Bonnet (1720–93) declared that 'this hypothesis of encapsulation is one of the greatest victories that pure understanding has won over the senses' (from the *Contemplation of Nature* [1764], quoted by Gould 1977, p. 21). This comment seems to justify Pascal's claim that the Cartesian system, putatively based on pure reason, was in reality a kind of romance of Nature.

While Malpighi was putting forward the idea of preformation in the ovum, another parallel theory was suggested in 1677 by Antoni van Leeuwenhoek (1632–1723). He discovered microscopic 'animalcules' in semen, later to be known as spermatozoa. In a famous drawing, Hartsoeker (1656–1725) sketched a tiny human being curled up in the head of a spermatozoon. This did not represent something he claimed to have seen, but was how he imagined the animalcule to look if a powerful enough microscope had been available. From this point, the late seventeenth century saw a fierce exchange between ovists and animalculists. Both groups of scientists believed in the preformation of the human being in the gamete. Both believed in the *emboîtement* of all future generations in the ancestral animal. Both believed that hereditary information passed down through only one sex. The only difference was that the ovists held the ovum to be all important, while the animalculists held the spermatozoa to be all important. The animalculists regarded the egg as a sort of empty house with one trapdoor into which the successful spermatozoon entered. The ovists tended to deny that the animalcules observed in semen had anything to do with generation! Perhaps they were simply parasites in the fluid, or perhaps they performed some function such as mixing the fluid, but without contributing anything to inheritance. From the early eighteenth century the ovists began to gain the upper hand, first after the observation of tiny animalcule-like organisms in water which obviously had nothing to do with generation and, more significantly, after the discovery of parthenogenesis in aphids (see Hankins 1985, p. 131). In a carefully controlled experiment Bonnet raised aphids for ten generations without any male being present. This clearly demonstrated that, at least in the case of aphids, everything necessary for generation could come solely from the female. Furthermore, aphids are viviparous and thus microscopic investigation was able to show the young like miniature adults within the body of their mother.

The context of the debate between the ovists and the animalculists was the dominance of the mechanical philosophy within the natural sciences. The attempts of Descartes and Gassendi to explain generation as a simple mechanical process were widely judged to have failed. Thus, while more and more scientists were coming to embrace the mechanical philosophy, there seemed an insuperable difficulty in applying mechanical explanations to the processes that generated animal forms. If biologists were not allowed to appeal to vital forces or to the soul, how could they explain the sudden emergence of this complexity? The only alternative seemed to be to assume that the complexity had been there all along. The idea of preformed animals present within the bodies of their parents since the beginning of the world thus took its place within a more general view of nature: the static clockwork image of the universe that was all-pervasive in the seventeenth and eighteenth centuries.

This was not to say that preformationism was without its critics. William Harvey had given an account of development in terms of epigenesis, and in the eighteenth century he was followed by other thinkers such as John Needham (1713-81) and Casper Wolff (1734-94). It is interesting to note that in many cases this rejection of preformation went hand in hand with a rejection of the mechanical view of living things. Wolff claimed that development was due not to mechanical processes but to an immanent vital force, the *vis essentialis*. It is possible then to see embryology during this period as a series of fights between polar opposites: between vitalism (broadly following Aristotle) and mechanism (broadly following Descartes); between epigenesis (gradual development) and preformation (everything present from the beginning); between ovism (preformation in the egg) and animalculism (preformation in the sperm). Strikingly, in each of these cases, for all the fire and fury of the debate, the final resolution tended to lie in a middle path.

> The solution to great arguments is usually close to the golden mean, and this debate is no exception. Modern genetics is about as midway as it could be between the extreme formulations of the eighteenth century. The preformationists were right in asserting that some pre-existence is the only refuge from mysticism. But they were wrong in postulating preformed structure, for we have discovered coded instructions. (Gould 1977, p. 18)

Before moving on to consider nineteenth-century embryology, we should consider what impact the embryological debates of the seventeenth and eighteenth centuries had upon theology, for some thinkers certainly drew theological conclusions from these ideas. Swammerdam thought that his observations had explained the doctrine of original sin (Needham 1959, p. 170). Leeuwenhoek's discoveries were seen by some Jewish writers as confirming the Talmudic view that the spilling of male seed is 'like murder' (Feldman 1974, p. 121). Malebranche was a Catholic priest and a leading advocate of preformation. However, for most Christians, original sin was thought to be passed down through the male line from Adam, or possibly through both parents, but certainly not only through the female line, as was implied by Swammerdam's ovism. Leeuwenhoek gave priority to the male lineage, and so might have supported some traditional theological beliefs, but his ideas were much less successful than ovism scientifically. 'Animalculism never really caught on' (Henry 1997, p. 71). Furthermore, there were problems for orthodox Jews in accepting it, for the Talmud spoke of both male and female seed. Malebranche was a prominent Catholic thinker, but he was regarded as something of a maverick. His reputation also suffered as a result of a controversial exchange with Bossuet and Arnauld on the theology of grace, after which certain of his works were censured by Rome. Cartesian philosophy of the sort espoused by Malebranche had an impact both within and beyond the Catholic Church, but it was viewed with caution and subject to criticism by many Catholic authors. Conservative theological opinion in the Order of Preachers (Dominicans) and the Society of Jesus (Jesuits) remained more or less wedded to the thought of Thomas Aquinas as understood through later commentators such as Cajetan and Suarez. This was not easily reconciled with the new mechanical philosophy. Thus there were some important theological inhibitors that prevented the new embryology from having the impact on theology one might have imagined.

An insight into the theological understanding of the embryo during the eighteenth century is provided by Fransisco Emmanuele Cangiamila (1701–63). His *Sacred Embryology* went through several editions in the latter part of the eighteenth century (Needham 1959, pp. 204–5; Connery 1977, pp. 201–9). On the question of ensoulment, Cangiamila considered the Aristotelian idea of delayed ensoulment to be antiquated. It seemed much simpler to posit one soul in the embryo from the beginning than a succession of different souls. Cangiamila also discussed the scientific theories of his own day. He was sceptical of animalculists but regarded the ovists as having some evidence on their side. In this context the opinion of Fienus and Zacchia was viewed as increasingly probable and also had the support of most physicians, though Cangiamila did not regard the case as proven. Donceel (1970, p. 94) is right to identify preformation as a factor favouring belief in immediate ensoulment in this period. However, the defence of this position by Fienus and Zacchia had not been due to Cartesian ideas. It stemmed, rather, from internal criticism within the Aristotelian tradition. Preformationism was not responsible for the initial revival of belief in immediate ensoulment in the early seventeenth century, but it probably helped to popularize this belief in the eighteenth century.

The final demise of preformation within scientific embryology was due, in part, to its inability to explain monstrous births (Needham 1959, p. 210). It also suffered as microscopy improved. In 1826 Carl Ernst von Baer observed the true ovum of a mammal, as opposed to the follicle, and in 1875 Wilhelm Hertwig observed the union of spermatozoon and ovum. The moment of fertilization was at last observed directly. Between von Baer and Hertwig other scientific theories had emerged that were to have a profound influence on embryology. In 1838, on the basis of microscopic observations, Matthias Schleiden and Theodor Schwann put forward the hypothesis that all living things were composed of cells. Cell theory soon became a unifying theme in biology and helped to explain the relationship between differentiation and growth in the embryo. All embryos begin as one cell, this cell divides and then the cells differentiate into those that will constitute the different tissues. This idea gave added content to epigenesis and seemed further to undermine preformation.

In 1859 Charles Darwin published his *On the Origin of Species by Means of Natural Selection: Or the Preservation of Favoured Races in the Struggle for Life*. Evolution became the paradigm of a new world-view. Rather than the static and mechanistic world of Descartes and Newton, this new view was historical and developmental. A year after publishing *Origin of Species*, Darwin wrote, 'embryology is to me by far the strongest single class of facts in favour of a change of forms' (Gould 1977, p. 70). The specific relationship between the embryo and evolution was given greater prominence due to the work of Ernst Haeckel (1834–1919). Haeckel believed that the development of the embryo should be understood in evolutionary terms, and that evolution should be understood by reference to embryology. He imagined the embryo as going through every form of life that comprised the evolutionary history of that animal. For example, the human embryo would start as a simple one-celled animal and then progress through fish, amphibian, primitive mammal and monkey forms until it reached the human form. This explains why, for example, the early human embryo appears to have a tail. Haeckel's system was similar in some ways to the Thomist–Aristotelian idea of a succession of souls, except that Haeckel had the extra ingredient of evolution. His slogan was 'ontogeny recapitulates phylogeny', meaning that the process of development of the embryo (ontogeny) repeats in itself the history of evolution (phylogeny). This was a very attractive idea because it combined two powerful stories: the story of the embryo and the story of evolution. It caught the imagination both of scientists and of non-scientists and helped to convince many people in the nineteenth century of the truth of evolution.

Haeckel believed that early stages in embryonic development repeated all the adult ancestral forms. However, the idea that this provided the key to understanding evolution was undermined by the progress of biology, and in particular, by the discovery of modern genetics. Biologists no longer believe that the stages of the embryo should be understood as repeating the history of evolution. It is true that human embryos appear more like embryos of other species in their class than they do to the adult members of their own species. This is because they are all moving from relatively undifferentiated embryo to the differentiated adult. It is also true that the embryonic form of an animal may show tell-tale signs of its ancestry. However, it is a confusion to think of the embryo as being like the adult form of another kind of animal. Embryos should be understood as immature forms of their own kind. In the sense in which Haeckel originally put it forward, it is simply not true to say that 'ontogeny recapitulates phylogeny'.

Haeckel's ideas influenced several theologians, most notable Pierre Teilhard de Chardin (1881-1955). Teilhard was both a priest and a palaeontologist and he attempted to produce a theology that would take evolution seriously. He has been criticized heavily both by scientists and theologians (for example Medewar, Gould, Pius XII: Benz 1966). Nevertheless, he was popular with a new lay readership and influential among some of the major Catholic theologians of the twentieth century (Jacques Maritain [1882-1973], Henri de Lubac [1896-1991], Karl Rahner [1904-84]). It is probably still too early to assess the extent of his legacy. For positive assessment see Haught (2000, pp. 81-3). Teilhard saw life, theology and metaphysics in developmental terms. Creation was less an event at the beginning of time and more a journey towards God. As human beings had already evolved from lower forms, they would continue to evolve socially and spiritually. It was natural for Teilhard to see the development of the embryo as a similar journey starting with the purely biological and culminating in the human. Rahner took up this idea in his essay on 'Hominization'. Elsewhere he explicitly invoked Haeckel's dictum 'ontogeny recapitulates phylogeny'.

Rahner saw himself as reviving the position once defended by Thomas Aquinas – that ensoulment occurs only after the organs of the embryo are properly formed. There are certainly echoes of Thomas in the views of Rahner, but it is important to distinguish the different theological and scientific contexts of these earlier and later versions of delayed ensoulment. Thomas worked within the framework of Aristotelian metaphysics and biology. Rahner combined Aristotle's metaphysics with philosophical approaches taken from Kant and Heidegger and Aristotle's biology with ideas taken from evolutionary biology. He strove to be aware of contemporary developments both in philosophy and science. However, in viewing the process of embryonic development as repeating evolution, Rahner was closer to Haeckel than he was to Darwin. His theological understanding of the embryo was founded on a mistaken scientific theory which, though it had been discredited among biologists, retained its sway upon the popular imagination: the seductive but misleading idea that the embryo retraces in its own development the evolutionary journey of the species.

A number of contemporary theologians have sought to apply the philosophical principles of Thomas Aquinas in a new scientific context in order to address the question of ensoulment. It cannot be assumed that Aquinas would have reached the same conclusions about the timing of ensoulment had he had access to modern biology. As Gould has stated with such clarity, modern genetics stands roughly midway between (Aristotlelian) epigenesis and (seventeenth-century) preformation. Hence the present state of embryology offers some solace both for the supporters of delayed ensoulment (in the gradual development of the organs: heart, brain, liver, etc.) and for the supporters of immediate ensoulment (in the genetic identity of the embryo from the time of fertilization). Nevertheless, it can no longer be denied that the process of embryonic development is truly a vital activity of the embryo. It is not the result of some force shaping the embryo from outside, as Thomas Aquinas believed. Development is as much an activity of the embryo as is growth, nutrition or respiration. However, if the organs of the embryo are shaped by an *intrinsic power* of development and not from outside by the continuing action of the father's seed then, according to Thomistic principles, the embryo must already possess a human nature, because the active powers that something possesses are determined by its nature. In the light of modern biological knowledge, it therefore seems that Thomas's principles would favour the view that the embryo is a human being from the time that the sperm and ovum fuse (Ashley 1976; Fisher 1991; Heaney 1992; Ashley and Moraczewski 1994; Johnston 1995).

For modern biology, the point of transition from unformed to formed, that is, from embryo to foetus, does not have the importance that it had for Aristotle. Still less is 'quickening', the first felt movements of the foetus, an event of great biological significance. In the nineteenth century, many people came to think that, 'if a moment had to be chosen for ensoulment, no convincing argument now appeared to support Aristotle or to put ensoulment at a later stage of life' (Noonan 1970, p. 38). Since then, scientists have consistently pointed to fertilization as the moment at which the life of a new biological individual begins. Nevertheless, in the late twentieth century, a line of argument was developed that severely qualified the significance previously given to fertilization. This argument relates to the phenomenon of twinning, an event that seems to occur a few days after fertilization. The various interpretations of twinning will be discussed in Chapter 14.

The biological story of the embryo has changed over time and it is likely to change in the future as our knowledge of development improves. Furthermore, even to the extent that we can be confident in our understanding of the biology, the philosophical interpretation of biological phenomena is not always obvious. Making human sense of the science requires reflection and argument. Nevertheless, any philosophical or theological account of the human embryo will have to be adequate to the best scientific evidence available if it is credibly to claim to reflect human reality.

In summary:

- The period between Aristotle (fourth century BCE) and William Harvey (seventeenth century CE) saw relatively modest progress in the field of embryology.
- William Harvey showed that the embryo was not formed from the mixing of two fluids as Hippocrates, Aristotle and Galen had supposed. His views also encouraged others to look for a human

ovum. Nevertheless, in regard to philosophy, Harvey remained broadly Aristotelian in outlook.

- The seventeenth century saw the rise of a mechanistic approach to nature in general. Descartes and Gassendi applied these mechanistic ideas to the embryo but with unimpressive results. After de Graaf identified what he thought was a human ovum, and Malpighi observed structure in the early chick embryo, mechanistically inclined philosophers suggested that the embryo was preformed inside the egg, and that earlier generations existed inside their female ancestors like a series of Russian dolls. Leeuwenhoek applied the same idea to the sperm and the male line.

- The idea of immediate ensoulment was revived in Catholic thought by Fienus and Zacchia within an Aristotelian framework, prior to the discovery of the ovum and the spermatozoon and prior to emergence of the theory of preformation. Nevertheless, preformation did play a role in helping to make their ideas more attractive.

- In the nineteenth century preformation was finally eclipsed and the dominant idea of the age was Haeckel's theory that embryology repeated the stages of evolution. This was discredited within biology but continued to influence popular and theological opinion. It provided the inspiration for a revival of the idea of delayed ensoulment in a Catholic context.

- Modern genetics stands midway between preformation and epigenesis and seems to offer a certain amount of support to opposite opinions about the timing of ensoulment, though on balance tends to favour ensoulment at fertilization.

What is perhaps most striking about the recent revival of the idea of delayed ensoulment is that, unlike its medieval counterpart, it has been invoked to justify the resort to abortion in a wide range of circumstances, outside the life-threatening (Donceel 1970). Similarly it has been used to justify the use of human embryos in scientific research (Rahner 1972, p. 236). To evaluate these shifts it is necessary to examine the Catholic ethical tradition dealing with difficult or disputed ethical cases: casuistry. We then need to consider the changing legal treatment of abortion and the debates surrounding embryo experimentation. Finally, it will be necessary to draw together the results of this enquiry and assess the implications of the Christian understanding of the human embryo.

12

Probable Sins and Indirect Exceptions

The devout Catholic bomber secures by a 'direction of intention' that
any shedding of innocent blood that occurs is 'accidental'. I know a
Catholic boy who was puzzled by being told by his schoolmaster that it
was an *accident* that the people of Hiroshima and Nagasaki were there
to be killed; in fact, however absurd it seems, such thoughts are
common among priests who know that they are forbidden by divine
law to justify the direct killing of the innocent.

(G.E.M. Anscombe, 'War and Murder')

In the year 1215, there was a general council of the Church at the
Lateran in Rome. It discussed matters of Christian doctrine and
published a creed, but its primary aim was to promote the pastoral
care of ordinary Christians, what was called at the time *cura animarum*.
The Fourth Lateran Council may be called the first great pastoral
council, comparable in scope and influence with the Council of
Trent (1545-63) and with the Second Vatican Council (1962-5). It
was held six years after Francis of Assisi founded the Order of Friars
Minor and one year before Dominic founded the Order of
Preachers. The friars were part of a spiritual revival, aspiring to
embrace poverty and to both live and preach the gospel. They were
missionaries, taking the gospel to people who had not heard it, but
they were equally concerned to minister to the spiritual needs of
those who were already Christians. Among the decrees of Lateran IV
was the requirement that all Catholics above the age of reason confess
their sins to a priest at least once a year (canon 21). This annual
obligation expressed the concern of the Church with the soul of every
Christian and not just with the spiritual lives of monks, nuns and
priests. It ensured that every Christian received not only forgiveness
but also individual spiritual and moral guidance from a priest.

The friars took up the work of hearing confessions and also wrote practical textbooks or manuals to inform and support confessors in their work. There had been *Summae Confessorum* since the eleventh century, but after Lateran IV manuals of this type were produced in increasing numbers. The Dominican friar Raymond of Pennaforte (c.1180–1275), who prepared the greatest work of canon law in the Middle Ages, the Decretals of Pope Gregory IX, also complied a book of particular legal and moral cases to instruct confessors: the *Summa de Casibus*. Around the same time his fellow Dominican Thomas Aquinas was writing the *Summa Theologiae*. The largest section of the *ST*, the second part, concerns moral theology understood in terms of the Christian virtues. Thomas deliberately placed moral theology within the context of creation (first part) and redemption (third part) so that ethical thinking would not be separated from Christian doctrine. However, even in Thomas's lifetime people had started to copy the middle part of the *ST* separately from the rest (Boyle 1982). In fact, most priests would have come across the works of Raymond and Thomas not directly but indirectly, through the hugely influential *Summa Confessorum* of John of Freiburg (Boyle 1974). Another important work in the same tradition was the mid-fifteenth century *Summa Moralis* of Antoninus of Florence (1389–1459). Later still, in the mid sixteenth century, there was a revival of moral theology among the Dominicans in Salamanca, of whom the most prominent figure was Francesco de Vittoria (1480–1546). The works of John of Freiburg, Antoninus and Vittoria combined commentary on the text on Thomas Aquinas with detailed examination of particular ethical questions or cases. The word 'casuistry' is sometimes used as a term of abuse, to mean dishonest thinking or sophistry, but originally it referred simply to the application of ethical principles to particular cases, as developed by these medieval writers.

Casuistry was an important element of ethical reasoning but was understood as just that, an element of a larger whole. Casuistry presupposed reflection on the ultimate aim of human life, on the nature of human action and on the importance of the virtues, of law and of grace in shaping human action. It also presupposed the ability to identify certain classes of act as virtuous or vicious, as lawful or unlawful. In its classical form, it assumed that there were some actions that could never be done, whatever the circumstances, because they were in themselves vicious and forbidden by divine law. Nevertheless, regardless of how clear someone's general understanding of law and virtue, it was necessary to ask whether in a particular case, the act was an example of one kind of action or of another. It was at this point that casuistry came in.

Casuistry concerns the resolution of cases by comparing them with other better understood cases and by teasing out the values or virtues at stake. Unlike theoretical questions, questions about particular practical matters commonly contain an element of uncertainty (*ST* IIIa Q.47 art. 9 ad 2). In this area rules of thumb can be useful and the insight of wise and experienced people is invaluable. Resolving dilemmas requires not only knowledge of principles but also a specific intellectual virtue that Aristotle called *phronesis* and Thomas Aquinas called *prudentia*. Jonsen and Toulmin (1988) have argued that though casuistry has fallen out of favour due to abuses in the past it should be reinstated as a method in ethical reasoning, especially in the complex area of bioethics. They define casuistry as follows:

> The analysis of moral issues, using procedures of reasoning based on paradigms and analogies, leading to the formulation of expert opinion about the existence and stringency of particular moral obligations, framed in terms of rules and maxims that are general but not universal or invariable, since they hold good with certainty only in the typical conditions of the agent and circumstances of the case. (Jonsen and Toulmin 1988, p. 257, quoted in Reich 1995, Vol. I, p. 348)

Jonsen emphasizes that, unlike modern 'situationism', casuistry in its classical form acknowledged the binding character of ethical principles. The concern of casuistry was to assess the relevance, applicability and limits of various principles to the particular case in hand. It was particularly concerned with borderline cases and thus, 'while [casuistry] may lead you to stretch a point on the circumference, it will not permit you to destroy the centre' (Anscombe 1981, p. 38). The centre is not defined by but rather presupposed by casuistry. The centre (the wrongfulness of murder, theft, adultery, etc.) is defined by divine law and virtue, by the nature of human beings and their highest good, which is God. In contrast, the circumference is constituted by uncertain cases where it is not clear how to understand or categorize a particular act.

The importance of the tradition of casuistry for the purposes of this book is that it embodied a great deal of discussion about abortion in the exceptional case where the mother's life is in danger. The first Christian reference to abortion in this circumstance is found in Tertullian (*On the Soul* 25). The passage is somewhat ambiguous. It describes a situation where the unborn infant blocks the entrance to the womb so that '[the infant] kills his mother, if he is not to die himself'. In such cases abortion seems a 'cruel necessity'. Nevertheless, as Tertullian describes the procedure, the 'dissection' of the child with 'unfaltering care', the 'violent delivery', the 'furtive robbery of life', the 'copper spike' that is called, 'the slayer of the infant' due to its 'infanticidal function', it is apparent his approval is laced with irony. This is a far cry from the Talmud in which there is explicit approval for embryotomy to save the mother's life.

> If a woman has difficulty in childbirth, one dismembers the embryo within her limb from limb because her life takes precedence over its life. Once its head (or the greater part) has emerged, it may not be touched, for we do not set aside one life for another. (*Mishnah, Oholot* 7.6)

The first Christians followed the Jewish ethical principle that 'we do not set aside one life for another'. However, they faced a difficulty in accepting that 'her life takes precedence over its life', for they saw the life of the unborn child as equally inviolable. The practical question of what to do in a situation in which a woman's life was threatened by her pregnancy was therefore extremely problematic for Christians. It is not altogether surprising that in the first thousand years of the Church's history, theologians preferred to pass over this difficulty in silence and to speak of abortion in circumstances where they were clear that it was sinful. It was not until the late Middle Ages that Christian theologians begin to address directly the question of abortion to save the mother's life.

One of the first to discuss this case was Antoninus of Florence. He declared that it was neither legitimate to kill the woman to save the child (by Caesarean section) nor to kill the infant to save the woman (by abortion). If the only way to save someone is by killing someone else, it is better to do nothing. However, he made one exception to this rule. Citing fellow Dominican John of Naples, he argued that before the soul was infused into the embryo (which, following Thomas Aquinas, he regarded as occurring at 40 days for males and 80 days for females) it was legitimate to abort the embryo to save the mother's life. This was not homicide, strictly speaking. However, an act that destroyed the early embryo and so prevented a child from coming to be was very close to homicide, therefore it could only be justified to save the mother's life. Furthermore, if it were doubtful whether or not the embryo possessed a human soul then it was not to be harmed. Antoninus only permitted abortion of the pre-ensouled embryo to save the mother's life. Nevertheless, it was very significant in explicitly allowing an exception to the traditional prohibition. Antoninus had great authority and was followed by several theologians such as Sylvester Prierias (d. 1523) and Martin Aspilcueta (1493–1586), more commonly known as Doctor Navarrus.

Early in the sixteenth century a Franciscan theologian called Antonius of Cordoba (1485–1578) proposed a different distinction for understanding the ethics of abortion. He saw no ethical distinction between killing an embryo before or after ensoulment. Both acts were forms of homicide. However, he saw an important difference between treatments which directly aimed at causing the death of the unborn infant (*de se mortifera*) and medicines that were directly intended to help the woman but which had a possible side-effect of causing an abortion (*de se salutifera*). The former included taking poison, cutting up the embryo in the womb or hitting the woman to cause a miscarriage. These were forbidden. The latter included treatments such as bleeding, baths and purgatives. These were legitimate. A woman had a duty to care for her child but she had a prior right (*ius potius*) to look after her own health. Nevertheless, this right would not justify a *direct* attack on the child who was an innocent and not an unjust aggressor.

Peter of Navarre (d. 1594) accepted this new distinction and gave the analogy of a pregnant woman fleeing from a wild bull. It was legitimate for her to run and leap to escape, even if this caused a miscarriage. The miscarriage is not her aim here, or even the means to an end, but is a tragic side-effect. It might be foreseen but it is not directly willed or intended. Peter also introduced another distinction. If the ensouled infant was capable of being born alive and baptized then he thought the woman should not take medicine that might cause a miscarriage, even where this would otherwise be legitimate. In his view, the spiritual welfare of the child was more important than the physical welfare of the woman. Baptizing a child, even if it died soon after birth, had great significance because of the received opinion that a child who died unbaptized could not enter heaven. This theme would recur in the tradition but it is important not to overstate its significance. The Jesuit theologian Gabriel Vasquez (1551–1604) followed Antonius of Cordoba in permitting *medicina sanative* that might indirectly cause abortion. However, he disagreed with Peter of Navarre about the requirement to forgo medical treatment because of the spiritual needs of the infant. The woman has no obligation to sacrifice her life for someone else's spiritual benefit. She might choose to do so, but she has no duty to do so.

In this context it is important to evaluate a claim made by a number of modern commentators (Fletcher 1954, p. 147; Williams 1957, pp. 193–5; Feldman 1974, p. 270) that early Christian objections to abortion were based on the fear that infants who died without baptism were subject to the fires of hell. Before Augustine the common Christian opinion seems to have been that infants who died before baptism were neither punished with hellfire nor enjoyed the bliss of heaven, but rather entered some neutral state (for example Gregory of Nazianzus, *Orations* 40, 23). However, in his struggle against the Pelagians, Augustine came to reject this doctrine: 'that person, therefore, greatly deceives both himself and others, who teaches that they [unbaptized infants] will not be involved in condemnation' (*On the Merits and Forgiveness of Sins, and on the Baptism of Infants* 21). His teaching was upheld by the local church council of Carthage in 418 and repeated by Fulgentius of Ruspe (*The Rule of Faith* 27). Augustine's thought had little influence on the Eastern Christian tradition and, over time, also came to be rejected in the West. After Thomas Aquinas, most theologians accepted that unbaptized infants entered a place of natural happiness called 'limbo' (from *limbus inferni*: the outskirts of hell; cf. *Commentary on the Sentences of Peter Lombard*, II, D. 33, Q.2, art.

2) see Toner (1913). From the seventeenth century, the fate of unbaptized infants came to be considered an open question 'simply, the argument is that God can save them without baptism if this is his will' (Connery 1977, p. 196).

A difficulty faced by those who wish to relate the opposition to abortion in the first three centuries of the Church to the practice of baptism is that there is notoriously little evidence of infant baptism at this time. To the extent that it existed it seems to have been the exception, not the rule. Augustine himself was not baptized as a child, despite being the son of a devout Christian woman. Furthermore, there is no text in the first millennium of the Christian tradition which makes a connection between abortion and infant baptism. Neither Augustine nor Fulgentius make this link. Pope Sixtus V seems to have been one of the first to do so in *Effraennatam* in 1588. From the sixteenth century, the fate of unborn children played some role in casuistic discussion on abortion and caesarean section. However, it was rarely invoked as a reason why abortion was forbidden in general.

Thomas Aquinas does not discuss the relevance of baptism for abortion, but he is clear that the children of non-Christian parents should not be baptized against the wishes of the parents, even if the infants are in danger of death (*ST* IIIa Q.68 art. 10). He is also clear that what makes killing wrong is not the fate of the victim after death but the injustice of depriving him or her of life. Indeed, all other things being equal, he regards it as worse to kill an innocent victim than a guilty sinner, notwithstanding the fact that the former is helped to heaven and the latter dispatched to hell (*ST* IIaIIae Q.64 art. 6 ad 2). The roots of the Christian rejection of abortion lie not in speculations about the fate of unbaptized infants but in the recognition that ending the lives of unborn children involves an injustice (see also Grisez 1970, pp. 232–3).

Let us return to the discussion of therapeutic abortion. Thomas Sanchez (1550–1610) revived the distinction drawn by Antoninus of Florence (concerning abortion before or after ensoulment) but combined this with the use of Antonius of Cordoba for abortion after ensoulment. He proposed that before ensoulment an embryo could be aborted directly to save the mother's life, but after ensoulment there could be no direct abortion although there could be use of *medicina salutifera* that caused a miscarriage indirectly. This view attracted a following including such figures as Paul Layman (1574–1635), Trullench (d. 1644) and Antonius Diana (1585–1663). However, it was also attacked vigorously by Leonard Lessius (1554–1623), Basilius Pontius (1569–1629), John de Lugo (1583–1660) and others. At this stage in the debate everyone accepted the legitimacy of indirect abortion, in the sense of taking life-saving medicines even if they had the side-effect of causing a miscarriage. Also, everyone was agreed that it was wrong directly to abort an embryo after ensoulment. What was controversial was whether it was legitimate directly to abort an embryo prior to ensoulment.

Antoninus had seemed to find this acceptable, but he did not have the advantage of a clear distinction between direct and indirect abortion. Sanchez had said yes, but he faced some difficult questions. If direct abortion was allowed to save the mother's life before ensoulment, why was it not allowed after ensoulment? Sanchez replied that before ensoulment the embryo was not a separate being but was part of the body of the mother (*pars viscerum mulieris*). However, if this were the case, why could the embryo not be aborted for other reasons prior to ensoulment? Sanchez answered that abortion is justified when the foetus directly threatens the mother's life as a quasi-aggressor, like a diseased limb, but if the threat comes from some other cause it would not be right to harm the embryo. (Here we see an echo of the doctrine of Maimonides.) But this line of argument brings us back to the place where we started. If the embryo can be called a quasi-aggressor before ensoulment, why can it not be called a quasi-aggressor after ensoulment? Thus, if direct abortion is permissible before ensoulment, it seems that it would be permissible after ensoulment. Yet it was agreed by all that direct abortion was not permissible after ensoulment, therefore it seemed that neither should it be permissible before ensoulment. Over time, especially after 1679, the position of Sanchez gradually lost its support.

The development of casuistry in the seventeenth century saw a great profusion of opinions on various ethical matters from the very cautious (rigorist) to the very permissive (laxist). In 1679, in an attempt to identify the limits of reasonable debate, the Holy Office condemned a set of 65 extreme laxist propositions. Two concerned abortion.

34 It is permissible to procure abortion before the ensoulment of the foetus lest the girl known to be pregnant be killed or disgraced.

35 It seems probable that all foetuses in the womb lack a rational soul and that they first begin to have one when they are born. Consequently it must be said that abortion never involves homicide.

The first proposition was apparently defended by Torreblanca (d. 1645), but it was associated with Sanchez inasmuch as several theologians argued that it followed from his position. This was in spite of the fact that Sanchez himself limited abortion before ensoulment to the situation where there was an intrinsic and serious health threat to the mother's life.

The second proposition, that the rational soul is given at birth, was defended by John Marcus, physician-general of the kingdom of Bohemia. Ensoulment at birth, with the first breath, was originally proposed by the Stoics, but does not seem to have found any supporters in the Christian tradition until Leonardo da Vinci. By the mid seventeenth century there were various views about the timing of ensoulment. The opinion of Thomas Aquinas taken from Aristotle, giving 40 days for males and 80 days for females, continued to have a major following. Others preferred Hippocrates' estimate of 35 days and 42 days or Augustine's figure of 46 days for both sexes. Fienus and Zacchia had proposed that ensoulment occurred at or within a few days of conception. Nevertheless, the idea that ensoulment did not occur until birth was unprecedented in the Christian ethical tradition and shocking even to the most liberal minds of the age. Caramuel Lobkowicz (1606–82), himself dubbed the 'prince of laxists' described the opinion as not only improbable but also intolerable.

The two condemned propositions do not touch on the question of abortion to save the mother's life. The evaluation of such procedures, and the circumstances, methods or intentions which served to justify them, was a matter left for discussion among theologians. Rome was concerned, at this time, only to condemn the most extreme positions. Nevertheless, theologians such as Dominic Viva (1648-1726) attempted to draw out the implications of these condemnations. This had the effect of reinforcing the view that direct abortion was never legitimate, even in the case of an embryo before ensoulment. Viva emphasized that early abortion should still be regarded as homicide in some sense: imperfect homicide. He also drew the analogy with the emission of seed. No theologian at the time accepted that it was legitimate for a man to emit seed outside the context of generation for the sake of his health. The destruction of seed contradicted the nature of generation and was forbidden on that basis (here we see again a similarity with Jewish thought). Direct abortion of an embryo before ensoulment was an even more serious sin, being a step closer to true or perfect homicide.

By the eighteenth century there were few theologians who followed Sanchez. In his *Theologia Moralis*, Alphonsus Liguori (1696-1787) sets out the two views about directly aborting the embryo before ensoulment to save a mother's life: that it is permitted (Sanchez) and that it is not permitted (Lessius). Both opinions are probable, in the sense of being supported by a number of theologians, but Alphonsus regards the second as the stronger and the safer position. Following Busenbaum (1609-68), he asks why anyone would cause an abortion directly when the mother's life could be saved by indirect abortion.

Another shift that occurred within moral theology between the seventeenth and the nineteenth century was the gradual acceptance of the view that ensoulment occurs at conception. Juan Cardenas (1613-84) is significant for saying that the opinion of Fienus was probable and thus, for reasons of safety, all foetuses should be treated as ensouled. To some theologians it seemed that the idea of ensoulment at conception was not at all probable, but as it was accepted by an increasing number of theologians it came to be regarded as at least probable. Thus writers such as Claudius LaCroix (1652-1714), Constantius Roncaglia (1677-1737) and Emmanuele Cangiamila (1701-63) all argued that abortion, at any stage, carried the danger of homicide. However, it is a curious fact that at this time debates about the timing of ensoulment had little practical effect. This is because after 1679 most authors held the view that direct abortion of an embryo was always forbidden, even before ensoulment.

By the early nineteenth century there was a consensus among theologians that the significant distinction when considering therapeutic abortion was not the stage of development of the embryo but the character of the treatment. Direct and intended abortion was never permitted at any stage of pregnancy, but medical treatment which caused an abortion as a side-effect could be legitimate to save the mother's life. The next major controversy concerned what counted as direct or indirect abortion.

In the 1860s two moral theologians, Jean Pierre Gury SJ (1801–66) and Antonio Ballerini (1805–81) proposed, for the first time in the Christian tradition, that direct abortion of an ensouled infant was justified to save a mother's life. How did they square this with the principle, accepted by all Catholic theologians, that 'we do not set aside one life for another'? Gury and Ballerini did not dispute the principle that a direct attack on the child was forbidden, even to save the mother's life. However, they drew a distinction between direct killing and direct abortion. The aim of therapeutic abortion was to speed delivery (*acceleratio partus*) in circumstances where delivery at the normal time would threaten the life of the mother. Even if the child was not viable, the aim of a therapeutic abortion was not to bring about the child's death but to remove the child from the womb. In allowing direct expulsion of the child, Ballerini did not allow procedures that involved killing the unborn child directly by cutting, crushing or poisoning. He had in mind only the induced delivery of the child before viability in order to save the mother's life.

While Ballerini had distinguished speeding delivery from actions that directly killed the child, a number of later authors would attempt to extend their principle still further. The early nineteenth century saw the re-emergence of the practice of craniotomy in cases where a child was not able to be delivered safely. It involved cutting, opening and breaking down the infant's head so that it could then be extracted from the womb. In 1872 an anonymous article appeared appended to the regular publication *Acta Sanctae Sedis* in which the author explicitly defended craniotomy on the basis of self-defence. Seven years later Daniel Viscosi published a 331-page work on craniotomy arguing the same case in much greater detail. Viscosi maintained that the embryo could be seen as an aggressor, even if its aggression was not voluntary or deliberate. It is legitimate to fend off an aggressor whether or not the aggression is culpable, as is clear from the case of someone who is attacked by a madman.

In a classic treatment of the subject, de Lugo had made the distinction between unintended killing and killing as a means to an end. It was legitimate in war to bombard an enemy, even though it is foreseen that innocent civilians including children, will be killed. However, it is not legitimate to kill children deliberately in an effort to demoralize the enemy. This argument was used to exclude any act directly aimed at harming the unborn infant, and thus excluded craniotomy. However, Viscosi argued that the aim in craniotomy was not to kill the child but only to remove it from the womb. From the perspective of intention, the death of the child is accidental. This is quite different from the case where the doctors intend the death of the child because, for example, it is disabled or unwanted.

Viscosi appealed to the principle enunciated by Ballerini: that directly intended abortion need not be directly intended killing. However, not everyone was convinced of Ballerini's arguments for speeding delivery before viability to save the mother's life. The assertion that deliberately cutting up the infant was not intended killing seemed to stretch the concept of intention past breaking-point. For this reason Viscosi's claims were highly controversial at the time and provoked criticism not only from other theologians such as Eschbach and Waffelaert but also from Rome. In 1884 the Holy Office was asked to respond to the question 'may it be safely taught in Catholic schools that craniotomy is permissible?' After consultation, its response was that craniotomy could not safely be taught. Further responses in 1889, 1895, 1898 and 1902 covered other procedures. The general rule was that any surgical procedure that was directly lethal (*directe occisiva*) to mother or child was not permitted. This rule would seem to permit, for example, the removal of a cancerous womb from a pregnant woman or the removal of a tube in the case of an ectopic pregnancy, but not operations involving cutting up a living embryo.

Since the beginning of the twentieth century the progress of medicine and, in particular, the possibility of safe caesarean section has resolved many conditions that once seemed to demand therapeutic abortion. In most cases doctors no longer face the dilemma of saving the mother or the child. Craniotomy is no longer common practice for obstructed delivery, though it is not unknown. However, the progress of medicine has not been able to resolve ectopic pregnancy. Continuing with the pregnancy threatens the life of the mother and there is virtually no hope for the child. The Catholic ethical tradition allows in such cases that actions may be taken that cause the death of the embryo indirectly, but not actions that aim at the death of the embryo either as an end or as a means. The difficult question is how to determine what counts as direct or indirect in this matter. It does not seem unreasonable to distinguish the intention of moving an embryo, in the case of ectopic pregnancy, from the unintended effect of its death. However, if a procedure involves dissecting or poisoning the embryo then it is difficult to see how this is anything other than an act of killing and, as such, is forbidden by the commandments. For a useful evaluation of different methods for managing ectopic pregnancy see Kaczor (1999).

The purpose of this chapter has been to explore the way that the Catholic casuistic tradition dealt with the human embryo. This historical perspective has become more important in recent years as a number of authors have invoked this tradition in order to defend a general right to early abortion or to support the use of human embryos for scientific experimentation. A good example of this approach is provided by Carol Tauer. She aims to show that 'there are "good and solid reasons", which appear at least as strong as those supporting the contrary position, for not including early human embryos under the full weight of the law against killing' (Tauer 1984, p. 33). Thus in the face of compelling 'or even adequate' reasons, early abortions should be permitted. Tauer does not make explicit what would count as adequate reasons, but we may suppose these extend beyond life-threatening situations.

Tauer's starting-point is the *Declaration on Abortion* published by the Sacred Congregation for the Doctrine of the Faith in 1974. In a key passage the SCDF argues that while there is no unanimity in the tradition about the timing of ensoulment it is possible to have moral certainty for the following reason: 'From a moral point of view this is certain: even if a doubt existed concerning whether the fruit of conception is already a human person, it is objectively mortal sin to dare to risk murder' (SCDF 1974, para. 11, quoted by Tauer 1984, p. 9). This argument can be seen to be an echo of that developed by Cardenas, LaCroix and others, but it also reflects a principle that was accepted as early as Antoninus of Florence: if there is uncertainty as to whether the soul has been infused, then it should be assumed for practical purposes that it has. It is unethical to risk homicide.

Against this argument Tauer appeals to the casuistic method known as probabilism. This approach was initially proposed by the Dominican Bartholomew of Medina who wrote: 'it seems to me that if an opinion is probable, it is lawful to follow it, even if the opposite opinion is more probable' (exposition of the *ST* IaIIae Q.19 art. 6). 'Probable' in this context meant: supported by persuasive arguments and by trustworthy authorities. A theory that was more probable was supported by better arguments and weightier authorities, but, of course, the more probable opinion might still be wrong. Probabilism focused on the tension between liberty and law. Cases of reasonable doubt should be resolved in the direction of liberty, not in the direction of obligation. However, Medina distinguished between speculative doubt and practical doubt. It was not a sin to act against a speculative doubt, but in the case of practical doubt, the benefit of the doubt should go to the potential victim. Medina's scheme was taken up by a number of Jesuit theologians. Francisco Suarez (1548-1617) made the distinction between a probable opinion of law and a probable opinion of fact. Opinions about facts should be weighed in terms of safety, but opinions about law should be weighed in terms of probability and freedom. On this basis, Suarez put forward the dictum: 'A doubtful law does not bind.'

The weight of Tauer's article is to show that the contemporary dispute about the status of the embryo is a speculative doubt, a doubt about law rather than a doubt about fact. If this is so, she argues, it should be resolved in terms of freedom, for a doubtful law does not bind. The opinion of a number of recent theologians (Rahner, Häring, Donceel) that the soul is infused two or three weeks after conception forms the basis of a probable opinion. Probabilism would then permit action to be taken on the basis of this opinion, for example, allowing experimentation on human embryos. 'The reasons in favour of experimenting might carry more weight than the uncertain rights of a human being whose very existence is in doubt' (Rahner 1972, p. 236, quoted in Tauer 1984, p. 29).

In assessing Tauer's argument it is necessary to address two questions: Is probabilism a reasonable basis for making ethical decisions? And would probabilism in its classical form support the conclusion that embryos may be used for experimentation? The present chapter began with a defence of the importance of casuistry. However, probabilism is only one method used by casuists and it was very controversial from the outset. Though it was originally suggested by a Dominican it was taken up by many Jesuits and heavily criticized by many Dominicans. The fundamental problem was that by concentrating on law and liberty probabilism took the focus away from the search for truth. 'Without fully realising it, Bartholomew of Medina and his followers had passed the frontier of reason, which naturally favours the opinion with the best reasons behind it' (Pinckaers 1995, p. 273). Conscience should act according to what seems to it most likely to be true. A second related criticism was that probabilism always tends in the direction of laxism, that is, it tends to permit everything. This was a criticism levelled not only by Dominicans but also by Protestants and even by other Jesuits (for examples see Stone 2003).

The method of probabilism was famously satirized by Pascal in his *Provincial Letters*. Pascal was a Jansenist. He tended towards the opposite extreme of rigorism and his satirical approach did not make for careful analysis. Nevertheless, at certain points his criticism is acute.

> 'But, father,' I replied, 'a person must be sadly embarrassed in choosing between them!' 'Not at all,' he rejoined; 'he has only to follow the opinion which suits him best.' 'What! If the other is more probable?' 'It does not signify,' 'And if the other is the safer?' 'It does not signify,' repeated the monk ... (*Provincial Letters* V, quoted from Pascal 1952, p. 33)

This passage highlights the way that probabilism deliberately sets aside any consideration of the relative probability of other opinions and also sets aside questions of relative safety. The defenders of probabilism held that if an opinion had solid reasons on its side, that sufficed to make it both probable and ethically safe. As noted above, this contrasted with practical opinion in which safety rather than probability was the major concern. However, it seems odd to say that the question 'what if I am wrong?' is relevant only to practical doubts and not at all to speculative doubts. In either case, if there is an alternative view that also has solid supporting arguments, then it seems reasonable to ask what would be the practical consequences of error. Tauer is surely right to say that safety is not the only consideration, especially in cases where the likelihood of error is very low. Nevertheless, the claim that neither the presence of a more probable alternative opinion, nor considerations of safety, are in any way relevant to questions of law is difficult to accept. Even in the twentieth century, probabilism still had its defenders (for example Davies 1946) but the ecclesial acceptance of probabilism has been qualified, especially since the time of Alphonsus Liguori.

> [The view accepted by the Catholic Church] is probabilism in a modified form with the strongest safeguards to prevent it from degenerating into laxism. The most important safeguards are (1) that the probable opinion must be 'solid' and (2) probabilism may not be adopted where the doubt concerns the validity of a sacrament or a vital interest whether of the agent himself or of somebody else. (Mortimer 1967)

When confronting questions about the use of embryos it is clear that the doubt does concern vital interests of the embryo. Tauer is right to say that the mere impossibility of disproving that the embryo might have a soul is not enough to justify acting as though it has one. That the embryo has a soul must be shown to be a reasonable opinion, supported by argument and authority. However, she seems to overinterpret the SCDF on this point. The *Declaration* does not rest the claim that the embryo may have a soul only on the impossibility of proving the opposite. Rather, it argues that there are solid reasons for thinking the embryo possesses a soul from conception. Tauer does not address their positive arguments, nor does she cite the many contemporary

Catholic theologians and philosophers who argue that the embryo has a soul from conception (for example Ashley and Moraczewski 1994; Barry 1989; Bracken 2001; Crosby 1993; Fisher 1991; Grisez 1989; Heaney 1992; Iglesias 1987; Johnston 1995; Tonti-Filippini 1992; Watt 1996). This list does not prove the case, for a counter-list would not be difficult to produce, but it demonstrates that there is a reasonable weight of opinion that needs to be acknowledged. If, however, the idea that the embryo may have a soul is probable, in the technical sense of being an opinion grounded in reasonable arguments and supported by a number of theologians, then the idea the embryo might have vital interests cannot be dismissed and must be taken into account.

A further point to note is that probabilism is concerned with opinions that have not been proscribed by the Church. A famous laxist principle of the seventeenth century was that it was legitimate to follow any position that was defended by a theologian and not yet condemned by the Church. However, even the laxists agreed that an opinion could not be held to be probable if it had been explicitly condemned by Rome. The development of a 'theology of dissent' by Curran (1969) and others needs to be evaluated on its own terms, but it is quite different from probabilism as traditionally practised and understood. The practical principle that 'life must be protected with the utmost care from conception' is based not only on the authority of individual theologians, or even of the Congregation of the Doctrine of the Faith (*Declaration on Abortion* 1975), but on the most recent ecumenical council of the Church (*Gaudium et Spes* 51), repeated in a papal encyclical devoted to the subject (*Evangelium Vitae* 61). It is therefore not possible to regard the opposite opinion as probable, in the sense of that term used in the tradition.

Finally, it should be noted that during the period when it was commonly believed that ensoulment occurred sometime after conception most theologians held that direct abortion of the embryo before ensoulment was unjustifiable (for example Cordoba, Vasquez, Lessius, de Lugo, Viva). Those who did allow direct abortion of the embryo before ensoulment (for example Antoninus, Sanchez) did so only if the mother's life was in danger. No orthodox theologian accepted that the embryo could be harmed for any lesser reason than the treatment of a pathological condition. Even if the embryo was not yet ensouled the deliberate destruction of it was regarded as a form of homicide. It was not just contraception, but lay midway between contraception and perfect homicide. It was, in Prummer's words, the destruction of a human being in the making (*homo in fieri*). The consensus of the tradition in protection of the embryo even before ensoulment is particularly significant because the method of casuistry relies on moving from agreed well-established cases to new and uncertain cases. The method established by the Catholic casuistic tradition as it actually existed historically could not justify the use of human embryos in experimentation or the deliberate abortion of a human embryo except where the life of the mother was directly threatened, as in ectopic pregnancy. Even in this case, it was commonly held that only procedures that led to the death of the embryo *indirectly* were acceptable, not methods involving deliberate dissection, as in craniotomy.

In Summary:

- The moral theology of the Catholic Church in the Middle Ages was shaped in part by the needs of confessors. This led to a tradition of detailed case law or casuistry. Casuistry concerned the resolution of difficult or doubtful cases, but assumed a background of agreed principles, authorities and cases.
- The discussion of abortion in the casuistic tradition focused on the case of abortion to save the life of the mother. Antoninus of Florence regarded even this sort of abortion as prohibited once the soul had been infused but allowed abortion to save the mother's life if it was certain that the soul had not yet been infused.
- Antonius of Cordoba introduced a distinction between causing an abortion directly and giving life-saving treatment which caused abortion as a side-effect. The first was prohibited at any stage of pregnancy, the second was permitted at any stage of pregnancy.
- Sanchez combined both views, arguing that direct abortion was allowed before infusion of the soul, but from that point only indirect abortion was allowed. Sanchez had his followers, but the majority view, following Lessius, was that direct abortion was

prohibited at any stage. The condemnations of laxism in 1679 encouraged this view. At the same time, other theologians began to argue that it was at least probable that ensoulment occurred at conception.

- The possibility that a child might live long enough to be baptized had some significance within the casuistical discussion of therapeutic abortion. However, there is no clear relation between Christian reflection on the fate of unbaptized infants and the traditional Christian opposition to abortion.

- In the nineteenth century a debate developed over what counted as direct abortion, and some theologians defended speeding delivery (*acceleratio partus*) and even craniotomy. Both these opinions were condemned, but the question of what counted as direct abortion remained, especially with regard to ectopic pregnancy.

- The attempt of Tauer and others to appeal to the casuistic tradition in order to justify embryo experimentation and early abortion is unconvincing. The tradition developed from and assumed a consensus on certain cases. The tradition never accepted the deliberate killing of the embryo other than in the context of saving the mother's life.

The context of contemporary Christian debates about the embryo is given not only by the Christian ethical tradition but also by recent developments in law and technology. We turn first to consider changes in abortion law in the UK and the USA and then go on to assess the impact that new reproductive technologies have had on the treatment and understanding of the human embryo.

13

The Justice of Miscarriage

Progress ... can be said to be an essential feature of all life. The whole point is to determine what constitutes progress.

(E.F. Schumacher, *Small is Beautiful*)

Before the nineteenth century, abortion in English law was not a matter of specific legislation but of common law, i.e. that law 'created by the *decisions of judges and the customs of the people*' (Williams and Smith 2002, p. 23). English legal authorities as early as the thirteenth century held that anyone who gave poison to procure abortion 'if the foetus is already formed and animated, and especially if animated, he commits homicide' (Bracton, *The Laws and Customs of England*, cited in Dunstan 1988, p. 47; also in Connery 1977, p. 102). The distinction of formed or unformed will be familiar from previous discussion of the timing of ensoulment. It may well have found its way into English common law from canon law. However, it should be noted that the English legal tradition subsequently focused on quickening – evidence of felt movement within the womb – rather than the determination as to whether the foetus was fully formed (Dunstan 1988, p. 47; Keown 1988, p. 3). This had the effect of delaying the stage at which killing the embryo would constitute homicide. The theological consensus of the early Middle Ages was that, at least in the case of the male foetus but possibly also in the case of the female, ensoulment occurred around or before the seventh week of pregnancy. In contrast, quickening, if understood as the first felt stirring of the infant in the womb, is seldom experienced before fourteen weeks.

Medieval legal authorities thus held abortion of an ensouled foetus to be homicide, though ensoulment later came to be identified with quickening. However, from the sixteenth century, many jurists began to question whether abortion was ever homicide. A revival of interest in Roman Law during the Renaissance promoted the Stoic view that the foetus became a (legal) person only after birth. This view can be seen in the continental jurists Menochius (d. 1583) and Tessaurus (d. 1590) (see Connery 1977, pp. 142-7) and also in their English contemporaries William Staunford (1509-58) and William Lambard (1536-1601) (see Keown 1988, p. 4). Nevertheless, where abortion was not regarded as homicide it was still a serious offence, 'a great misprison' (Edward Coke, *Third Part of the Institutes of the Law of England*, cited in Connery 1977, p. 146). Furthermore, according to Coke (1552-1634), if the aborted child were born alive and subsequently died as a result of the injuries it sustained *in utero* then this would constitute homicide. Coke's opinion was not held by all his contemporaries but seems to have prevailed both among commentators and in subsequent case law (Keown 1988, pp. 10-11).

The attitude of English common law to abortion at the beginning of the nineteenth century was thus as follows: abortion which produced live birth but subsequent death of the child was regarded as homicide; abortion that led to stillbirth was a 'great misprison', at least if this occurred after quickening; the legal status of abortion prior to quickening was debated. Some held that abortion before quickening was an indictable offence (this view was upheld by the Supreme Court of Pennsylvania and by the Supreme Court of North Carolina in the mid nineteenth century), but most held that it was not indictable. Nevertheless, even those who held that it was not itself an offence did not therefore regard it as lawful behaviour. Actions can be unlawful, and thus the basis of other offences, even though they are not themselves criminal offences.

> Chief Judge Shaw of Massachusetts in 1845 stated the position plainly: any attempt to induce an abortion on a consenting woman prior to quickening is not only wicked but also an act done 'without any lawful purpose' and therefore, if it happens to result in the woman's death, it is murder, notwithstanding that it was intended to help her and she fully consented to the risk. (Finnis 1994, p. 10)

It is thus wholly unsustainable to claim (*pace* Means 1971) that before the nineteenth century British subjects and American citizens enjoyed a 'common law liberty' to procure abortion at any stage of pregnancy. On the contrary, there is ample evidence both from jurists and from case law that abortion, at least after quickening, was regarded as a common law offence and as such was subject to prosecution.

Though there was no *de jure* liberty to procure abortion under the common law, it could be argued that there was something like a *de facto* liberty in the sense that abortion cases were notoriously difficult to prosecute. 'The Abortionist's case' of 1348 shows that abortion was regarded as worthy of criminal prosecution even in the Middle Ages, but in the event the alleged perpetrator was acquitted because of the difficulty in determining the cause of the child's death. There was also a procedural fault in that the indictment failed to specify a baptismal name (Keown 1988, p. 4). In a case from 1504, *R.* v. *Lichefeld*, the defendant stood accused of 'feloniously entertaining' one Joan Wynspere knowing that she had taken poison to procure abortion. However, it was judged that he did not have a case to answer because 'the principal to whom he was an accessory, was dead' (ibid., p. 6). The case of Eleanor Beare, tried at the Derby Assizes in 1732 was remarkable for securing a conviction. She used a metal rod to induce a miscarriage in her servant, Grace Belfort. The case was unusual in that Grace gave testimony against her mistress, as did other servants. Beare was sentenced to two days in the pillory and three years in prison (ibid., pp. 8–9). It is possible to find cases from England and also from colonial America and from the newly independent USA where abortion was prosecuted under common law. Nevertheless, according to any reasonable estimate of the actual prevalence of abortion, these cases were exceptional and, even when brought, frequently failed to result in conviction. The common law at the turn of the nineteenth century thus not infrequently failed to deter what was, or at least was perceived to be, an increasingly frequent occurrence.

Legislation to proscribe abortion was first introduced in England in 1803 as an element of Lord Ellenborough's Malicious Shooting Bill. Abortion was treated alongside shooting, stabbing, poisoning and other forms of malicious assault. The primary purpose of the Bill was to tidy up the law. A number of offences which had once been dealt with under the common law were thus brought into the ambit of statute. In dealing with abortion, Ellenborough held that abortion after quickening should be a capital offence. Abortion before quickening was a serious offence punishable by pillory or transportation, but was not capital. In what represented a significant development on the previous common law, the Bill emphasized intention. If poisons were given with the intention of causing abortion, an offence had been committed. It was no longer necessary to prove that the actions of the defendant were the cause of the death of the unborn child. It was enough to show that an unlawful attempt had been made to bring about an abortion. It was also significant that the Bill referred to the 'unlawful' attempt to bring about abortion. This left the door open to the lawful inducing of abortion for therapeutic purposes – to preserve the mother's life.

It has been argued that the prohibition of abortion in Lord Ellenborough's Act was 'less to do with the protection of foetal life than with the desire to protect women from the dangers of enforced abortion' (Brookes 1988, p. 24) so that 'abortion could be construed as a form of murder in which the victim was *not the foetus* but the woman' (McLaren 1990, p. 191, emphasis added). It is important to examine this claim, for it is one that has also been made in connection with later statutes on abortion. It is certainly true that an important concern of the law was to punish unlawful acts that resulted in the deaths of many women. Even where a woman survived, abortion could be seen as a form of reckless endangerment. Nevertheless, this legislation clearly built upon the common law, which was certainly concerned with the protection of the unborn child. This is explicit in the language of earlier jurists such as Bracton and Coke and is also evident from the fact that, under the common law, the woman herself could be indicted for abortion. Lord Ellenborough's Act was not concerned only with 'enforced abortion' as the consent of the woman had no bearing on the criminality of the act. Furthermore, the appeal to quickening in Ellenborough's Act seems to reflect the medieval distinction between abortion before or after ensoulment. Inasmuch as this is so, it represents a return to Bracton's view that killing of an ensouled foetus constitutes homicide. This reading is also supported by the fact that the final clause of this section relates to infanticide. It seems, then, that 'the primary aim of these sections was the protection of children' notwithstanding their concern also 'to safeguard women from hazardous attempts at abortion' (Keown 1988, p. 20). The claim that nineteenth-century anti-abortion legislation was not concerned to protect the unborn child is untenable.

Ellenborough's Bill was passed with little comment, but the sections dealing with abortion were subsequently much criticized by physicians. The principle concern of these criticisms was not that the Bill represented a novel development in criminalizing abortion. Rather, it was seen as anachronistic in retaining the significance of 'quickening' and an implied medieval/Aristotelian account of ensoulment. From a nineteenth-century medical perspective, quickening did not have the significance in science that it enjoyed in contemporary popular opinion: 'During no period of gestation does any sudden revolution or change take place; and what is called quickening, is merely the motions of the child becoming sensible to the mother' (from the *Edinburgh Medical and Surgical Journal* 1810, cited in Brookes 1988, p. 25). Some authors (such as McLaren 1990) have detected in this attitude an unwillingness to allow the woman's subjective feelings of quickening determine the status of the embryo. This has also been linked to the desire on the part of physicians to shore up claims of professional competence. It is certain that the medical profession in the nineteenth century, both in Britain and in America, were keen to enhance their professional standing. This is seen in the founding of the Provincial Medical and Surgical Association (the precursor of the British Medical Association [BMA]) in 1832, and in the founding of the American Medical Association (AMA) in 1847. Both bodies were concerned to secure proper standards of medical care through the regulation of both of physicians and unqualified or irregular practitioners. Nevertheless, the desire to exercise control does not explain why the medical establishment should have pressed for stronger laws against abortion. If the primary problem were simply dangerous and unqualified abortionists the solution would more naturally have been to decriminalize abortion and place it in the hands of qualified and licensed professionals. The political pressure brought by physicians in the nineteenth century for more effective laws against abortion cannot be adequately explained unless it is understood that they were concerned to protect unborn children as well as to protect women and to uphold their own professional standards. This is indeed reflected in the many statements of physicians of the time (see comments made by Ryan, Burns, Bartley, Hutchinson, Beck and Dunlop, Severn and Thompson, cited in McLaren 1990, pp. 193-4).

The 1803 law in relation to abortion was amended in 1828 (Lansdowne's Act), 1837 (Offences Against the Person Act) and 1861 (Offences Against the Person Act). The OAP Act of 1837 abolished the distinction between abortion prior to quickening and abortion of a quickened foetus. This was in line with what many doctors had argued since the passing of Lord Ellenborough's Bill. The OAP Act also abolished the death penalty for abortion, a move in line with a Criminal Law Commissioners' report of 1836, which concluded that for many offences the death penalty rendered convictions difficult to secure and undermined the deterrent effect of the law (Keown 1988, p. 29). The maximum term given for the abortion was thus reduced to three years. In 1861 the maximum term was raised to life imprisonment, the woman's liability for self-abortion was clarified and a new statutory offence was created of supplying means knowing that they would be used to procure an unlawful abortion. In 1929 the Infant Life Preservation Act closed a final loophole by prohibiting the killing of a child before birth who was capable of being born alive (a condition which the law presumed to be attained at the 28th week of pregnancy). Before this Act, it was abortion to kill the child before birth and homicide to kill it after it was born alive, but no offence whatever to kill it during birth. Though the Acts of 1861 and 1929 remain in force, they have been heavily qualified by the 1967 Abortion Act (as amended by the Human Fertilization and Embryology Act of 1990) which permits abortion in a wide range of cases.

The pattern of legislation in the USA followed a similar path to that in the UK, though the story is complicated by the fact that it was played out severally in the various states. Prior to 1820, all states accepted the English common law and regarded abortion after quickening as an offence. There was a general consensus that abortion before quickening was not an indictable offence. As with Ellenborough's Act, the first American legislation proscribing abortion, enacted in Connecticut in 1821, invoked the common law category of abortion subsequent to quickening (though, whereas Ellenborough punished abortion before quickening, the Connecticut statute did not). Again, as in the UK, later legislation abandoned the terminology of quickening as unscientific and anachronistic. Connecticut introduced a law in 1860 making no mention of quickening, clarifying the woman's liability and proscribing the advertising or provision of abortifacients. By 1880 most states had enacted anti-abortion statutes which prohibited pre-quickening abortion (Mohr 1978, pp. 200–25).

Both in England and in the USA, the views of physicians exercised a strong influence over the shape of this legislation, but there was a significant difference between the two situations. In the UK, though medical and medico-legal writers regularly called for the tightening of the law, neither before the 1803 Act nor before the subsequent legislation of 1828, 1837 or 1861 was there any concerted political *campaign* to change the law. Abortion legislation in the UK during the nineteenth century represented not a sustained political campaign but rather a series of measures to clarify and bolster previous laws, albeit measures that were informed both by medical opinion and by general public opinion. The early period of American abortion legislation (1820–60) proceeded in a similar fashion. However, in 1857 an American physician called Horatio Robinson Storer launched what was most definitely a campaign to secure more effective legislation against abortion. He wrote to physicians around the country to enquire about their state law on abortion and to solicit their support. In 1859, as a result of his efforts, the AMA resolved 'publicly to enter an earnest and solemn protest against such unwarrantable destruction of human life'.

James Mohr, in his work on the history of abortion in America (Mohr 1978), devotes a chapter to 'The Physicians' Crusade against Abortion, 1857–80'. In characterizing the motivation for the physicians' crusade, he focuses first on the issue of enhancing the status of the medical profession and only secondarily on protection of the unborn child. However, as the sources Mohr quotes reveal, the physicans' central reasons for opposing abortion, and the public expressions of the crusade were very much concerned with the unborn child. The final paragraph of the Report on Criminal Abortion submitted to the AMA in 1859 is worth quoting in full:

> In accordance, therefore, with the facts in the case, the Committee would advise that this body, representing, as it does, the physicians of the land, publicly express its abhorrence of the unnatural and now rapidly increasing crime of abortion; that it avow its true nature, as no simple offence against public morality and decency, no mere misdemeanor, no attempt upon the life of the mother, but the wanton and murderous destruction of her child; and that while it would in no wise transcend its legitimate province or invade the precincts of the law, the Association recommends, by memorial, to the governors and legislatures of the several States, and, as representing the federal district, to the President and Congress, a careful examination and revision of the statutory and of so much of the common law, as relates to this crime. For we hold it to be a thing deserving all hate and detestation, that a man in his very originall, whiles he is framed, whiles he is enlived, should be put to death under the very hands, and in the shop, of Nature.

Storer appealed to physicians as a body arguing that as they were concerned for the life and health of both mother and child, and as they were more aware than the general public of the nature of the embryo as a living being, they should endeavour to persuade people and politicians of the need to introduce more effective legislation against abortion. His first objective was to promote the cause among physicians and to identify the protection of unborn life with ethical and professional conduct. In this he was remarkably successful. Even after he left America in 1872 the crusade did not lose momentum and the core of political opposition to abortion remained the AMA. Storer's attempt to gain the support of the clergy was less conspicuous in its success. As a Protestant he complained that the Catholic clergy were more effective in their support than those of his own congregation. The greatest difficulty he faced was not outright opposition but indifference or inertia. The churches were broadly supportive of the physicians' campaign but they did not supply many activists; these were drawn disproportionately from the medical profession itself.

How did the early feminist movement react to the campaign to restrict abortion? 'Given their basic assumptions, many feminists found themselves ultimately in the anomalous [*sic*] position of endorsing ... anti-abortion legislation' (Mohr 1978, p. 113). Feminists emphasized the toll of abortion upon women and tended to view abortion as a symptom of male oppression of women rather than a means of liberation. Men made women pregnant and then pressed them, or abandoned them, to the risks of the abortionists and to a disproportionate share of the guilt and grief of the abortion. Thus 'the vast majority of feminist spokeswomen were unwilling to condone abortion or encourage its practice' (Mohr 1978, p. 111). For early feminists such as Susan B. Anthony or Elizabeth Stanton, what was in dispute was not the nature of abortion as the killing of an unborn child but rather the causes of and remedies for this terrible act. Matilda Gage asserted that 'this crime of "child murder", "abortion", "infanticide" lies at the doors of the male sex' (cited in Mohr 1978, p. 112). It was held within these circles that only the emancipation of women could overcome the problem of abortion. The law should continue to proscribe abortion, but women should be granted equality of respect and, in particular, be free to refuse the sexual advances of men. To tackle the problems of unwanted pregnancy, abortion and maternal death in childbirth 'they advocated "voluntary motherhood", primarily through sexual abstinence' (Tribe 1990, p. 33).

The introduction of legislation against abortion in the nineteenth century was expressive of a moral consensus among Christians that abortion was a serious injustice against the unborn child. The groups most influential in the introduction and the subsequent shape of legislation against abortion were professional bodies of physicians. Nevertheless, the move was not opposed by lawyers, clerics, early feminists or the general public. There was no resistance to or backlash against the moves and a counter-movement seeking to repeal these laws did not emerge in the UK until the 1920s and in the USA until the 1950s. In the nineteenth century there was a widespread belief in a common Christian morality shared by Catholic, Anglican and Nonconformist alike.

Having acknowledged the medical, legal, political and religious consensus that promoted anti-abortion legislation on both sides of the Atlantic in the nineteenth century, it is necessary to examine the movement that would eventually largely negate these laws. It is not possible to identify a coherent movement in favour of legalizing abortion until well into the twentieth century. Nevertheless, many elements that would much later fuel or shape that movement were already present in the nineteenth century or even before. One such element is the emphasis on personal liberty or autonomy expressed in different ways in the writings of John Locke and Jean Jacques Rousseau, in the American Bill of Rights and in the French Revolution. This is not to say that before the twentieth century anyone asserted a 'liberty to abort'. Still less is it to say that the right to an abortion is implicit in the American Constitution. Nevertheless, the rhetoric of 'choice' or of 'reproductive rights' clearly gains its force from this earlier tradition and for that reason is more prevalent and more persuasive in an American context than, for example, in a British context.

A quite different school of thought which was to have a profound influence on the later abortion debate has its origin in the writings of Thomas Malthus. Though he opposed both contraception and abortion, holding that the population should be controlled by delaying marriage and by self-restraint, Malthus nevertheless popularized the idea that poverty is caused by overpopulation. This fundamental idea was to lead to the promotion first of contraception and later of abortion. Marie Stopes was typical of the first generation of birth-controllers who sought to emphasize the distinction between contraception and abortion, and to see contraception as part of the solution to abortion. She waged a campaign against the advertising of abortifacient drugs (Brookes 1988, p. 99, n. 9) and strongly opposed what she characterized as 'the evil practice of murderous abortion' (Letter to Pope Pius IX, see Hall 1977, p. 271). However, others later came to regard abortion as a necessary element of birth control when contraception failed. Thus the organization that bears her name, Marie Stopes International, now advertises itself as 'one of the UK's leading abortion-providers'. It is also noteworthy that Janet Chance, first chairman of the Abortion Law Reform Association, and Stella Browne, vice-chairman, had both been active members of the Malthusian League (Brookes 1988, pp. 84, 85, 89). An important element in the eventual shift of public opinion towards accepting abortion in the 1960s was 'fear of overpopulation' (Brookes 1988, p. 134). This was heralded dramatically as early as 1954 by Hugh More in his pamphlet *The Population Bomb* (which would later provide the title for a book by Paul Ehrlich).

Marie Stopes called her birth control organization 'The Society for Constructive Birth Control and Racial Progress'. The second half of this title reveals another element of her concern: eugenics. This term was coined by Francis Galton, a cousin of Charles Darwin: '[eugenics] is the science which deals with all influences that improve the inborn qualities of a race; also with those that develop them to the utmost advantage' (Galton 1904). The political practice of eugenics focused on encouraging people with 'superior qualities' to breed and on preventing those with 'inferior qualities' from doing so. During the 1930s several countries instituted sterilization programmes to prevent certain sections of society (particularly the mentally ill) from having children. This occurred not only in Nazi Germany but in Sweden (Armstrong 1997) and in America (Boisaubin 1998). Eugenics touched abortion first as a form of birth control that should be offered to those who were unfit to have children, the 'racially inferior'.

A second and more enduring legacy of eugenics is the provision of abortion for the sole reason that the child suffers from a physical or mental disability. This represents a revival of the ancient pagan custom of killing or exposing infants who were regarded as not worth rearing. The British Abortion Act of 1967 specifically allows abortion in cases where 'there is a substantial risk that if the child were born it would suffer from such physical or mental abnormalities as to be seriously handicapped'. The background to this clause was the thalidomide disaster. This sedative launched in 1959 was found to cause serious disability in children if taken during pregnancy. The drug was withdrawn, but not before hundreds of children had been affected. There was great public sympathy for women who had taken the drug and then wished to have an abortion rather than give birth to a disabled child. According to the advocates of abortion, 'thalidomide was the motor that reinvigorated the Abortion Law Reform Association and which paved the way for reform' (Simms and Hindell 1971, p. 108). In other respects, the latter part of the twentieth century has seen moves towards greater recognition and legal rights for people with disabilities. However, this contrary movement has as yet had little impact on the detection and destruction of the disabled unborn. In the 1990 amendments to the Abortion Act of 1967 the Infant Life Preservation Act of 1929 was neutralized: the time-limit for abortion was removed altogether in cases of disability. The viability of the child is thus no longer legally significant in cases where the child is thought to be 'seriously handicapped'. No criteria have ever been supplied to explain the phrase 'seriously handicapped'. A case is currently before the British courts in which an abortion was conducted on a child later than 24 weeks because the child suffered from a cleft palate. The case, an application for judicial review of the police failure to investigate the matter, has been brought by an Anglican priest who was herself born with cleft palate.

Perhaps the most important shift between the nineteenth and twentieth centuries occurred within the feminist movement and in left-wing politics. In the nineteenth century feminists had generally opposed abortion as a degradation of women. Furthermore, socialists were suspicious of Malthusian ideas as these seemed to blame the poor for their poverty and express a bourgeois concern about social control. However, in the early twentieth century a number of women on the political left began to identify access to abortion with women's emancipation. One such was Stella Browne. Throughout the 1920s she continued to promote the idea that abortion was an element of women's emancipation. She concentrated on changing attitudes in the birth control movement, in the Communist Party and the Labour Party and in the women's movement. In 1936 she was one of the founder members of the Abortion Law Reform Association. The executive committee was limited to women. Even at this time many in the feminist movement continued to oppose abortion. Nevertheless, by the 1960s abortion had become symbolic for many of women's emancipation. While, in the general population, women are as divided on this issue as are men, within the British Labour Party or the US Democratic Party there is very little room for women who are unhappy with the idea of abortion as emancipation. The path of a 'pro-life feminist' is currently a very hard and lonely road indeed.

The emergence of pro-abortion feminism in the 1930s was shaped in part by the practice of abortion during this period. The extent of illegal abortion at this time is difficult to gauge, but it seems to have been widespread. Illegal abortion was not necessarily unsafe (Brookes 1988, p. 42), for due to medical advances, maternal mortality both from abortion and from childbirth declined steadily throughout the first half of the twentieth century. Nevertheless, there were risks in abortion and these fell disproportionately on the poor.

In addition to illegal abortion there was a rise in abortion performed for therapeutic reasons. Throughout the nineteenth century therapeutic abortion was not unknown and it seems to have been lawful (see Keown 1988, pp. 49–83). However, during the first half of the twentieth century some physicians began to interpret the idea of therapeutic abortion with ever greater latitude. By including danger to health as well as life, and danger to mental as well as physical health, it could be stretched to encompass abortion for social or personal reasons. The difference between a therapeutic and a criminal abortion was, or at least appeared to many to be, 'often a matter of the patient's ability to pay a specialist's fees' (Brookes 1988, p. 65). When, in 1938, the law was finally tested, in the Bourne case (*R* v. *Bourne* [1938]), it was no great surprise that lawful abortion was determined to include not only life-saving treatment but abortion done for the sake of the health of the mother, whether physical or mental. The Bourne decision did little more than clarify existing law but it may well have served to encourage physicians who were inclined to, to perform abortion in an increasingly wide variety of circumstances.

The enactment of legislation against abortion had occurred roughly at the same time on both sides of the Atlantic, but in slightly differing ways, reflecting variations in social and political cultures. The same can be said of the reversing of this legislation. In Britain the Abortion Act of 1967 was passed by Parliament. It was a private member's Bill introduced by a member of the Liberal Party (David Steel) and subject to a free vote, but it became law largely because of the support of the ruling Labour Party. It enshrined no general right to abortion, but made abortion conditional on the judgement of two physicians that the balance of risk to the woman's life or health favoured abortion. It can be seen as but an extension of the case law allowing therapeutic abortion for the sake of the mother's general health. On paper, it did not amount to a great change in the existing law, and pro-abortion activists continue to complain that it leaves the decision in the hands of doctors (Brookes 1988, p. 156). Nevertheless, in practice the number of abortions in England and Wales rose steadily from 23,641 (2.7 per cent of pregnancies) in 1968 to 167,149 (14.1 per cent of pregnancies) in 1973. The figure for 2001 was 186,274 which represented a staggering 22.8 per cent of pregnancies. It is clear that legal abortion since the 1967 Act has been very widely performed.

In the USA, the pro-abortion (or 'pro-choice') movement of the 1960s made relatively little impact in the state legislatures. Between 1967 and 1973 nineteen states reformed their abortion laws to varying degrees, the most radical being New York which allowed abortion for non-medical reasons up to 24 weeks. However, there was also a reaction. The New York Legislature sought (unsuccessfully) to repeal the statute. Between 1970 and 1973, over 30 states considered and rejected such laws; these included North Dakota and Michigan which held referenda on the issue. Rather than a gradual state by state change, abortion law in the USA was revolutionized by a decision of the Supreme Court. In 1973, in *Roe* v. *Wade*, the Supreme Court, by a majority of 7:2, struck down anti-abortion legislation across the country. Holding that the Constitution contained a right to abortion, the Court ruled that a state could proscribe abortion only after foetal viability and not even then if abortion was in the interests of the woman's health. In short, the Court created a right to abortion, radically subversive of the Anglo-American legal tradition. Those who made this decision were drawing on ideas of liberty and privacy, which clearly have an important place in the American political–legal tradition. However, the discovery of a constitutional right to abortion was itself without precedent and would likely have been widely rejected prior to the 1960s. In analysing abortion as a question of privacy, that is, a matter that does not harm others, the court begged the central question. By default, it denied to the embryo any human or moral status that might ground legal protection.

Britain enacted an abortion law that was, by and large, the will of the people, and expressed itself in the elastic but very traditional language of threat to physical or mental health. The law of the USA was decided by the Supreme Court and framed in terms of fundamental constitutional rights. Public opinion in the USA remains much more bitterly and much more evenly divided than public opinion in Britain. It is apparent even to supporters of abortion that 'the [US] public is deeply divided on abortion in elective circumstances' (Cook, Jelen and Wilcox 1992, p. 35). Indeed approximately 47 per cent oppose legal abortion for social reasons, while 37 per cent are in favour (ibid.). There is also a racial difference, with support for legal abortion far stronger among whites than African-Americans (p. 45). However, despite the strong identification of the pro-choice movement with feminism, there is 'practically no relationship between gender and attitude towards abortion' (p. 44). If anything women are 'slightly less supportive' of legal abortion than men. An interesting image of the continuing ambivalence to legal abortion in the USA was provided by the conversion of Norma McCorvey, the anonymous Jane Roe of the *Roe* v. *Wade* case, to the pro-life cause. She now regrets the role she played in American legal history. Her change of heart has no bearing on the law, of course, but it serves to show that the law remains controversial even among some of those who might be presumed to support it.

The pro-abortion movement in Britain in the 1920s and 1930s was neither large nor mainstream, but it was successful in linking abortion to the birth control movement, to feminism and to left-wing politics. Most fundamentally it altered the perception of the problem of illegal abortion. For nineteenth-century reformers illegal abortion was seen as harming both mother and child. Compassion towards women harmed by abortion was translated into criticism of abortionists and, among early feminists, criticism of the situations that led women to seek abortion. Compassion for the women whose lives were endangered by illegal abortion was thus wholly compatible with compassion for their unborn children. Anti-abortion reform, like anti-slavery reform and legislation against child-labour was perceived as progressive and compassionate. However, a new generation of activists in the early twentieth century began to argue that abortion was inevitable and the only realistic solution for women was to make it safe and freely available. What was significant here was less the rhetoric of rights than the shift in perspective from abortion as an act harming women and their children, to abortion as a solution for a woman in a desperate situation. This allowed the practice of abortion to be viewed as a form of compassionate concern and thus to attract the sympathy of various groups in society, including many Christians.

The early promoters of legal abortion such as Havelock Ellis, Stella Browne and Janet Chance were almost uniformly hostile to religion. Chance declared that, whereas abortion was no crime 'religious creeds are intellectual crimes' (Grisez 1970, p. 216). Nevertheless, in the second half of the twentieth century many Christians began to accept a perspective according to which abortion could be seen as an act of compassion. In 1954 the Revd Joseph Fletcher, an Episcopalian minister, published a volume on *Morals and Medicine*. Here he claimed that the human person was defined by the possession of freedom and knowledge and thus the foetus (along with the new-born infant, the mentally disabled adult and various others) was not a person. He went on to defend abortion on a wide range of grounds. To understand these claims, which were highly novel in theological or philosophical terms, it is necessary to place them in context. Fletcher's theology was reshaped by a new social context in which abortion was perceived, at least by some, as a compassionate response. The importance of this perceived moral context is made more explicit in his later work *Situation Ethics* (1966).

From the 1960s a number of prominent Christian voices began to express support for free access to abortion. Perhaps the most notable was the Clergy Consultation Service on Abortion in the USA. This group, founded in May 1967, offered to refer women for abortion, even though at that time abortion was still a serious criminal offence. Between 1967 and 1970 a number of Protestant bodies (including the Episcopal Church, the United Methodist Church and the American Baptist Convention) made declarations which, to varying degrees, advocated the relaxation of abortion laws. The American Baptist Convention and the Unitarian Universalist Association were among organizations which sent delegates to the convention of 1969 which launched the National Association for

Repeal of Abortion Laws. The United Methodist Church, which had offices opposite the Supreme Court, also leased space to the Religious Coalition for Abortion Rights.

In the UK, the Anglican Church had made clear its opposition to abortion in the Lambeth Conferences of 1931 and 1958, but by the 1960s it too was divided. John Robinson, Bishop of Woolwich, strongly advocated a repeal of the existing abortion laws. Others, including the Archbishop of Canterbury (Michael Ramsey), opposed abortion for social reasons and were concerned that lax legislation might open the way to abortion on demand. Nevertheless, the prevailing mood in the country clearly favoured reform of the abortion laws, so the Church Assembly Board for Social Responsibility set up a committee to consider the matter. Its report, published in 1965 under the title *Abortion: An Ethical Discussion*, was a compromise document unsatisfactory to both sides. Though a number of Anglican bishops sit in the House of Lords they were reluctant to exercise their votes on this issue. Only seven voted, less than a third of those eligible to do so. Most of these favoured moderate reform but opposed abortion for social reasons. Only one bishop, Dr Ian Ramsey, Bishop of Durham, voted for the social clause (Hindell and Simms 1971, pp. 90–94). This was not the only public show of support for the social clause by prominent Christians: Lord Soper, former president of the Methodist Conference, was in favour. It is also noteworthy that David Steel MP, sponsor of the 1967 Abortion Bill was a practising Christian and the son of a Church of Scotland minister.

This litany of Christian involvement in the moves to permit abortion does not imply that all Christians supported these changes. Christians, particularly but not exclusively Catholics, were in the forefront of opposition. Nevertheless, when these laws were passed, the witness of the Christian churches on abortion was very mixed. It is necessary to re-emphasize at this point that the acceptance of abortion by many Christians during and since the 1960s represents a quite radical departure from the Christian tradition. Not only the Catholic tradition and that of the Early Church, but the fathers of the Reformation, and indeed of the whole Christian tradition, Orthodox, Catholic and Protestant, Evangelical and Liberal, up until the mid twentieth century had opposed abortion for other than strictly therapeutic reasons (and even then, according to the Catholic tradition, abortion was justified only if it was 'indirect'). The suggestion of the present chapter is that the reasons for this dramatic shift do not lie in speculations about ensoulment or in sudden realization of the cumbersome character of the law, but that it stems from a re-imaging of abortion as an act of compassion, or even, an act of liberation (on the important difference between abortion as justified by compassion and abortion as liberation see Harrison 1995 and Gorman and Brooks 2003). However, this powerful social myth effectively excludes any consideration of the unborn child. What is most invidious is not the arguments put up against the moral status of the embryo, but the redirecting of attention so that any serious consideration of the child is viewed as a failure to identify with the mother.

The clash between pro-abortionists and anti-abortionists, or, in their own self-designations, pro-choice and pro-life Christians, lies not in the details but in the perspective. There are legitimate detailed questions to ask about the usefulness and effectiveness of particular laws and amendments. There are questions about how the issue of abortion is best presented both among Christians and in the wider public forum. There are questions about how best to support women with unwanted pregnancies and how to comfort and reconcile those who have undergone an abortion. Nevertheless, before addressing questions of detail it is necessary to gain an adequate ethical and theological perspective. Christian morality is based on compassion and on an identification with those in need. It should not exclude but include. It should seek ways to avoid violent conflict. The perspective of the tradition is that Christian compassion must embrace *both* mother and child, must acknowledge both, must not deny the humanity of either. Only if this can be done can the details of law, politics and justice be discussed fruitfully among believers.

In summary:

- Under the English common law, abortion was a serious offence, at least after quickening. Before quickening it appears not to have been a crime but neither was it a proper lawful action to which citizens could claim a right. Nevertheless, abortion was very difficult to prosecute successfully before the nineteenth century.

- In the nineteenth century both England and the USA enacted statutes restricting abortion. The first of these was Lord Ellenborough's Act 1803 which imposed the death penalty for abortionists who gave drugs to cause an abortion after quickening. Subsequent English legislation removed any reference to quickening and imposed a life sentence for causing an abortion. Legislation in the USA began in Connecticut in 1821. This law also contained reference to quickening but, as in England, later laws abandoned this distinction. By 1880 most states had enacted laws against abortion irrespective of quickening.

- Both in England and in America, opposition to abortion was strongest among physicians. However, in England this opposition did not amount to a campaign whereas the USA witnessed a crusade against abortion led by the physician Horatio Storer. Other groups were less conspicuous as activists but there was general support for anti-abortion legislation among the clergy, lawyers and early feminists.

- The movement to repeal the anti-abortion laws began in Britain in the 1920s in the UK and had its roots in the birth control movement, though not all members of the birth control movement advocated abortion. The sea change in public opinion on abortion in the 1960s was due to many factors including concerns about overpopulation, acceptance of eugenic abortion (especially in the wake of thalidomide) and more generally, in a change of perspective in which abortion was seen as a compassionate and practical solution to the plight of women with unwanted pregnancies.

- Christians, having opposed abortion consistently until the mid twentieth century, then began to divide on the issue. Some continued to oppose abortion as contrary to the doctrine of the sanctity of all human life. Others saw the legalization of abortion as the compassionate answer to a difficult question. Nevertheless, by accepting abortion as a solution, they effectively denied the humanity of the unborn child.

The present chapter has considered the changing pattern of abortion law in Britain and the USA, from the common law to the laws of the nineteenth century and their repeal in the late twentieth century. This is relevant to the present book because, for most of Christian history, the question of the theological understanding of the embryo has had a moral impact primarily in the area of abortion, and abortion has been subject to legal restrictions since the Middle Ages. However, in 1978 the world entered a new era, as Louise Brown was born: the first new-born child to have been conceived outside the womb. *In vitro fertilization* opened up the possibility of freezing, storing, testing, selecting and even experimenting on human embryos. It led in the 1980s to a fierce debate on the ethics of experimenting on embryos, a debate which considered the status of the embryo in very different context.

14

The Embryo in Isolation

The Second principle is that of division into species according to the natural formation, where the joint is, not breaking any part as a bad carver might.

(Plato, *Phaedrus*)

When in vitro fertilization (IVF) led to the first successful human birth in 1978 it was proclaimed as a technological triumph and an answer to the anguish of many childless couples. However, some feared that it was the beginning of the *Brave New World* foreseen by Aldous Huxley in his dystopian novel of 1932. The phrase 'test-tube baby' evoked the image of human life being created, and perhaps controlled, by scientists. Such fears generally subsided only to resurface in connection with the human genome project – which in 1990 began to compile a map of the entire human genetic sequence. This was completed ahead of schedule in 2003. The social dangers implicit in such a project were explored in the 1997 science-fiction film *GATTACA*. They were also mirrored in the language of the popular press, which shifted from 'test-tube baby' to 'designer baby'. The reproductive technology that has provoked the strongest public reaction is that of cloning, a prospect which can no longer be regarded as pure science fiction. The questions raised by IVF, by the human genome project and by human cloning are certainly not identical, but all these activities belong to a new biotechnological context which has challenged society to reflect seriously on what it is to be human. It is outside the scope of the present enquiry to consider all the theological and ethical implications of these technologies. Our task here is specifically to consider the impact of these technologies on the treatment of the human embryo.

In principle, IVF need not involve the deliberate destruction of

214

embryos. It is possible to fertilize one ovum in vitro, allow the embryo to develop for a few days and then introduce it into the womb where it could implant and progress successfully to term. Of course, there would be a risk that the embryo might not implant, but such a risk is present in every pregnancy. In principle, therefore, IVF does not necessarily imply an attack on early human life. However, while one can imagine an ideal case in which no human embryos are harmed, in practice, there are strong practical considerations that have favoured the production of many more embryos than are transferred to their mother's womb. The fundamental reason for this is to increase the chances of successful pregnancy. Before the woman can bring a child to term it is often necessary to have several cycles of treatment, with two or three embryos transferred in each cycle. It is not regarded as practical to conceive only as many embryos as will be transferred in one cycle because of the difficulty of obtaining human ova. The ova have to be extracted from the woman by laproscopy, generally after she has been given super-ovulatory drugs. This is an intrusive procedure and clinicians prefer not to repeat it. Furthermore, unlike sperm, it has not yet proved possible to freeze ova successfully. Thus, in order to give the woman a greater chance of giving birth, it is usual to conceive a relatively large number of embryos in vitro and freeze those who are not transferred immediately. In time, all the frozen embryos could be transferred, but it is common for some to remain after the treatment has come to an end. These 'spare' embryos, if not transferred to the womb, face eventual destruction. Every year, many thousands of embryos are consigned to this fate.

There are at least two further reasons why IVF clinicians feel the need to produce more embryos than will eventually be transferred to the mother: The first is the need, or perceived need, to screen embryos prior to transferring them. Screening prior to transfer relieves the mother of the prospect of abortion and relieves the clinician from ethical and perhaps legal responsibility for the birth of a disabled child. For parents with inheritable diseases, pre-implantation screening can allow the selection of offspring who are free from the disease. All this implies, of course, the destruction of embryos who are thought unworthy of rearing.

The second reason why clinicians prefer to produce more

embryos than will be transferred is in order to provide embryos for research purposes. The development of IVF has required a constant supply of embryos. Moreover, since embryo experimentation was first permitted, a quite different branch of medicine has become interested in making use of human embryos. It has been suggested that 'stem cells' from human embryos could, in the future, provide medical treatment for a whole host of diseases. English law currently permits the creation of human embryos purely for research purposes. However, such is the great supply of 'spare' embryos that experimenters rarely feel the need to conceive more embryos.

The ethics of overproducing embryos that will either be discarded or used in scientific experiments depends on the ethical status of the human embryo. In this respect IVF raises some of the same issues as abortion. However, the context of IVF is in many respects quite different from the context of abortion. Abortion usually addresses the crisis of an unwanted pregnancy. IVF addresses the ongoing inability of a couple to conceive a child. The embryo who is about to be aborted exists within the body of his or her mother and is wholly dependent upon her for survival. The embryo conceived by IVF exists, at least for a time, outside the body of his or her mother. In an important sense, the IVF embryo exists in isolation. Furthermore, there is no equivalent with IVF to the problem of unsafe illegal abortions. Several of the considerations that have swayed legislators to permit abortion (whether rightly or wrongly) do not obtain in the case of IVF. It is therefore imaginable that a state might decide to grant legal protection to the embryo outside the womb by banning embryo experimentation, without extending this protection to the embryo inside the womb in the case of abortion. This somewhat paradoxical situation exists in a number of states in the USA (Louisiana, Pennsylvania, Massachusetts, Michigan, Minnesota, South Dakota and arguably Maine, North Dakota and Rhode Island). It came close to occurring in the UK in 1985 when the Unborn Child (Protection) Bill was approved for its second reading. It has come to exist in Italy where a law regulating IVF was passed as recently as 2004. The use of embryos for experimental purposes cannot be justified simply on the basis that the law permits abortion.

On the other hand, the IVF embryo that is discarded or used in experiments is much younger and much less developed than the embryo threatened by abortion. It is often not until the fifth or sixth week of pregnancy that the woman realizes she is pregnant. By this time the embryo can be seen on ultrasound and already possesses a beating heart, arms and legs, even fingers and toes. It has the appearance of a tiny baby. In contrast, the embryo produced by IVF, if not transferred to the womb is frozen after only a few days. At this stage it is scarcely visible to the human eye. It has no blood, no heart and no nervous system. It does not look like a baby.

There has been some support for embryo experimentation, especially in the USA, from those who regard abortion as a right and fear that recognition for the embryo in the context of experimentation will lead to restriction of abortion. This could be described as tactical support. However, the most sustained political pressure in favour of experimentation on human embryos has come from the medical and scientific community. In the UK, shortly after the second reading of the Unborn Child (Protection) Bill, an organization was founded to lobby parliament and to use the media to promote the cause for embryo experimentation. The name of the organization was 'Progress' (now the Progress Educational Trust). Opposition to embryo experimentation was thus depicted as opposition to scientific and medical progress.

The story of the politics of the embryo experimentation debate in the UK in the mid 1980s has been well told by Mulkay (1997). Despite initial successes for those who opposed experimentation, the eventual legislation, the Human Embryology and Fertilization Act (1990), allowed embryo experimentation under licence. In the 1990s the experimentation debate was repeated in relation to embryonic stem cell research and 'therapeutic cloning'. The idea of embryonic stem cell research is to take 'stem cells' from human embryos and use them to treat diseases. The embryos would be destroyed in the process. In the case of therapeutic cloning the embryo would be produced not by fertilization but by cell nuclear transfer (the technique used to produce Dolly the sheep: the first cloned mammal) so that it would be genetically identical, or nearly identical, to an existing adult. This clone embryo would then be dissected for its stem cells.

The embryonic stem cell debate was broken-backed in the sense that the principle of allowing embryo experimentation had already been conceded. If embryos could be used and destoyed in research on infertility, why could they not be used for (stem cell) research on incurable diseases? The case for more experimentation was defended on the basis that embryonic stem cells represented the 'Holy Grail' which promised a cure for diseases such as Parkinson's and Alzheimer's diseases. Such defences tended both to exaggerate the present state of research and to underplay the potential of alternative lines of research and treatment, most notably those involving adult stem cells, or stem cells taken from the umbilical cords of new-born infants. Nevertheless, experimentation on human embryos was supported by a number of charities representing people suffering from various diseases. The only new element in this debate was the fear that a clone embryo would be allowed to be born. Most people were deeply unhappy about cloning as a method of fertility treatment. In 2001 the Human Fertilization and Embryology Act was amended to allow experimentation on embryos for a wider range of reasons. Cloning human embryos for medical research purposes was permitted, but in a separate piece of legislation, the Human Reproductive Cloning Act (2001), it became an offence to 'place in a woman a human embryo which has been created otherwise than by fertilization (i.e. a clone embryo)'.

In the USA the debate over embryo experimentation largely focused on the question of federal funding. Experiments on embryos are permitted by most states, but they cannot receive federal funding. This situation is similar in some ways to the legal stalemate over abortion. No state can prohibit abortion in the first trimester, but there is no obligation on states to fund abortions, and federal funding for abortion is limited to cases of rape, incest or danger to the mother's life. Such compromises satisfy neither side, but are products of an activist judiciary, a deeply divided public and a health-care system funded largely by private insurance. This contrasts with the UK where the decisions to permit and to fund are more closely connected. Most abortions are funded by the NHS, and the Medical Research Council can and does fund embryo experimentation. On the question of cloning there is no federal law but a number of states have enacted legislation prohibiting cloning for reproductive purposes (Arkansas, California, Iowa, Louisiana, Michigan, New Jersey, North Dakota, Rhode Island and Virginia) and some also for therapeutic purposes (Arkansas, Iowa, Michigan, North Dakota). This mirrors the uneven pattern of state legislation on embryo experimentation.

The issue of embryo experimentation brings the ethical status of the human embryo into focus in a particularly sharp fashion. In this case, the embryo is not within the body of his or her mother but exists in the outside world, a separate and isolated living being. What may be done to such an embryo turns on how the human embryo is understood. Some frame the issue in terms of when human life begins. Others prefer to start with a definition of 'person'. The Warnock Committee, which was established by parliament to inquire into the issue, claimed that it was possible to resolve the practical issues without directly addressing such questions.

> Although the questions of when life or personhood begin appear to be questions of fact susceptible of straightforward answers, we hold that the answers to such questions in fact are complex amalgams of factual and moral judgements. Instead of trying to answer these questions directly we have gone straight to the question of *how it is right to treat the embryo*. (Warnock 1984, para. 11.9, emphasis in the original)

Nevertheless, while the Warnock Committee refrained from any detailed exploration of when human life or personhood began, their conclusions imply that they had come to a judgement on these matters. In para. 11.15, the Committee endorsed the 'more generally held position' that 'the human embryo is entitled to some added measure of respect beyond that accorded to other animal subjects, [though] that respect cannot be absolute'. This seems to be based on the judgement that the human embryo is 'a potential human being' (11.22) and thus neither a non-human animal nor an actual human being. Given the importance of this judgement to the argument as a whole, it would surely have been better for the Committee to grasp the nettle and inquire directly into the question of whether the embryo is an actual human being and, if not, when it becomes an actual human being.

In the light of scientific developments, by the 1950s most Christians had come to believe that human life begins when sperm and ovum fuse at fertilization, and that God breathes in the soul at that moment. However, since the 1960s there has been a revival, among some Christians, of the medieval view that the soul is infused at some time after conception. This seems to have been driven less by any discoveries in science, and more by the political and ethical debates surrounding abortion. The desire to permit abortion, inspired by the re-imaging of abortion as an act of compassion, led many Christians to reconsider the character of the embryo. If the embryo were not fully human then it would be much easier to justify abortion. Joseph Fletcher was an early example of this strand of thought. He argued that whereas the embryo is a human being, it is not a human person. What sets human beings apart from other animals is their possession of reason or the capacity for free decisions. This is what grounds human dignity and is signified by the term 'person'. If the human embryo is not a human person then it does not merit legal protection.

At first sight, Fletcher's account of the person seems similar to that of Thomas Aquinas. Like Aquinas, Fletcher held that a person is a rational being. Like Aquinas, Fletcher held that the early human embryo is not a person. However, there are also significant differences between these two thinkers. Aquinas did not think it was possible to be a human being without being a human person, whereas Fletcher thought that it was possible to be a human being without being a human person. For Aquinas, the embryo was not a person because it did not possess a human nature. It was not a human being, nor did it possess any intrinsic or natural capacity to become a human being. It did not belong to the human species. For Fletcher the embryo was a member of the human species, but it was not a person because it could not exercise intellectual capacities. Aquinas believed that the embryo was shaped not from within but from without, by the power of the father's seed, and that it only became human after the organs were formed when God infused a rational soul into it. It has been argued above (Chapter 11) that, in the light of modern biology, Aquinas's principles favour the view that the human embryo is a human being, and hence a human person, from conception. However, Fletcher, by focusing on the actual powers that someone could display, explicitly described even new-born infants as nonpersons. Lastly, it should be noted that Fletcher regarded it as ethical to destroy human nonpersons, if there was some benefit to persons. In sharp contrast, Aquinas held that the deliberate destruction of the embryo was always unethical, even before ensoulment.

The root difference between Aquinas and Fletcher is that, for Aquinas, a person is defined as 'an individual being of a rational nature': *persona est rationalis naturae individua substantia* (*ST* Ia Q.29, quoting Boethius *On the Two Natures of Christ*). Aquinas believed that new-born infants have only an imperfect use of reason on account of the wetness of their brains (*ST* Ia Q.101 art. 2). Nevertheless, he held that they possess a rational nature from the time the organs of the embryo are fully formed. This is equally true of a formed foetus, a new-born infant, a mentally disabled adult or someone who was asleep or unconscious. If they possess a human nature, they possess a rational nature, even if they are unable freely to exercise their reason at a certain time. For Fletcher, to be a person, someone must be able to exercise his or her reason.

The approach of Fletcher was based not on Aquinas, Aristotle or Boethius but on the English philosopher John Locke. Locke defined a person as '... a thinking, intelligent being, that has reason and reflection, and can consider itself as itself, the same thinking thing, in different times and different places' (*An Essay Concerning Human Understanding* Book II, Chapter 26 para. 9). These abilities obviously involve a high degree of self-awareness. Fletcher showed that a definition of this sort implies that new-born infants are nonpersons. From there it is but a short step to embracing infanticide, at least in certain cases. Fletcher explicitly accepted this conclusion, as have the secular philosophers Jonathan Glover (1977), Michael Tooley (1983) and Peter Singer (1994), who follow a similar path of reasoning. However, an ethic that allows infanticide seems entirely contrary to the Christian tradition of care for the weak and the vulnerable (Wyatt 1998, pp. 221ff.). In the ancient world, opposition to infanticide sharply distinguished Jews and Christians from most of their pagan contemporaries. Given the purposes of the present enquiry, it is reasonable for the sake of argument to take as a starting-point the rejection of infanticide. If Christians ought to reject infanticide, then they ought to reject arguments which presuppose that infanticide is acceptable. Therefore, given that Christians ought to reject infanticide, they also ought to reject arguments from personhood of the sort exemplified by Fletcher. The point is well expressed by the Lutheran theologian Gilbert Meilaender.

> Personhood arguments, exclusive rather than inclusive in their understanding of human community, seem in many ways to have turned against the long and arduous history in which we have slowly learned to value and protect – for Christians, to see Christ in – those who are 'least' among us. (Meilaender 1997, pp. 32–33).

This is not to deny that it is possible, for various purposes, to define 'person' in the way that Locke does. His definition would include all adults who are alert and awake, but would exclude those who were mentally incapacitated and those who were disorientated. There is ethical and legal significance in distinguishing those who are able to exercise autonomy from those who are unable. For example, in discussing the need for consent in medical treatment, the law distinguishes competent persons who are able to make decisions for themselves from those who are not competent. Nevertheless, definitions of personhood based on the ability to exercise autonomy systematically degrade or even exclude altogether those human beings who are unable to speak or act for themselves. As concern with rights or justice' focuses on need rather than on power, it is incongruous to say that someone who cannot exercise the power of reason is excluded from legal protection or ethical concern. We generally regard those who are immature, mentally disabled or temporarily unconscious as meriting more not less protection. As they cannot defend themselves, their parent, guardian, carer, next of kin or the court should act to protect their best interests. If we are to use the term 'person' in Locke's sense, then it is not only human 'persons' whose lives are precious, sacred or inviolable. It is all human beings.

Fletcher followed Locke and thus argued that the human being becomes a person only when he or she becomes self-aware. In a similar fashion, some other theologians have argued that the human embryo does not become a human being until he or she becomes self-aware. Karl Rahner was one of the most prominent Catholic theologians of the late twentieth century. He was a deliberately speculative theologian who wished to engage with contemporary thought and culture. In his reflections on the human embryo he was influenced less by Locke and more by the evolutionary ideas of Teilhard de Chardin. Rahner preferred to talk not of ensoulment or personhood but of 'hominization'. He thought that the process of embryonic development was parallel to the evolutionary history of human beings in that it proceeded in stages from the nonhuman to the human. It has been argued above (in Chapter 11) that this idea rests on a mistaken biology. Nevertheless, Rahner influenced a number of other theologians, including Bernard Häring, Joseph Donceel, and Michael Coughlan.

Aside from questions of evolutionary biology, the fundamental problem with the approach of Rahner, Donceel and others is that the demand for the embryo to possess a functioning brain seems at once too weak and too strong. If what is distinctive about human life is the ability to reason, then why place the end-point of human development with the appearance of the brain? Many other animals possess a brain. On the logic of this argument, the end-point should surely be identified with the time when the child shows real evidence of rational thought in a way that surpasses other animals, that is, when he or she begins to talk. This point is emphasized by Ford: 'One weakness in Donceel's position is the unjustified demand for the formation of sense organs and of the brain for rational ensoulment once it is admitted there are no actual rational functions performed for two years' (Ford 1988, p. 52). If a human being is characterized in terms of actual thoughts or free actions, then it seems that this definition of a human being will suffer from the same problems as Fletcher's definition of personhood. It will exclude new-born infants and others whom Christians have always counted as part of the human community. If, on the other hand, being human is defined, for example, in terms of capacity to acquire the power of thought, then it can be asked why the early embryo does not also possesses this. Surely, since the embryo has the potential to develop into a new-born baby, 'it has the potential to acquire whatever characteristics the baby has the potential to acquire' (Foster 1985, p. 36). If it is said that the embryo might die before birth, it could equally be said that a new-born infant might die before exercising the ability to think. If being human is restricted to those who can use their reason, then it will exclude many whom we are accustomed to view as human beings. On the other hand, if being human involves having a rational nature, and this is expressed in terms of capacity or active potentiality, then it seems that this is already possessed by the human embryo.

It is now necessary to turn our minds directly to the question: is the human embryo a human being? If human being is defined biologically, and not in terms of personhood in the restrictive sense outlined above, then it seems reasonable to say that a human being is an individual living being of the species *homo sapiens*. On the face of it the human embryo would fall under this definition. The embryo is clearly a living being, is an individual and is human. It is not only a part of a human being (like the organs of the body) nor is it a potential part of a human being (like the gametes). From the moment of fertilization the embryo is a complete whole, a living being in the process of developing. If it is asked when the life of a particular human being began, the most obvious answer would usually be: at the moment of fertilization. The significance of this transition has been emphasized in a number of official Catholic documents: 'From the time that the ovum is fertilized, a life is begun which is neither that of the father or the mother; it is rather that life of a new human being with his [or her] own growth' (John Paul II 1995, para. 60, *Declaration on Procured Abortion*, No. 12).

Nevertheless, a number of commentators, while acknowledging that the human being should be given a biological definition, have resisted the conclusion that the embryo is a human being. One significant stumbling-block, both for philosophers and theologians (Anscombe 1985; Ford 1988), is the occasional formation of identical (or monozygotic) twins. Little is known about the process of twinning, but it seems that in a small percentage of cases (0.3 per cent), the early embryo divides to give two individuals. This process occurs within the first fourteen days or so after fertilization, before the emergence of the primitive streak: the first sign of what will become the spinal cord. Furthermore, it is widely believed that twinning could be induced artificially by dividing or agitating the human embryo. The multiplication of embryos in this way has been done many times with other species of animal, and was first done with sea urchin embryos over a century ago. The phenomenon of twinning poses obvious difficulties in relation to the individuality of the early embryo. It was prominent in the deliberations of the Warnock Committee and lies behind its recommendation that experimentation only be allowed prior to the emergence of the primitive streak. 'This marks the beginning of the *individual* development of the embryo' (Warnock 1984, 11.22, emphasis added).

If the human embryo can split in two, is it truly an individual living being? This question gets its force from the fact that in general human beings do not multiply by dividing in two, or by a new human being budding off one who already exists. Human beings multiply by sexual reproduction. However, if we turn from human beings to other organisms we see that many living things multiply both sexually and asexually. This is true not only of plants but of starfish, certain worms and various other simple animals. We are familiar with taking cuttings from a plant to generate new plants. In the case of these species we do not deny that they are individual living beings simply because they can be multiplied by being divided. We count individual starfish and individual rosebushes without difficulty. So also, scientists who deal with human embryos treat them as biological individuals. They count them, screen them, freeze them or transfer them. It makes perfect sense to say, for example, that two embryos were transferred to the womb (i.e. two individuals), even though, potentially, each of these embryos could generate twins.

The strong inclination of scientists to treat embryos as individuals was further illustrated by the reaction of the scientific community to the term 'pre-embryo'. This term was coined in the mid 1980s to give more rhetorical force to the case for research on early human embryos. Its justification rested, among other things, on the supposed lack of individuality of the 'pre-embryo'. However, while many scientists favoured allowing research on human embryos, they were highly critical of this novel terminology (Nature [1987] 327:87, 'IVF remains in legal limbo'). It seemed arbitrary to redefine embryo to exclude the earliest stages of embryonic development: the zygote and blastocyst. Plato once said species should be divided 'according to the natural formation, where the joint is, not breaking any part as a bad carver might' (*Phaedrus*). We should beware of creating artificial concepts that cut across natural continuities. The widespread rejection of the term pre-embryo, even by those who favoured experimentation on embryos, bears witness that the early human embryo is indeed an embryo, that is, the first stage of life of an individual living being.

From a biological perspective, there is no difficulty in saying that, during the first stage of human development, some individuals divide to produce twins. For secular philosophers the occasional multiplication of human embryos in this way should be no barrier to counting the embryo as a human being, at least in the biological sense. However, the perplexity surrounding identical twins is exacerbated in a Christian context by the doctrine of the spiritual and immortal soul. Bodies can be cut into pieces, but the spiritual soul is supposed to be one and indivisible. It is the soul that gives unity to the body, not vice versa. Furthermore, according to the dominant tradition in Catholic theology, it is the simplicity of the soul that ensures its survival after the death of the body. For this reason, a number of theologians have held that the soul is not infused until after the time when twinning become impossible, that is, until fourteen days or so after fertilization (Ford 1988; see also Häring 1972, p. 79; Mahoney 1984, pp. 62–3; Meilaender 1997, p. 31).

The difficulty in telling a convincing 'soul story' about twinning is due, at least in part, to uncertainty in regard to the precise biological mechanism of the process. Is twinning genetically predetermined or determined by the fertilization event? In which case, the early embryo could be thought of as conjoined twins (Sutton 2003, p. 28). Is twinning asymmetrical? In which case it could be understood as one embryo generating a second (Watt 2000, p. 60). Is twinning symmetrical? In which case it could be thought of as the destruction of one individual to give rise to two new individuals (Watt 2000, p. 59). Some consider this last story unbelievable, for the embryo that ceases to exist would leave no corpse (Coughlan 1990, p. 72). However, imagine a sixteen-cell embryo that was shaken apart to produce sixteen single-celled embryos. If this ever happened then it would be natural to say that the sixteen-cell embryo had ceased to exist and sixteen new embryos had begun to exist. The problem with twinning seems less our inability to tell a 'soul story' and more the inability to judge between these stories. Until more is known empirically, it is difficult to know what sort of story to tell.

My own view is that monozygotic twinning shows that human embryos possess certain powers that are lost later in life. An embryo has the power of a starfish that, when divided, can generate new individuals from its separated parts. At the turn of the twentieth century, Hans Dreisch (1867-1941) first induced twinning by agitating the embryos of sea urchins. He was so impressed by this phenomenon that he abandoned mechanical theories of life in favour of a form of vitalism. It seemed to him that the embryo must possess something like a soul because, when it was divided, it did not die or produce two half-beings but rather developed into two complete individuals. Aristotle said something similar in relation to animals that continue to live when divided 'in each of the two [separated] parts, all the parts of the soul are present' (*On the Soul* I.5). It is somewhat ironic that twinning, which Dreisch thought was evidence for the presence of a soul, is now taken as evidence for the absence of a soul. What impressed both Aristotle and Dreisch was the way that the whole was present in each of the parts such that the separated parts became new wholes. Catholic theology, following Aquinas, holds that where there is a whole unified organism, there is a soul. The soul is not multiplied *by* the body, but souls are multiplied *according to* the number of bodies (*ST* Ia Q.76 art. 2). This is not contradicted by procreation, which generates a new body. As the new body is generated, God gives a new soul. Yet surely something similar could be said about twinning. As twinning results in a multiplication of human embryos, then God gives new souls appropriately (Fisher 1991; Flannery 2003).

Another consideration that has made some Christians hesitate to identify fertilization as the beginning of a human being is the discovery that many embryos are lost before implantation occurs. This consideration was put forward by Karl Rahner as a reason for doubting that ensoulment occurred at fertilization. 'Will today's moral theologian ... be able to accept that 50 per cent of all "human beings" - real human beings with "immortal" souls and an eternal destiny – will never get beyond this first stage of human existence?' (Rahner 1972, p. 226). Could it be imagined that the next world is mainly populated by human beings who have lived only a few days? 'Although this is logically possible, it is also rather counterintuitive' (Meilaender 1997, p. 31). Nevertheless, though this argument has been much repeated, it is very weak. It amounts to saying that because many embryos do not survive, they are not valuable in the eyes of God. As such, 'it does not appear very different, if at all, from arguing from the statistics in some countries, or in earlier centuries, of infant or perinatal mortality to the conclusion that the tragically large number of children who die, or have died, at birth could not possibly be all possessed of an immortal soul' (Mahoney 1984, p. 61).

The argument gains its force from the difficulty we experience in trying to imagine what heaven will mean for those who have died before birth. This is not a new problem but has perplexed Christians since ancient times. Augustine says, 'As for abortions, which have been alive in the mother's womb but have died there, I cannot bring myself either to affirm or to deny that they will share the resurrection.' But he immediately goes on to say, 'And yet, if they are not excluded from the number of the dead, I cannot see how they will be excluded from the resurrection of the dead' (*City of God* XXII, Ch. 13). Much of the difficulty we have in imagining embryos in heaven is also found in trying to imagine new-born babies in heaven. Yet the Christian tradition strongly affirms that the souls of babies who die after baptism are received immediately into heaven. Augustine is brave enough to speculate about the resurrected bodies of such infants – he thinks that the body will appear as it would have been had they lived to maturity (*City of God* XXII, Ch. 14). This still leaves the question of how glory can be experienced by someone who died before they even learned to talk. This is not an easy question.

> I doubt very much whether we can do more than plead that we know so little of what glory means for any of the elect, that it would be foolhardy to exclude the possibility of even such little experience as foetuses have being glorified. If there can be such a thing as glorified inexperience, maybe the Victorians were not being totally stupid in treating dead children as angels. (Tugwell 1990, p. 169)

As Christians are required to say that there are very many new-born infants in the life of the world to come then they should remain open to the possibility that there will also be many human embryos. If they are human and they have died, then they will be raised from the dead, though we cannot say what that will be like.

If, from the moment of fertilization, the human embryo is a human being, then the decision to terminate pregnancy is the decision to end the life of a human being. Clearly this affects how we should understand it and what terminology we should use to describe it. For example, abortion is often referred to as termination of pregnancy. It is certainly true that abortion brings pregnancy to an end; however, pregnancy is also brought to an end by delivery and live birth, but in this case people do not refer to 'termination of pregnancy'. The reason for this is surely that the langauge is known to be euphemistic and there is no need to use euphemisms when describing welcome events. The language of termination of pregnancy is used precisely because it disguises the fact that what is terminated in this case is the life of an unborn human being. 'Abortion' is a more accurate term because it alludes to the expulsion of the foetus from the womb. This brings a primary consequence of the procedure into focus, its effect upon the unborn child. In medical usage the term 'abortion' can also refer to miscarriage: 'spontaneous abortion'. However, in common language the word abortion is reserved for the deliberate expulsion of the foetus. The common usage is helpful in that though spontaneous and induced abortions may be similar from a medical point of view they carry a very different human and ethical significance. Both events are tragic and distressing, but the second is also a human action and thus a matter of decision, virtue and justice.

Terminological questions also surround the categorization of birth control measures that act, not by preventing fertilization, but by preventing the embryo from implanting in the womb. Should drugs such as 'the morning-after pill' be classified as contraceptives or as abortifacients? Even in countries where abortion is permitted, this classification has political importance, because the legal regulation of abortion is generally much stricter than the regulation of contraception. When the English law on this question was tested in 2002, Justice Munby turned to contemporary medical usage for a definition of pregnancy. He asserted that pregnancy was generally regarded as beginning at implantation. The morning-after pill was therefore declared not to cause a miscarriage in the terms of the 1861 Offences against the Person Act (*Smeaton* v. *Secretary of State* [2002]), but for the other side of the argument see Keown 1984. When moral theologians take the opposite view and define anti-implantation agents as abortifacient they are sometimes criticized for ignorance of medical terminology and thus failing to base their concepts on biological realities. On the other hand, opponents of abortion have seen in the recent definition of pregnancy as beginning at implantation the effects of social distortion upon a biological concept. It allows drugs that prevent implantation to be classified as contraceptives and thus dispensed more widely.

In assessing this issue, it is important to note that the adequacy of a concept should be judged by reference to its context and use. Those physicians who define pregnancy as beginning with implantation do so, at least in part, because this is the earliest point at which pregnancy can be detected. Standard pregnancy tests measure the level of a hormone that is produced by the embryo after implantation (human chorionic gonadotropin). This does not occur until the embryo is attached to the womb. It may also be noted that fertilization and pregnancy are distinct concepts. This is clear from the example of IVF where, immediately after fertilization, the embryo already exists but the woman is not yet pregnant. It may be said, paradoxically, that someone can thereby become a mother before she becomes pregnant! The definition of pregnancy that dates it from implantation has become common among physicians. Nevertheless, if asked about the *age* of the foetus, the physician will generally begin not with implantation but with fertilization. A different question brings a different answer. It is plausible to see this as reflecting the significance of implantation for the woman (and the gynaecologist) over and against the significance of fertilization for the embryo (and embryologist).

In a curious way, this contemporary emphasis on implantation seems to represent a return to the pre-scientific idea that conception consists primarily in the planting of the seed in the passive woman. In contrast, from Hippocrates to von Baer, most biologists have emphasized that the woman provides not just a place but something analogous to the man's semen. In identifying the beginning of the embryonic life, the most significant event has consistently been seen as the fusing of male and female elements, whether seed and seed (Hippocrates), seed and blood (Aristotle) or sperm and ovum, (von Baer). Implantation is certainly an important marker for pregnancy, but embryologists continue to understand the process of development as beginning with the union of sperm and ovum and to date the age of the embryo from this point.

From an ethical point of view, the reason for the distinction between abortion and contraception is that abortion destroys something (whether this something is called an embryo, a foetus or an unborn child), whereas contraception prevents this being from coming to be in the first place. Even those who do not object to abortion in principle should recognize that there is an ethically significant distinction between agents that prevent fertilization (contraceptives in the uncontroversial sense of the word) and agents that act to prevent implantation. It is therefore misleading to describe anti-implantives as 'emergency contraception'. If an agent can act both as a contraceptive-proper and as an anti-implantive then both these actions should be acknowledged and it should be stated which of these actions is predominant. For example, the standard oral contraceptive is predominantly contraceptive, but sometimes acts as an anti-implantive, whereas the morning-after pill is predominantly anti-implantive but sometimes acts as a contraceptive (if taken just before ovulation). If anti-implantives are not distinguished from contraceptives proper, then the law will continue to be distorted, the public misinformed and physicians and pharmacists stripped of the protection of conscience that obtains in cases of abortion.

Terminological battles occur not only in relation to the embryo ('pre-embryo'), abortion ('termination of pregnancy') and anti-implantives ('emergency contraceptives') but also in relation to human cloning. It has become common to distinguish two forms of cloning: reproductive cloning and therapeutic cloning. In the first case an embryo is cloned and transferred to the womb in order to give birth to a clone child. Cloning is here envisaged as a form of fertility treatment, perhaps for couples who cannot produce gametes and do not want to use donor gametes. In the second case an embryo is cloned and then dissected so that embryonic stem cells can be obtained. Current English law reflects the ethical opinion that reproductive cloning is bad and should be banned, whereas therapeutic cloning is useful and should be permitted. Other countries have prohibited cloning whether for reproductive or therapeutic purposes, and the word 'clone' continues to evoke unease in many people.

For this reason some scientists and government organizations prefer to talk not of therapeutic cloning but of Cell Nuclear Replacement (CNR) or of Somatic Cell Nuclear Transfer (SCNT). This is quite justifiable in a scientific context to the extent that it accurately describes the method employed in producing the clone embryos. However, in both therapeutic and reproductive contexts it is the same method employed and a human embryo is produced. This is recognized in UK law by the fact that it is an offence to 'place in a woman a human embryo [*sic*] which has been created otherwise than by fertilization'. Despite great efforts on the part of scientists, governments and lobbyists, the language of 'therapeutic cloning' remains with us, so that, if someone talks about SCNT or CNR they have then to explain that what they are referring to is therapeutic cloning. The survival of the term 'therapeutic cloning' is to be welcomed in that it reminds us that SCNT/CNR involves the production of a human embryo. Embryonic stem cells are derived from embryos.

Some moral theologians have pointed out that terminology of therapeutic and reproductive cloning is, however, flawed for other reasons. On the one hand, all cloning is reproductive in the sense that it generates new human embryos. On the other hand, the language of therapeutic cloning obscures the important ethical distinction between research that is therapeutic for the subject of research and research that is helpful for others. The clone embryo is not the beneficiary of the therapy but is used for the sake of others. If the human embryo is recognized as a human being then it should immediately be seen that, contrary to common opinion, cloning for medical/research purposes is *worse* than cloning for reproductive purposes. It contradicts the most fundamental principles of ethical research. 'In research on man the interests of science and society should never take precedence over consideration relating to the well-being of the subject' (Helsinki Declaration).

The debates surrounding embryo experimentation, the morning-after pill and human cloning have focused, in part, on terms and definitions. Should Christians adopt a definition of person according to which some human beings are nonpersons? What is a human being? Is the human embryo rightly called a human being? Is the being that comes into existence at fertilization rightly called an embryo? Should we date the development of the embryo from implantation or from fertilization? Are drugs that prevent the embryo from implanting rightly termed contraceptives? Should a more specific term be used to distinguish anti-implantives from contraceptives proper? Is therapeutic cloning rightly called cloning? Is it rightly called therapeutic? In all these cases we can see that it is important to choose terms that *both* accord with biological realities *and* reflect distinctions that are humanly and ethically significant.

In summary:

- While in principle IVF need not involve discarding or destroying human embryos, in practice it generates many more embryos than are transferred to the womb. From the beginning, the development of the technique was supported by experimentation on embryos.
- IVF raises the question of the ethical status of the embryo in a much sharper way than abortion does. In the case of IVF the embryo is not within the womb of his or her mother. The question of what to do with the embryo is thus more directly related to what it is, in itself, and not only in relation to its mother.
- The term person can be understood in different senses. The classical definition coined by Boethius refers to an individual being of a rational nature. In contrast, Locke defined person as one who is 'a thinking, intelligent being, that has reason and reflection, and can consider itself as itself, the same thinking thing, in different times and different places'. New-born infants are persons in the Boethian sense, not in the Lockean sense. Locke's definition of person will not tell us which beings should be the objects of human solidarity, care or legal protection.

- Rahner's account of the hominization of the embryo was not based on Locke's definition of the person, but, as Ford points out, it suffers from some of the same problems. It is not clear why new-born infants (who cannot yet reason) are classified as human beings while embryos (who cannot yet reason) are not classified as such. If immediate ability to reason is the test then it seems that neither should be classified as human, but if potential to develop the power to reason is the test, then it seems that both should be classified as human.
- Some have questioned whether the embryo is an individual living being, given that an embryo might divide to produce identical twins. This is a perplexing issue and can be approached in different ways. Twinning should probably be thought of as analogous to reproduction, with souls being multiplied according to bodies. Others have doubted that early embryos are human beings because so many are lost, but this is a very weak argument. The human embryo is an individual living being of the species *Homo sapiens*: a human being in the biological sense of that term.
- Current UK law and common medical usage defines pregnancy as beginning at implantation. In part, this is because pregnancy cannot be detected before implantation. However, the age or stage of development of the foetus is generally dated from conception. Agents that prevent implantation should be distinguished in terminology and in law from those that prevent fertilization. It is misleading to describe anti-implantives as contraceptives.
- The language of 'reproductive cloning' and 'therapeutic cloning' is open to criticism, but it does highlight the fact that both processes involve the generation of cloned human embryos. If the human embryo is a human being, as argued in this chapter, then cloning for research is worse than cloning for reproductive purposes.

This enquiry began with the Hebrew Scriptures and ancient Greek embryologists and has extended to the twenty-first century debates over embryo experimentation, 'emergency contraception' and stem cell research. It has been a complex story, but its connection with the developing reality of Christian doctrine and practice has given it an underlying coherence. There have been some fundamental claims that have remained unchanged and some themes that have been repeated in different contexts. There has been a constant interplay of law, science, philosophy, ethics and theology. The tradition has been the setting for a number of significant debates and arguments. Taken as a whole it constitutes a sustained and ongoing reflection on the theological meaning or status of the human embryo. It is now necessary to review the implications of this tradition for our central question: In the light of a critical reading of the Christian tradition, how ought a Christian to regard the human embryo?

15

The Least of these Little Ones

And in this he showed me something small no bigger than a hazelnut,
lying in the palm of my hand, as it seemed to me, and it was as round
as a ball. I looked at it with the eye of my understanding and thought:
What can this be? I was amazed that it could last, for I thought that
because of its littleness it would suddenly have fallen into nothing. And
I was answered in my understanding: It lasts and always will, because
God loves it; and thus everything has being through the love of God.
(Julian of Norwich, *Showings*, Chapter 5)

The aim of this book has been to seek illumination from the
Christian tradition on the human significance or ethical status of the
human embryo. To do this it has been necessary to examine legal,
scientific, philosophical, ethical and theological sources within a
continuous history of more than two millennia. We have seen that,
in all of these areas, there has been change and development over
the centuries. Thus, as the tradition has developed, arguments that
appeared secure in one age have later been shown to rely on unsafe
premises. Similarly, the insights of a previous age have sometimes
been obscured by the mistakes or confusion of a later age. This is
as true for science as it is for ethics and philosophy. Nevertheless,
the benefit of critically engaging with these sources, and of seeking
to tell a coherent story of the tradition, is that it gives us a much
greater perspective through which to find understanding. The
Warnock Committee was right to say that 'the questions of when
life or personhood begin ... are complex amalgams of factual and
moral judgements' (Warnock 1984, para. 11.9). However, they
were wrong to think that such judgements could be sidestepped. If
we are to make human sense of the exact but abstract truths of the
natural sciences then we need to interpret, and interpretation
requires perspective, and this is given, in part, by a sense of
intellectual history.

The legal story

In practice, the status of the human embryo is often treated as a question of law: abortion law and the regulation of IVF and embryo experimentation. Laws vary between jurisdictions and can change considerably over time. As outlined in Chapter 13, causing a miscarriage was an offence under English common law when done after 'quickening', that is, after the unborn child was felt to move. Nevertheless, the common law on abortion was difficult to enforce and led to few convictions. In the late nineteenth century, both in the UK and the USA, statutes were enacted against abortion and the distinction relating to quickening was abandoned. This was due primarily to the ethical concerns of physicians, but was supported by clergy, lawyers, early feminists and public opinion. It was not until the 1960s that laws permitting abortion for a wider variety of reasons were enacted in England and in various states of the USA. The Abortion Act of 1967 effectively allowed abortion for personal or social reasons where two physicians agreed that it was indicated. In the USA, the Supreme Court overturned existing statute law in the landmark case *Roe* v. *Wade* [1973] and created a constitutional right to abortion. Law on embryo experimentation has been more fragmentary. In the UK it is permitted under licence from the Human Fertilization and Embryology Authority. In the USA it is subject to various funding restrictions and is forbidden in some states. There is no state-wide ban, but neither has the Supreme Court struck down laws protecting the embryo from destructive experimentation.

The 1967 Abortion Act and *Roe* v. *Wade* [1973] both appealed to precedent, but in neither case is the appeal convincing. Both clearly involved radical legal change and, at least in this sense, were wholly unprecedented. It is a matter of dispute whether this change represents progress or decline. Some see the current shape of legislation as a civilized and compassionate advance on previous laws. Others regard it as a return to the brutality of a pre-Christian age. What we regard as progress will depend on what we regard as right or wrong, helpful or harmful, just or unjust.

The 1967 Abortion Act fairly embodied the will of the people in that it reflected changes in attitudes within society on the subject of abortion. Nevertheless, public opinion on its own is not enough to determine the justice or injustice of the law. The justice or injustice of the law depends on its success or failure to protect whoever stands in need of its protection. The issue of justice is even more apparent in the case of *Roe* v. *Wade*. That decision was not based on the will of the people, which was and remains divided, nor on any very clear precedent, but rather on an interpretation of legal principles drawn directly or indirectly from the Constitution. The Supreme Court determined that abortion was henceforth to be treated as a matter of privacy and, for this reason, granted the status of a constitutional right. However, this conclusion follows if, and only if, the human embryo can be disregarded as a potential victim of injustice. The legitimacy of the decision of the Supreme Court thus involves much wider considerations than legal precedent or due process. The appropriate application of principles of liberty and justice turns on the question of the philosophical and ethical understanding of the human embryo. Law exists to promote justice and liberty, to prevent or discourage injustice and to protect the weak. A proper evaluation of the law thus requires us to determine who are the weak.

The scientific story

Since ancient times, philosophical discussion has been shaped, in part, by the current scientific account of human development. The writings of Hippocrates and Aristotle from the fourth/fifth century BCE (see Chapter 2) dominated scientific thought well into the seventeenth century CE and exercised a great influence on philosophical and legal thinking even into the nineteenth century. Though they did not possess the microscope and had only the most rudimentary knowledge of the chemistry of life, the ancient embryologists made remarkable achievements. Hippocrates systematically observed the development of the chick embryo and Aristotle collected observations from a great variety of animals: invertebrates and vertebrates, egg-laying animals and those that gave birth to live young. On this basis they characterized the formation of the embryo as a gradual process of differentiation and growth. The organs were not believed to pre-exist in the seed but to be formed sequentially as development proceeded, a view later called 'epigenesis'.

To many, Aristotle's account of embryology seemed to imply that the human being came to exist at some point between conception and birth. Abortion subsequent to this would constitute homicide, but prior to this it would not be the killing of a human being. This opinion did not inform Roman law, which did not regard any abortion as homicide, but it influenced an important strand of Jewish thought seen in Philo and in the Septuagint and thence entered the Christian tradition (see Chapters 4 and 5). It reached its maximum influence in the canon law and theology of the Middle Ages but its indirect influence could still be seen in abortion law up to 1837 in the continuing legal relevance of 'quickening'.

The theories of Hippocrates and Aristotle contained important elements of truth and the idea of a process of gradual development is still with us. Nevertheless, their theories suffered a heavy blow from the discoveries of William Harvey (Chapter 11). He showed that, immediately subsequent to conception, the womb was not full of a mixture of fluids, as the ancient embryologists had thought. Harvey also suggested that all animals begin with an egg: a hypothesis that encouraged others to look for and eventually to identify the human ovum. The invention of the microscope and the influence of the new mechanical philosophy at first led embryology to embrace a preformationism that now seems absurd: the idea that the first woman contained all subsequent generations in her ovaries like a series of Russian dolls. Nevertheless, even preformation played its role in the development of scientific understanding. Stephen J. Gould has pointed out that modern embryology stands midway between the epigenesis of Aristotle and the preformation of Bonnet. The embryo formed by the union of sperm and ovum already has the genetic information to guide development (preformation), but the organs and the structures of the human body develop gradually (epigenesis). From the seventeenth century, physicians became increasingly resistant to the idea that a fundamental transition from pre-human and human occurred at some point during gestation. This did not seem to accord with the smooth process of development they observed. With the observation of the sperm and ovum in the nineteenth century, and even more so with the discoveries of modern genetics in the twentieth century, it was fertilization that came to be regarded as the single most significant biological transition in human reproduction.

It is the well-recognized significance of the union of sperm and ovum that has been invoked by various Catholic authorities in defence of their position that human life is to be protected from conception: 'From the time that the ovum is fertilized, a life is begun which is neither that of the father or the mother; it is rather that life of a new human being with his [or her] own growth' (John Paul II 1995, para. 60). In response, in the context of fierce political and ethical debates, the biological significance of fertilization has been questioned. There has been a great deal of discussion of the phenomenon of monozygotic twinning, as well as an emphasis on the extent of early embryo loss (discussed in Chapter 14). There have been efforts to portray implantation as a more significant marker especially with regard to defining pregnancy. Nevertheless, embryologists continue to date the process of development from fertilization. It is partly for this reason that so many scientists rejected the term 'pre-embryo' for the earliest stages of the human embryo. An acknowledgement of the significance of fertilization as the beginning of human life is also implicit in the language even of those who defend experimentation on embryos: 'The Bill, as it has come to us from another place, proposes research up to 14 days. My first question is, 14 days after what?' (Sir Bernard Braine, House of Commons Hansard Debates, 2 April 1990, col. 933).

From a biological perspective, if we set aside the exceptional cases of identical twins and of human cloning, there is a great deal of support, both from scientists and nonscientists, for the idea that the life of an individual human being can be traced back to fertilization. Human beings begin as human embryos and human embryos are generated by fertilization. What is far more controversial is the question of what ethical conclusions, if any, can be drawn from this. What is the ethical significance of the point at which the life of the human organism begins? Should we be starting with this question or with other questions, for example: What makes human beings valuable? or What constitutes a human person? Such questions are not the direct concern of science but of philosophy, ethics and ultimately of theology.

The philosophical story

The decisions people come to on philosophical matters are partly shaped by social, political and cultural influences. For example, in Chapter 13 we saw how in the mid twentieth century abortion was reconstrued as an acceptable practical solution for women with unwanted pregnancy. Since then it has become difficult to support the struggle for women's emancipation without accepting the legitimacy of abortion. In the case of embryo experimentation (Chapter 14), scientists did not to want to close off promising avenues of research and those suffering from incurable illnesses looked to medical progress in search of hope. Such strong social and cultural forces make it difficult to give serious and unprejudiced thought to the ethical status of the human embryo. Nevertheless, people rightly seek to justify their beliefs by rational arguments, both in order to persuade others and in order to be more ethically reflective and self-critical.

Most prominent among the philosophical arguments invoked to justify the destruction or use of human embryos have been arguments from 'personhood': The qualities that distinguish human beings from other animals, and what we most value in human beings, seem not to be biological features so much as intellectual, emotional and spiritual characteristics. These qualities seem to be captured, at least to a first approximation, by John Locke's definition of a person: 'a thinking, intelligent being, that has reason and reflection, and can consider itself as itself, the same thinking thing, in different times and different places'. A number of thinkers have argued that human embryos, while they may or may not be human beings, are certainly not persons, according to this definition of the word, and thus they do not merit the full protection that is due to a person.

It would be no exaggeration to say that an argument based on a definition of the person which would exclude the human embryo is the most influential form of justification given in defence of unrestricted access to abortion and of destructive embryo experimentation. It is therefore very important to notice a serious defect in this form of argument. The definition of person given by Locke is best exemplified by strong and self-conscious adults who are able to exercise their freedom and assert their autonomy. It

therefore excludes the weak, the semi-conscious and the
incompetent who are precisely those in greater need of protection.
Such definitions also exclude new-born infants from full human
status and open the way to infanticide. For this reason they are
incompatible with any ethos founded on protection of the weak
including, amongst others, the Christian ethical tradition.

It was noted in Chapter 14 that the definition of person used in
most contemporary discussion is of a very recent origin and that
there is an alternative account provided by an older tradition.
According to Boethius a person is an individual being of a rational
nature. This focuses on the nature that is shared by all members of
the same species, rather than the powers someone possesses at a
particular time. According to this understanding, a human person is
nothing more or less than a living human being. The human
solidarity we feel with the very young, the very old and those who
are sick is not only a matter of irrational sentiment. It is a matter of
recognizing fellow human beings as those with whom we share a
common nature, as kin, as brothers and sisters. This has provided
the grounding not only for modern discussion of human rights but
for many different ethical systems throughout the ages. In the
ancient world, as well as Christians and Jews, the Stoics, for
example, emphasized the virtue of *philanthropia* – love of fellow
human beings on account of their humanity.

A human embryo may look like the embryo of a dog or cat, but
it possesses a potential that the embryo of another species does not
possess. As argued in Chapter 14, the human embryo is an
individual living being of the species *Homo sapiens*. We should
therefore ask what is it that prevents us from extending to it the
ethical and legal status of a human being? Without Locke's account
of personhood it is difficult to see how human embryos can be
excluded from that ethical concern that is proper to human beings.
From a Boethian perspective, the human embryo, like the new-
born baby, is not a 'potential person' but a person with potential.

The ethical story

One reason given above for preferring a Boethian definition of
person to that given by Locke was that Locke's definition had

unacceptable ethical consequences with regard to the treatment of mentally incompetent adults. However, this may seem circular. If ethical conclusions are justified by their conformity to reason, how can we weigh up the adequacy of reasons by reference to their ethical implications? We can test reasoning by its implications because, at least in some cases, we can have more confidence in a conclusion than we have in a theoretical argument. It is by no means easy to argue from first principles in ethical matters. Ethical reasoning often involves the interrelating of many principles as well as a subtle analysis of what is ethically relevant in a particular situation. It was because of the difficulty of attempting to argue from first principles in subtle and difficult ethical problems that the method of casuistry, as outlined in Chapter 12, was developed. This is based on the idea that unknown and complex cases are best understood by relating them to better known and simpler cases.

In practice, people learn to make ethical decisions within a particular tradition of thought and practice. This tradition will include not only the presentation of certain ethical principles (for example respect for the person, harm, benefit, fairness) but also specific virtues of character, moral fables, examples of heroes and villains, and particular judgements on paradigm cases. People can be critical of elements of the received tradition, but they learn to be so only with the help of other aspects of that same tradition. From a Christian perspective, Christians have an added reason to look to their own particular ethical tradition. This has been generated and sustained by the Scriptures within the context of the Christian community. Christians therefore see in the principles, virtues, stories and judgements of this tradition the guidance of the Holy Spirit. This does not mean that every ethical judgement becomes straightforward, for the needs of a particular situation are not always obvious. Mature judgement requires not only knowledge but also experience and the right dispositions of character. Nevertheless, in the context of the tradition, certain starting-points including principles, virtues and particular judgements can be relied upon.

An important particular judgement of the Christian tradition, as outlined in Chapters 3–5 of this book, is the rejection of infanticide. This practice, which was almost routine in pagan society, was strongly rejected both by Jews and by Christians. The slaughter of the innocents by Pharaoh (Exodus 1:15-22), repeated much later by Herod (Matthew 2:16-18) was a paradigm for godlessness. The Scriptures valued marriage, procreation and children, but also, and more fundamentally, emphasized the importance of protecting of the weak. In early Christianity this was seen not only in relation to infanticide but also in the care for the sick, and in the establishments of hospitals, asylums and orphanages. Those who had little or no social value in pagan society were taken in by the Church. It was in this context that early Christians understood abortion. They did not accept abortion for the same reason that they did not accept infanticide, because it represented an injustice against a weak and vulnerable child. 'For us murder is once for all forbidden; so it is not lawful for us to destroy even the child in the womb' (Tertullian, *Apology*, 9:8).

The present enquiry has demonstrated the remarkable consistency in Christian attitudes to early human life. We saw in Chapter 5 that, far from being a new teaching, the claim that 'life must be protected with the utmost care from conception' (*Gaudium et Spes* 51) represents the teaching of the Early Church, of the Greek East and the Latin West. It was not altered in its fundamentals by the collapse of the Roman empire or the barbarian invasions of the Dark Ages. As seen in Chapters 10, 11 and 12, it remained substantially unchanged through the Renaissance, the Reformation, the scientific revolution and the Enlightenment. Like other social evils, abortion was still practised by Christians, and the Church struggled to find ways of defending the unborn while remaining a community of reconciliation. The particular shape of the legal and penitential structures of the Church varied through the ages, but in every age, depriving the unborn child of life was considered a serious sin, and in every age there was some way in which this sin could be acknowledged and forgiveness received, as in the case of every sin, by the grace of God. Chapter 13 explored the way in which, in the mid twentieth century, some Christians came to embrace the opinion that abortion could be considered as an act of compassion, or even of liberation. However, it was urged that this recent Christian reconstrual of abortion should be seen as a distortion of the ethical reality of the situation. It imagines a compassion that can be extended to a woman while excluding her child. It therefore fails to acknowledge the need of the unborn child for care and protection which had hitherto been the hallmark of the whole Christian tradition.

While the Christian understanding of abortion, so strikingly different from pagan attitudes, remained unchanged in its essentials from the time of Christ to the mid twentieth century, there were three aspects of the issue that were subject to debate and variation. In the first place, from the Middle Ages until the present, Christian writers have debated the issue of therapeutic abortion. Most theologians have held that 'indirect' abortion is permissible in cases where the life of the mother is seriously threatened (see Chapter 12). Nevertheless, this tradition only considered abortion in circumstances in which pregnancy is a threat to a mother's life. It cannot provide a justification for the use of abortion as the solution to unwanted pregnancy. A second variable element was the timing of ensoulment. The view of the earliest generation of Christians was that God gives a soul to the human embryo as soon as it comes into existence, at conception. However, for much of Christian history, and particularly in the Latin West in the Middle Ages, it was believed that the soul was given some time later than conception. This topic has been discussed in a number of contexts (see Chapters 5, 7, 8, 9, 10, 11, 14) and will be considered further below (see p. 247). The third variable element, highlighted in Chapter 5, is the great divergence of the penalties attaching to abortion in the penitential and legal systems of the Church from time to time and place to place. In particular, under the influence of theories of delayed ensoulment, canon law has sometimes prescribed different penalties for early and for late abortion.

It was the variable penalties given for early and late abortion that were invoked by G.R. Dunstan to support his view that the embryo should not be accorded an 'absolute' ethical status. '[T]he claim to absolute protection for the human embryo "from the beginning" is a novelty in the western, Christian and specifically Roman Catholic ethical traditions. It is virtually a creation of the later nineteenth century' (Dunstan and Sellars 1988, p. 40). Dunstan's argument has been widely influential, being repeated, for example, by Richard Harries, Anglican Bishop of Oxford, in relation to embryonic stem cell research and by Archbishop Peter Carnley, Primate of the Anglican Church in Australia, in the context of the Australian stem cell debate. However, as argued in Chapter 5, Dunstan's argument rests on a fallacy, for different penalties do not imply a relative ethical status. Should we argue, for example, that if an offence is not punished by capital punishment then it is not 'absolutely' wrong but only 'relatively' wrong? Should we argue that if one offence is punished more harshly than another then the 'lesser' offence is not really a crime or an injustice? Surely what matters is not whether we can think of an even worse offence, but rather, whether or not this particular act is an injustice. Comparisons should not be used to obscure the fact that some acts involve real harm or injustice towards the victim.

The earliest canonical authorities did not regard the stage of development of the embryo as ethically or legally relevant to the question of abortion. In contrast, in the Middle Ages, church law generally considered late abortion to be a more serious offence than early abortion. Nevertheless, behind this variation there has been an enduring desire to protect the human embryo. This attitude has been extraordinarily constant through two millennia of Christian thought and practice. Deliberate destruction of the human embryo, apart from medical interventions to save a mother's life, have consistently been considered gravely wrong. Christians have never regarded the destruction of a human embryo in the same way as they regarded the killing or consuming of a non-human animal. In the Middle Ages the human embryo was regarded as having a somewhat ambiguous status: forming but not yet fully formed; alive but not yet rationally ensouled; a human (*humanus*) but not yet a man (*homo*). Nevertheless, this ambiguity was always resolved in favour of the embryo. If not regarded as actual homicide, destruction of the human embryo was regarded as something very close to homicide: the killing of a man-in-the-making (*homo in fieri*).

The desire to protect the human embryo from its very beginnings represents that spirit of concern for 'the least of these' (Matthew 25:40) that so characterizes the gospel. In the Early Church, it showed itself in a concern to care for new-born infants who were abandoned or disabled and equally in a concern to protect unborn infants even though hidden in the womb. This attitude, shaped by the gospel and evident everywhere in the tradition, is fundamental to Christian ethical understanding. It is much more significant than the variations in penalties and penances also evident through the tradition. It has recently been argued that in our appreciation of the human embryo we make a mistake if we think that it is possible to move 'from observation first to fellowship second' (O'Donovan 1984, p. 66). In the ethical resolution of ambiguities of status or claims to recognition, the Christian attitude is, or should be, to give priority to love over knowledge, to favour inclusive accounts of human community and solidarity, and to give priority to the ethical claims of the weak:

> The Gospel emphasis upon the prior moral claim of the weak ... needs to be taken a great deal more seriously by Christian theologians and moralists than hitherto ... In short the 'leastness' of the embryo and its relative weakness in the human community, far from being an argument for its exploitation, may be the one consideration that should make adult humans draw back from the exercise of power. (Clarke and Linzey 1988, pp. 60–61)

The theological story

In ethical questions there is a constant interplay between practical application and speculative understanding. This is seen in moving from legal to scientific to philosophical to ethical discussion. The task that remains is to place these interrelated stories in the context of Christian belief. The perspective of theology has provided the unifying narrative for our enquiry and it is through this perspective that we have hoped to discover a deeper appreciation of the human embryo.

One prominent theme in theological reflection on the human embryo, both ancient and modern, is the question of the nature and origin of the soul. According to Tertullian, in the second century CE, 'we allow that life begins with conception, because we contend that *the soul also begins from conception*; life taking its commencement at the same moment and place that the soul does' (*On the Soul* 27, emphasis added). On the other hand, in the thirteenth century Thomas Aquinas asserted that 'It is in this way that through many generations and corruptions we arrive at the

ultimate substantial form, both in man and other animals ...
therefore the intellectual *soul is created by God at the end* of human
generation' (*ST* Ia Q.118 art. 2 ad 2, emphasis added). In the early
seventeenth century Thomas Fienus and Paolo Zacchia argued that
the rational soul was given immediately after conception. As
recently as 2002 the *Report of the House of Lords Select Committee on
Stem Cell Research* recalled this debate remarking that 'the Christian
tradition, for so much of its history ... thought of the human
person in the full sense coming only with a *delayed ensoulment*'
(Appendix 4: The Moral Status of the Early Embryo: Reading the
Christian Tradition, emphasis added).

In much contemporary discussion there has been a tendency to
identify arguments concerning personhood with debates over the
timing of ensoulment. It has been pointed out above, and in Chapter
14, that there are important differences between the modern
definition of person in the tradition of John Locke and the ancient
and medieval definition in the tradition of Boethius. It should also be
pointed out that even in the ancient context the language of soul is
subtly different from the language of person. Christians have talked
about the soul in various ways, but the soul has been understood first
and foremost as the principle of *life*. What has life has soul. Plants
and animals are not soulless, but they possess souls different in kind
from the human rational and spiritual soul. This conception of the
soul was shared by Christian thinkers as diverse as Tertullian,
Gregory of Nyssa, Augustine and Thomas Aquinas. It was eclipsed
in the seventeenth century due to the rise of mechanistic thinking in
the natural sciences and Cartesian mind–body dualism in philosophy. However, a number of twentieth-century philosophers have
provided more holistic accounts of the human being in which
context it has again become possible to talk of a principle of life and
not just a principle of mind or thought (see Chapter 6).

If the soul is the principle of life, the presence of the soul will
generally be evident from the presence of life, though it should
borne in mind that life might exist in a latent form before it
manifests itself in the motions of the living being (Augustine,
Enchiridion 86). As outlined in Chapter 11, the idea of a succession
of different souls in the embryo, each brought into being by the
power of the parent, is hard to defend outside the context of

medieval biology. In the context of modern biology it seems most natural to say that human life begins when the human embryo first comes into existence, at fertilization. From the perspective of the Christian tradition, if human life begins with fertilization, then this is when the soul begins, for in Christian usage, life and soul are correlates. This is so even if the higher powers of the soul are not exercised until much later in life.

Soul talk concerns life and thus biology. Nevertheless, in the Christian tradition 'soul' has primarily been concerned not with life in relation to the body but with life in relation to the ultimate source of life, the Creator. Even for Plato and Aristotle the question of the origin of the soul lay ultimately with the divine. For Christians, soul talk has been inseparable from the relation of human beings to God as Creator and as Redeemer. God forms man from the dust and breathes into him the breath of life and Adam becomes a living being (Genesis 2:7). At death the dust returns to the earth as it was and the breath returns to God who gave it (Ecclesiastes 12:7). The origin and destiny of the soul lies with God. Theologians have discussed the timing of ensoulment, but a more pressing and deeper question has been the origin of the soul. What is implied by the giving of the soul by God? Were all souls created together in the beginning when God finished his work on the sixth day? Or are new souls specially created by God when they are needed? And are the souls of children generated by the parents in cooperation with God? If there is some truth in each of these suggestions, as argued in Chapter 7, this greatly strengthens the view that the soul is present from conception. If the parents are involved in the procreation of the soul it seems that this must occur when the male and female elements fuse, at fertilization. So also the pre-existence of the soul in the mind of God the Creator reminds us of the destiny to which each is called from the first moment of his or her existence. All days that are formed for us are already written in God's book when God sees us in embryo (Psalm 139:16, see Chapter 1).

The great contribution of the theologians of the Reformation to the understanding of the human embryo lay in emphasizing that all human life should be understood primarily in relation to God as Creator and Redeemer, rather than in relation to human achievements or capacities (Chapter 10). God creates from nothing

(*ex nihilo*) and apart from God all creatures would come to nothing.
Every creature is created with a destiny hidden in the will of God.
In redemption, also, the initiative lies with God who rescues sinners
from the emptiness of sin and death and gives them new life in
Christ. Without the grace of God human beings cannot be justified.
They are saved not through their power but in their need. The
dependence of all things on the mercy of God, both in the sphere
of creation and of redemption, is a doctrine common to Reformed
and Catholic Christians. It is evident, for example, in the writings of
Julian of Norwich.

> I was amazed that it could last, for I thought that because of its
> littleness it would suddenly have fallen into nothing. And I was
> answered in my understanding: It lasts and always will, because God
> loves it; and thus everything has being through the love of God.
> (Julian of Norwich, *Showings*, Chapter 5)

In this theological context the significance of the human embryo lies
not in the powers or capacities he or she possesses but in relation to
the Creator and also, Barth has reminded us, in relation to his or her
parents. The human embryo exists within these relationships from
the very first, is in need from the very first, and for this reason
Christians should care for and protect the embryo from the very first.

Reflections on the origin of the soul, on creation, providence
and predestination all illuminate the theological significance of the
embryo. However, from a Christian perspective, the strongest form
of argument is that taken directly from the example of Christ. The
considerations set out in Chapter 9 thus provide a focus through
which to draw together these theological elements into a distinctive
Christian vision. Jesus, through whom we understand what it is to
be human, began life as a human embryo in the womb of Mary.
Though he was in the form of God he humbled himself and was
found in human form (Philippians 2:7). The ethical message of
concern for 'the least of these' (Matthew 25:40) is rooted in the act
of God in coming to be among us as the least. In Christian
understanding, the incarnation does not contradict the doctrine of
creation but includes it. In the incarnation God enters the littleness
of the world. The creation and destiny of each human being is
henceforth seen in relation to Christ. The implications of this for
our appreciation of the human embryo are well expressed by the

Scottish theologian Thomas Torrance:

> Every child in the womb has been brothered by the Lord Jesus. In becoming a human being for us, he also became an embryo for the sake of all embryos, and for our Christian understanding of the being, nature and status in God's eyes of the unborn child. (Torrance 2000, p. 4)

The language of the soul should direct us to the origin of the soul in God, to creation and to the redemption of every human creature in Christ. It is in the littleness of Christ as an embryo in the womb of the Virgin that we should understand the human embryo rather than in the varying penances for abortion given in the past or in recent definitions of personhood. The human embryo is a new creature, called and destined to be a child of God, a brother or sister of Christ. There is never a time when he or she is unrelated to God or beyond the scope of human solidarity. In the perspective given by the embryonic Christ, it is difficult to see how the systematic use and destruction of human embryos in scientific research can be regarded as ethical.

This enquiry has been concerned specifically with a Christian story. It has sought to determine what a critical engagement with legal, scientific, philosophical, ethical and theological aspects of the Christian tradition has to teach us about the human embryo. Nevertheless, it is hoped that there is much of interest here for those who are not adherents of Christianity. The recognition that human life is a gift from God, that human beings possess a soul that is given by God, is common to Jews, Muslims and many other religious traditions. Many of those who are not practising members of any faith community also acknowledge a spiritual dimension to life, a dimension beyond the material. What has been described here in the concrete and sometimes obscure theological language of Christianity relates fundamentally to the mystery of human existence. The existence of each human being is not only a puzzle to be solved or an ambiguity to be resolved but is an unfathomable mystery. Therefore, the origin of the human being should also be recognized as a profound aspect of our common humanity. The human embryo, even while it consists of a single cell or just a few cells, is nothing less than the hidden or enfolded beginning of a new human being. To grasp this is to appreciate more deeply who we are, where we came from and on whom we depend.

Bibliography

Primary sources

Alighieri, Dante 1984 *The Divine Comedy: Pergatory*, trans. M. Musa (Harmondsworth: Penguin).

Ambrose of Milan *On Death as a Good Thing*, English trans. M.P. McHugh, 'Death as a Good Thing' in P.M. Peebles *et al.* (eds) 1972, *Saint Ambrose: Seven Exegetical Works*, *The Fathers of the Church, A New Translation*, Vol. 65 (Washington DC: The Catholic University of America Press).

Aristotle *De Anima (On the Soul)*, English trans. H. Lawson-Tancred 1987 (Harmondsworth: Penguin).

Aristotle *On the Generation of Animals*, Loeb 366 (Aristotle, Vol. XIII), trans. A.L. Peck 1942, repr. 1979 (Cambridge, MA: Harvard University Press).

Aristotle *History of Animals 7–10*, Loeb 439 (Aristotle, Vol. XI), trans. D. Balme 1991 (Cambridge, MA: Harvard University Press).

Aristotle *Parts of Animals*, Loeb 323 (Aristotle, Vol. XII), trans. A.L. Peck 1993 (Cambridge, MA: Harvard University Press).

Augustine *City of God*, trans. H. Bettenson 1984 (Harmondsworth: Penguin).

Augustine *Enchiridion*, trans. J.F. Shaw in P. Schaff (ed.) 1887, *St Augustine: On the Holy Trinity, Doctrinal Treatises, Moral Treatises*, Nicene and Post-Nicene Fathers, Series I, Vol. III (Grand Rapids, MI: Eerdmans).

Augustine *On the Soul and its Origin*, trans. P. Holmes in P. Schaff (ed.) 1887, *St Augustine: Anti-Pelagian Writings*, Nicene and Post-Nicene Fathers, Series I, Vol. V (Grand Rapids, MI: Eerdmans).

Basil the Great *Letters and Select Works*, trans. H. Wace and R. Geare in P. Schaff and H. Wace (eds) 1894, Nicene and Post-Nicene Fathers, Series II, Vol. VIII (Grand Rapids, MI: Eerdmans).

Bede 1990 *Ecclesiastical History of the English People*, trans. L. Sherley-Price (ed.) D.H. Farmer (Harmondsworth: Penguin).

Calvin, J. *Commentaries on the Last Four Books of Moses*, trans. C. Bingham (repr. Grand Rapids, MI: Eerdmans, n.d.).

Calvin, J. *Institutes of the Christian Religion*, trans. H. Beveridge 1845 (Edinburgh: Calvin Translation Society).

Clement of Alexandria *Excerpts from Theodotus (also called Prophetic Eclogues)*, trans. H. Wilson in A. Roberts and J. Donaldson (eds) 1871, *Fathers of the Third and Fourth Centuries*, Ante-Nicene Fathers Vol. VIII (Grand Rapids, MI: Eerdmans).

Dillenberger, J. (ed.) 1961 *Martin Luther: Selections from his Writings* (London: Anchor Books).

Gregory of Nyssa *On the Making of Man*, trans. H. Wilson and W. Moore in P. Schaff and H. Wace (eds) 1892, *Gregory of Nyssa: Dogmatic Treatises; Select Writings and Letters*, Nicene and Post-Nicene Fathers, Series II, Vol. V (Grand Rapids, MI: Eerdmans).

Gregory of Nyssa *On the Holy Spirit, Against the Followers of Macedonius*, trans. H. Wilson and W. Moore in P. Schaff and H. Wace (eds) 1892, *Gregory of Nyssa: Dogmatic Treatises; Select Writings and Letters*, Nicene and Post-Nicene Fathers, Series II, Vol. V (Grand Rapids, MI: Eerdmans).

Gregory of Nyssa *On the Soul and the Resurrection*, trans. C.P. Roth 1993 (Crestwood, NY: St Vladimir's Seminary Press).

Hippocrates *The Seed and The Nature of the Child*, trans. I.M. Lonie 1978 in G.E.R. Lloyd (ed.) 1983, *Hippocratic Writings* (Harmondsworth: Penguin).

Hippocrates *On Nutriment*, Loeb 147 (Hippocrates, Volume I), trans. W.H.S. Jones 1923 (Cambridge, MA: Harvard University Press).

Hippolytus *Refutation of All Heresies*, trans. J.H. Macmahon in A. Roberts and J. Donaldson (eds) 1885, *Fathers of the Third Century*, Ante-Nicene Fathers Vol. V (Grand Rapids, MI: Eerdmans).

Irenaeus of Lyons *Against Heresies*, trans. J.H. Macmahon in A. Roberts and J. Donaldson (eds) 1885, *The Apostolic Fathers with Justin Martyr and Irenaeus*, Ante-Nicene Fathers Vol. I (Grand Rapids, MI: Eerdmans).

Jerome *Letters and Select Works* in P. Schaff and H. Wace (eds) 1892, Nicene and Post-Nicene Fathers, Series II, Vol. VI (Grand Rapids, MI: Eerdmans).

Julian of Norwich, 1978 *Showings*, trans. E. College and J. Walsh (Mahwah, NJ: *Paulist* Press).

Lactantius *On the Workmanship of God, or the Formation of Man*, trans. W. Fletcher in A. Roberts and J. Donaldson (eds) 1885, *The Fathers of the Third and Fourth Centuries*, Ante-Nicene Fathers Vol. VII (Grand Rapids, MI: Eerdmans).

Minucius, Felix *Octavius*, trans. R.E. Wallis in A. Roberts and J. Donaldson (eds) 1885, *The Fathers of the Third Century*, Ante-Nicene Fathers Vol. IV (Grand Rapids, MI: Eerdmans).

Pascal, B. 1952 *The Provincial Letters* (Chicago, IL: Encyclopaedia Britannica Inc.).

Peck, A.L. 1942 Introduction, notes and translation of Aristotle *On the Generation of Animals*, Loeb 366, repr. 1979 (Cambridge, MA: Harvard University Press).

Schaff, P. and H. Wace (eds) 1899 *The Seven Ecumenical Councils*, Nicene and Post-Nicene Fathers, Series II, Vol. IV (Grand Rapids, MI: Eerdmans).

Soranus of Ephesus *Gynecology*, trans. O. Temkin 1992 (Baltimore, MD: Johns Hopkins University Press).

Tertullian *Apology*, trans. S. Thelwall in A. Roberts and J. Donaldson (eds) 1885,

Latin Christianity: Its Founder, Tertullian, Ante-Nicene Fathers Vol. III (Grand Rapids, MI: Eerdmans).

Tertullian *On the Soul*, trans. P. Holmes in A. Roberts and J. Donaldson (eds) 1885, *Latin Christianity: Its Founder, Tertullian*, Ante-Nicene Fathers Vol. III (Grand Rapids, MI: Eerdmans).

Thomas Aquinas *Summa Theologica*, trans. Fathers of the English Dominican Province 1911 (London: Burns, Oates) repr. 1981 (New York: Thomas More Publishing).

Wollstonecraft, M. 1989 (1790) *A Vindication of the Rights of Women* (Amherst, NY: Prometheus Books).

Secondary sources

The following historical studies are particularly useful: Connery 1977; Dunstan 1990; Feldman 1974; Grisez 1970; Keown 1988; Mohr 1978; Mulkay 1997; Needham 1959; Noonan 1965; Saward 1993. They are not all written from the same ethical or theological perspective, but they contain useful source material.

Alberts, B. *et al.* 2002 *Molecular Biology of the Cell* 2nd edn (New York: Garland).

Allen, L.C. 1983 *Word Biblical Commentary Psalms 101–150* (Waco, TX: Word Books).

Althaus, P. 1981 (1968) *The Theology of Martin Luther* (Philadelphia, PA: Fortress Press).

Anderson, A.A. 1972 *New Century Bible Commentary: The Book of Psalms II, Psalms 73–150* (Grand Rapids, MI: Eerdmans).

Anscombe, G.E.M. 1961 'War and Murder', in Anscombe 1981.

Anscombe G.E.M. 1981 *Ethics, Religion and Politics: Collected Philosophical Papers Volume III* (Oxford: Basil Blackwell).

Anscombe, G.E.M. 1985 'Were you a Zygote?' in A. Phillips Griffiths (ed.) *Philosophy and Practice* (Cambridge: Cambridge University Press).

Armstrong, C. 1997 'Thousands of Women Sterilized in Sweden without Consent', *British Medical Journal* 315:563.

Ashley, B. 1976 'A Critique of the Theory of Delayed Animation' in D. McCarthy and A. Moraczewski, *An Ethical Evaluation of Fetal Experimentation: An Interdisciplinary Study* (St Louis, MO: Pope John XXIII Center.

Ashley, B. and Moraczewski, A. 1994 'Is the Biological Subject of Human Rights Present from Conception?' in P. Cataldo and A. Moraczewski, *The Fetal Tissue Issue: Medical and Ethical Aspects* (Braintree, MA: Pope John Center).

Balme, D. 1990 'Human is Generated by Human' in Dunstan (ed.) 1990.

Barnes, J. (ed.) 1995 *The Cambridge Companion to Aristotle* (Cambridge: Cambridge University Press).

Barr, J. 1992 *The Garden of Eden and the Hope of Immortality* (London: SCM).

Barry, R. 1989 'The Personhood and Individuality of Unborn Human Life' in R. Barry *Medical Ethics* (New York: Peter Lang).

Barth, K. 1961 *Church Dogmatics*, trans. G.W. Bromiley and T.E. Torrance (Edinburgh: T & T Clark).

Benz, E. 1966 *Evolution and Christian Hope* (New York: Doubleday).

Berry, C. 1993 *Beginnings: Christian Views of the Early Embryo* (London: CMF).

Berry, R.J. 1996 *God and the Biologist* (Leicester: Apollos).

Board for Social Responsibility *Personal Origins: The Report of a Working Party on Human Fertilization and Embryology of the Board for Social Responsibility* (London: CIO Publishing).

Boisaubin, E.V. 1998 'Nazi Medicine', *Journal of the American Medical Association* 279:1496.

Bonhoeffer, D. 1955 *Ethics*, trans. Neville Horton Smith (New York: Macmillan).

Bonner, G. 1985 'Abortion in Early Christian Thought' in Channer 1985.

Bouwsma, W. 1988 *John Calvin: A Sixteenth-century Portrait* (Oxford: Oxford University Press).

Boyle, L. 1974 'The *Summa Confessorum* of John of Freiburg and the Popularization of the Moral Teaching of St. Thomas and of some of his Contemporaries' in *St Thomas Aquinas 1274–1974 Commemorative Studies*, A. Mauer *et al.* (eds) (Toronto: Pontifical Institute of Mediaeval Studies).

Boyle, L. 1982 *The Setting of the* Summa *of St Thomas Aquinas*, The Etienne Gilson Series 5 (Toronto: Pontifical Institute of Mediaeval Studies).

Bracken, C. 2001 'Is the Early Embryo a Person?' *Linacre Quarterly* 68.1:49-70.

Braine, D. 1993 *The Human Person: Animal and Spirit* (London: Duckworth).

Brookes, B. 1988 *Abortion in England: 1900–1967* (London: Croom Helm).

Brown, P. 1988 *The Body and Society: Men, Women and Sexual Renunciation in Early Christianity* (New York: Columbia University Press).

Cameron, N. (ed.) 1987 *Embryos and Ethics: The Warnock Report in Debate* (Edinburgh: Rutherford House).

Carrick, P. 1985 *Medical Ethics in Antiquity* (Dordrecht: D. Reidel).

Carrick, P. 2001 *Medical Ethics in the Ancient World* (Washington, DC: Georgetown University Press).

Cassuto, U. 1967 *Commentary on Exodus*, trans. I. Abrahams (Jerusalem: Magnes).

Catechism of the Catholic Church 2002 (London: Burns & Oates/Continuum).

Channer, J.H. 1985 *Abortion and the Sanctity of Life* (Exeter: Paternoster Press).

Charlton, W. 1987 'Aristotle on the Place on Mind in Nature' in Gotthelf and Lennox (eds) 1987.

Clarke, S. 1975 *Aristotle's Man* (Oxford: Clarendon Press).

Clarke, P. and Linzey, A. 1988 *Research on Embryos: Politics, Theology and Law* (London: Lester Crook).

Cockburn (ed.) 1991 *Human Beings* (Cambridge: Cambridge University Press).

Congregation for the Doctrine of Faith 1974 *Declaration on Procured Abortion* (Vatican City).

Congregation for the Doctrine of the Faith 1987 *Instruction on Respect for Human Life in its Origin and the Dignity of Procreation* (*Donum Vitae*) (Vatican City).

Connery, J. 1977 *Abortion: The Development of the Roman Catholic Perspective* (Chicago, IL: Loyola University Press).

Cook, E.A., Jelen, T.G. and Wilcox, C. 1992 *Between Two Absolutes: Public Opinion and the Politics of Abortion* (San Francisco, CA: Westview Press).

Copleston, F. 1946 *A History of Philosophy Volume I: Greece and Rome* (Westminster, MD: The Newman Press).

Corream, J., Sgreccia, E. 1998 *Identity and Statute of Human Embryo* (Vatican City: Liberia Editrice Vaticana).

Coughlan, M. 1990 *The Vatican, the Law and the Human Embryo* (London: Macmillan).

Crosby, J. 1993 'The Personhood of the Human Embryo', *Journal of Medicine and Philosophy*, 18.4:399–417.

Crosby, J. 1996 *The Selfhood of the Human Person* (Washington, DC: Catholic University of America Press).

Cullman, O. 1958 *Immortality of the Soul or Resurrection of the Dead* (New York: Macmillan; London: Epworth Press).

Curran, C. 1969 *Dissent in and for the Church: Theologians and 'Humanae Vitae'* (New York: Sheed and Ward).

Dahood, M. 1970 *The Anchor Bible: Psalms III 101–150* (Garden City, NY: Doubleday).

Davidson, D. 1980 *Essays on Actions and Events* (Oxford: Oxford University Press).

Davis, H. 1946 *Moral and Pastoral Theology* (London: Sheed & Ward).

Donceel, J. 1970 'Immediate Animation and Delayed Hominization', *Theological Studies* 31: 75–105.

Draper, J.A. 1996 *The Didache in Modern Research* (Leiden: Brill).

Dunstan, G.R. 1988 'The Human Embryo in the Western Moral Tradition', in Dunstan and Sellars 1988.

Dunstan, G.R. (ed.) 1990 *The Human Embryo: Aristotle and the Arabic and European Traditions* (Exeter: University of Exeter Press).

Dunstan, G.R. and Sellars, M. 1988 *The Status of the Human Embryo: Perspectives from Moral Tradition* (London: King Edward's Hospital Fund).

Durant, W. 1939 *The Story of Civilisation* (New York: Simon & Schuster).

Dworkin, R. 1993 *Life's Dominion: An Argument about Abortion and Euthanasia* (London: HarperCollins).

Elton, B. 2000 *Inconceivable* (London: Black Swan).

English, R. 2002 'Nuclear Cell Transfer of Statutory Language', *New Law Journal* 152.7018 (February): 161.

Feldman, D. 1974 (1968) *Marital Relations, Birth Control and Abortion in Jewish Law* (New York: Schocken Books).

Finnis, J. 1994 '"Shameless acts" in Colorado: Abuse of Scholarship in Constitutional Cases', *Academic Questions*, 7 (Fall 1994): 10–41.

Fisher, A. 1991 'Individuogenesis and a Recent Book by Fr Norman Ford', *Anthropotes* 7.2 (December): 199–244.

Fitzmyer, J. 1981 *The Gospel According to Luke I–IX*, Anchor Bible 28 (Garden City).

Flannery, K. 2003 'Aristotle and Contemporary Embryology', *The Thomist* 67.2:249–78.

Fletcher, J. 1954 *Morals and Medicine* (Boston, MA: The Beacon Press).

Ford, N. 1988 *When Did I Begin? Conception of the Human Individual in History, Philosophy and Science* (Cambridge: Cambridge University Press).

Foster, J. 1985 'Personhood and the Ethics of Abortion' in Channer 1985.

Freeland, C.A. 1987 'Aristotle on Bodies, Matter and Potentiality' in Gotthelf and Lennox (eds) 1987.

Galton, F. 1904 'Eugenics: Its Definition Scope and Aims' *The American Journal of Sociology* 10.1:1-6.

Gilbert, S. 1997 *Developmental Biology*, 5th edn (New York: Sinauer Assoc.). *The Human Fertilization and Embryology Act 1990*.

Ginzberg, L. 1909-38 *The legends of the Jews, by Louis Ginzberg; Translated from the German Manuscript by Henrietta Szold*. 7 vols. (Philadelphia, PA: The Jewish publication society of America).

Glover, J. 1977 *Causing Death and Saving Lives* (Harmondsworth: Penguin).

Golden, M. 1988 'Did the Ancients Care when their Children Died?', *Greece and Rome*, 35:152-63.

Gorman, M. 1982 *Abortion and the Early Church* (New York: Paulist Press).

Gorman, M. and Brooks, A. 2003 *Holy Abortion? A Theological Critique of the Religious Coalition for Reproductive Choice* (Eugene, Oregon: Wipf & Stock).

Gotthelf, A. (ed.) 1985 *Aristotle on Nature and Living Things* (Bristol: Bristol Classical Press).

Gotthelf, A. and Lennox, J. 1987 (eds) *Philosophical Issues in Aristotle's Biology* (Cambridge: Cambridge University Press).

Gould, S.J. 1977 *Ontogeny and Phylogeny* (Cambridge, MA: The Belknap Press of Harvard University Press).

Grene, M. 1963 *A Portrait of Aristotle* (Chicago, IL: University of Chicago Press).

Grisez, G. 1970 *Abortion: The Myths the Realities and the Arguments* (New York: Corpus Books).

Grisez, G. 1989 'When Do People Begin?', *Proceedings of the American Catholic Philosophical Association* 63:22-47.

Hall, R. 1977 *Maire Stopes: A Biography* (London: André Deutsch).

Hankins, T.L. 1985 *Science and the Enlightenment* (Cambridge: Cambridge University Press).

Häring, B. 1972 *Medical Ethics* (Slough: St Paul's Publishing).

Harries, R. (Chair) 2002 *Report of the House of Lords Select Committee on Stem Cell Research* (London: HMSO).

Harrison, B.W. 1995 'Abortion: Religious Traditions: Protestant Perspectives' in Reich 1995.

Haught, J. 2000 *God after Darwin: A Theology of Evolution* (Boulder, CO: Westview Press).

Heaney, S. 1992 'Aquinas and the Presence of the Human Rational Soul in the Early Embryo', *The Thomist* 56:1.

Henry, J. 1997 *The Scientific Revolution and the Origins of Modern Science* (London: Macmillan).

Hewson, A. 1975 *Giles of Rome and the Medieval Theory of Conception* (London: The Athlone Press).

Hoekema, A. 1994 *Created in God's Image* (Grand Rapids, MI: Eerdmans; Carlisle: Paternoster Press).

Iglesias, T. 1987 'What Kind of Being is a Human Embryo?' in Cameron 1987.

Iglesias, T. 1990 *IVF and Justice* (London: Linacre Centre).

Jakobovits, I. 1965 'Jewish Views on Abortion', repr. In F. Rosner and D. Bleich *Jewish Bioethics* (New York: Santedrin Press, 1979).

Jakobovits, I. 1988 'The Status of the Embryo in the Jewish Tradition' in Dunstan and Sellers (eds) 1988.

Jackson, B. 1973 'The Problem of Exodus 21:22-5', *Vetus Testamentum* 23:273-304.

James, W. 2000 'Placing the Unborn: On the Social Recognition of New Life', *Anthropology and Medicine* 7.2 (August): 169-85.

John Paul II 1981 *Familiaris Consortio* (London: Catholic Truth Society).

John Paul II 1995 *Evangelium Vitae* (London: Catholic Truth Society).

Johnston, M. 1995 '*Delayed Hominization*: Reflections on Some Recent Catholic Claims for Delayed Hominization', *Theological Studies* 56: 743-63.

Jones, D. 2001 'The Status of the Embryo in the Christian Tradition' submission to *House of Lords Select Committee on Stem Cell Research*, repr. in *Ethics and Medicine* 17.3 (Fall 2001).

Jones, W.H.S. 1924 *The Doctor's Oath* (Cambridge: Cambridge University Press).

Jonsen, A. and Toulmin, S. 1988 *The Abuse of Casuistry* (Berkeley, CA: University of California Press).

Kaczor, C. 1999 'Is the "Medical Management" of Ectopic Pregnancy by the Administration of Methotrexate Morally Acceptable?' in Gormally (ed.) *Issues for a Catholic Bioethic* (London: Linacre Centre).

Kass, L. 1988 *Toward a More Natural Science: Biology and Human Affairs* (London: The Free Press).

Keil, K.F. and Delitzsch, F. *Biblical Commentary on the Old Testament: Volume 2, The Pentateuch*, trans. J. Martin (Grand Rapids, MI: Eerdmans, n.d.).

Kelly, K. 1987 'What are the Churches Saying about IVF?' in K. Kelly *Life and Love: Towards a Christian Dialogue on Bioethical Questions* (London: Collins Liturgical).

Kennedy, A. 1997 *Swimming against the Tide: Feminist Dissent on the Issue of Abortion* (Dublin: Open Air).

Kennedy, I. and Grubb, A. 1998 *Principles of Medical Law (with Cumulative Supplements)* (Oxford: Oxford University Press).

Kenny, A. 1973 *The Anatomy of the Soul: Historical Essays in the Philosophy of Mind* (Oxford: Basil Blackwell).

Keown, J. 1984 'Miscarriage: A Medico-Legal Analysis', *Criminal Law Review*: 604-14.

Keown, J. 1988 *Abortion, Doctors and the Law: Some Aspects of the Legal Regulation of Abortion in England from 1803 to 1982* (Cambridge: Cambridge University Press).

Kerr, F. 1986 *Theology after Wittgenstein* (Oxford: Basil Blackwell).

King, H. 1990 'Making a Man: Becoming Human in Greek Medicine' in Dunstan (ed.) 1990.

Kline, M. 1973 '*Lex Talionis* and the Human Fetus', *Journal of the Evangelical Theological Society* 20.3 (1977): 193–202.

Lee, P. 1996 *Abortion and Unborn Human Life* (Washington, DC: Catholic University of America Press).

Lennox, J. 2001 *Aristotle's Philosophy of Biology* (Cambridge: Cambridge University Press).

Lewis, N. 1983 *Life in Egypt under Roman Rule* (Oxford: Clarendon Press).

Little, C.H. 1933 *Disputed Doctrines, A Study in Biblical and Dogmatic Theology* (Burlington, IA: The Lutheran Literary Board).

Mahoney, J. 1984 *Bioethics and Belief* (London: Sheed & Ward).

Maienschein, J. 2002 'What's in a Name: Embryos, Clones, and Stem Cells', *American Journal of Bioethics* 2.1 (Winter): 12–20.

McCabe, H. 1987 *God Matters* (London: Geoffrey Chapman).

McCabe, H. 2002 'The Logic of Mysticism' in *God Still Matters* (London: Continuum).

McCarthy, B. 1997 *Fertility and Faith: The Ethics of Human Fertilization* (Leicester: InterVarsity Press).

McGrath, A. 1993 *Reformation Thought: An Introduction* (Oxford: Blackwell).

McGrath, A. 1994 *Christian Theology: An Introduction* (Oxford: Blackwell).

McLaren, A. 1990 'Policing Pregnancies: Changes in Nineteenth-century Criminal and Canon Law' in Dunstan (ed.) 1990.

Means, C. 1971 'The Phoenix of Abortional Freedom: Is a Penumbral or Ninth-Amendment Right about to Arise from the Nineteenth-century Legislative Ashes of a Fourteenth-century Common-law Liberty?' *New York Law Forum* 17:335.

Meilaender, G. 1995 *Body, Soul and Bioethics* (Notre Dame, IN: University of Notre Dame Press).

Midgley, M. 1979 *Beast and Man* (Hassocks: Harvester Press).

Mohr, J.C. 1978 *Abortion in America: The Origins and Evolution of National Policy* (Oxford: Oxford University Press).

Mortimer, R.C. 1967 'Probabilism' in Macquarrie, J. (ed.) *A Dictionary of Christian Ethics* (London: SCM).

Mulkay, M. 1997 *The Embryo Research Debate: Science and the Politics of Reproduction* (Cambridge: Cambridge University Press).

Munitz, M.K. 1965 *The Mystery of Existence* (New York: Appleton-Century-Crofts).

Musallam, B. 1990 'The Human Embryo in Arabic Scientific and Religious thought' in Dunstan (ed.) 1990.

Needham, J. 1959 *A History of Embryology* (Cambridge: Cambridge University Press).

Newman, J.H. 1990 (1845, rev. 1878) *An Essay on the Development of Christian Doctrine* (Notre Dame, IN: University of Notre Dame Press).

Noonan, J.T. 1965 *Contraception: A History of its Treatment* (Cambridge, MA: Harvard University Press).

Noonan J.T. 1970 'An Almost Absolute Value in History' in J.T. Noonan (ed.) *The Morality of Abortion: Legal and Historical Perspectives* (Cambridge MA: Harvard University Press).

Nussbaum, M. 1978 *Aristotle's De motu animalium: Text with Translation, Commentary, and Interpretive Essays* (Princeton, NJ: Princeton University Press).

Nutton, V. 1990 'The Anatomy of the Soul in Early Renaissance medicine' in Dunstan (ed.) 1990.

O'Donovan, O. 1984 *Begotten or Made?* (Oxford: Clarendon Press).

O'Mahoney, P. 1990 *A Question of Life: Its Beginning and Transmission* (London: Sheed & Ward).

Origen *De Principiis* in A Roberts and J. Donaldson (eds) 1885, *The Fathers of the Third Century*, Ante-Nicene Fathers Vol. IV (Grand Rapids, MI: Eerdmans).

Peck, A.L. 1942 Introduction, notes and translation of Aristotle *On the Generation of Animals*, Loeb 366, repr. 1979 (Cambridge, MA: Harvard University Press).

Pence, G.E. (ed.) *Flesh of my Flesh: The Ethics of Cloning Humans: A Reader* (Lanham, MD: Rowman & Littlefield 1998).

Pinckaers, S. 1995 *The Sources of Christian Ethics* (Edinburgh: T & T Clark).

R v. *Bourne* [1938] 3 All ER 615.

R (Smeaton) v. *Secretary of State for Health* [2002] EWHC 610 (Admin), [2002] 2 FLR 146, [2002] 2 FCR 193, 66 BMLR 59.

R (Quintavalle) v. *Secretary of State for Health* [2002] EWCA Civ 29, [2002] 2 All ER 625, [2002] 2 WLR 550, [2002] 2 FCR 140, 64 BMLR 72.

Rahner, K. 1972 *Theological Investigations Volume IX* trans. by G. Harrison (London: Darton, Longman & Todd).

Reich W.T. (ed.) 1995 *Encyclopedia of Bioethics (rev. edn)* (New York: Simon & Schuster/Macmillan).

Ryle, G. 1949 *The Concept of Mind* (London: Hutchinson).

Sacred Congregation for the Doctrine of the Faith 1974 *Declaration on Abortion* (Washington DC: US Catholic Conference).

Saward, J. 1993 *Redeemer in the Womb* (San Francisco, CA: Ignatius Press).

Schumacher, E.F. 1989 (1973) *Small is Beautiful: Economics as if People Mattered* (New York: Perennial (HarperCollins).

Siegfried, F.P. 1913 'Creationism' in *The Catholic Encyclopedia* (New York: Encyclopedia Press).

Simms, M. and Hindell, K. 1971 *Abortion Law Reformed* (London: Peter Owen).

Singer, P. 1994 *Rethinking Life and Death* (Melbourne: Text Publishing).

Smith, W.D. 1979 *The Hippocratic Tradition* (Ithaca, NY: Cornell University Press).

Stone, M. 2003 'Scrupulosity and Conscience: Probabilism in Early Modern Scholastic Ethics' in H.E. Braun and E. Vallances (eds) *Contexts of Conscience in Early Modern Europe, 1500–1700* (London: Palgrave).

Sutton, A. 2003 *Infertility* (London: Linacre Centre and The Catholic Truth Society).

Tate, M.E. 1990 *Word Biblical Commentary Psalms 51–100* (Dallas, TX: Word Books).

Tauer, C. 1984 'The Tradition of Probabilism and the Moral Status of the Early Embryo', *Theological Studies* 45:3–33.

Teichman, J. 1974 *The Mind and the Soul: An Introduction to the Philosophy of Mind* (London: Routledge & Kegan Paul).

Thompson, D'Arcy W. 1913 *On Aristotle as a Biologist* (Oxford: Clarendon Press).

Toner, P. 1913 'Limbo' in *The Catholic Encyclopedia* (New York: Encyclopedia Press).

Tonti-Filippini, N. 1992 'Further Comments on the Beginning of Life', *Linacre Quarterly* 59.3:76–81.

Tooley, M. 1983 *Abortion and Infanticide* (Oxford: Oxford University Press).

Torrance, T.F. 2000 *The Being and Nature of the Unborn Child* (Lenoir: Glen Lorien Books).

Tribe, L. 1990 *Abortion: The Clash of Absolutes* (New York: W.W. Norton).

Tugwell, S. (ed.) 1988 *Albert and Thomas: Selected Writings* (New York: Paulist Press).

Tugwell, S. 1990 *Human Immortality and the Redemption of Death* (London: Darton, Longman & Todd).

Warnock, M. (Chair) 1984 *Report of the Committee of Inquiry into Human Fertilization and Embryology* (London: HMSO).

Warnock, M. 1987 'Do Human Cells Have Rights?', *Bioethics* 1:1–12.

Watt, H. 1996 'Potential and the early Human', *Journal of Medical Ethics* 22: 222–6.

Watt, H. 2000 *Life and Death in Healthcare Ethics: A Short Introduction* (London: Routledge).

Westermarck, E. 1906–8 *The Origin and Development of the Moral Ideas* (London: Macmillan).

Wiggins, D. 1980 *Sameness and Substance* (Oxford: Basil Blackwell).

Williams, G. 1957 *The Sanctity of Life and the Criminal Law* (New York: Alfred A. Knopf).

Williams, G.H. 1970 'Religious Residues and Presuppositions in the American Debate on Abortion', *Theological Studies* 31.1: 10–75.

Williams, G. and Smith, A.T.H. (eds) 2002 *Learning the Law (12th edn)* (London: Sweet & Maxwell).

Wittgenstein, L. 2001 (1922) *Tractatus Logico-Philosophicus* (London: Routledge).

Wolpert, L. 1998 *Principles of Development* (Oxford: Oxford University Press).

Wolpert, L. 1991 *The Triumph of the Embryo* (Oxford: Oxford University Press).

Wood, P. and Good, J. 2001 'Human Reproductive Cloning–Nipped in the Bud?', *New Law Journal* 151.7010 (November): 1760.

Wyatt, J. 1998 *Matters of Life and Death: Today's Healthcare Dilemmas in the Light of Christian Faith* (Leicester: InterVarsity Press).

Index

Scripture Index